by BERNARD B. FALL

THE VIET-MINH REGIME

LE VIET-MINH

STREET WITHOUT JOY

THE TWO VIET-NAMS

THE VIET-NAM READER (co-author)

VIET-NAM WITNESS

HELL IN A VERY SMALL PLACE

LAST REFLECTIONS ON A WAR

ANATOMY OF A CRISIS

Bernard B. Fall

ANATOMY OF A CRISIS

The Laotian Crisis of 1960–1961

Edited with an Epilogue by
Roger M. Smith
University of Michigan

DOUBLEDAY & COMPANY, INC., GARDEN CITY, NEW YORK

1969

Maps based on originals by Roger M. Smith

Contents

Preface   11

Part One: THE BACKGROUND

  I. Prelude At Sop-Nao   17

 II. Some Glimpses From the Past   23
    The Country and Its People   23
    Early History   25
    The French Arrive   28

III. From War to War   30
    "Pax Gallica"   30
    The Japanese Coup   33
    "Free Laos"   34
    The Struggle for Control   35
    Constitutional Government   39
    The Exiles   40
    "Pathet Lao"—Round One   43

 IV. The Road to Geneva   46
    The Invasion   46
    The Winter Offensive   54

  V. Phony Peace   58
    Showdown at Geneva   58
    The Lao as a Negotiator   64
    Grinding Down the Pathet Lao   66
    Travels to the East   71

The 1957 Accords   75
The 1958 Elections   81

Part Two: THE CRISIS

VI.   The Pendulum   93
     Swing to the Right   93
     The UCPL Integration Crisis   98

VII.   "The Laos Fraud"   107
     The Early Phase   107
     "Pathet Lao"—Round Two   112
     The Diplomatic Byplay   119
     The Summer Campaign   122
     The Second Wave   126
     September High Tide   133
     September Fog   134
     Mission on the Spot   143
     Second Thoughts   146
     "Why They Called Off the Dogs"   151

VIII.   The American Stake   157
     From Bastion to Buffer   159
     Why America in Laos?   161
     Graft and Corruption   164
     Rationale for a Policy   166

IX.   New Turmoils   173
     The Year of the Sword   173
     That "UN Presence"   177
     The 1960 Elections   181
     Souphanouvong's Escape   183

X.   Coup and Countercoup   184
     The Kong-Lê Phenomenon   184
     Neutrality's Narrow Path   188

The Parsons Mission 192
"Polarization" 195

Part Three: THE SOLUTION

XI. Internationalizing the Crisis 203
   Civil War 203
   Neutrality Plans 208
   Aligning the Allies 213
   Geneva Once More 219
   The Souvannaphouma Incident 221
   Three Wandering Princes 224
   The End of the Road or: This Is Where We Came In 227

XII. Epilogue 232

   Notes 239
   Appendixes 248
   Bibliography 264
   Index 267

Preface

————◄◆►————

The process of writing a book about a current crisis is always delicate, for one runs the risk of either being overtaken or, worse, contradicted by events. That does not mean that the process itself is unworthwhile; on the contrary, it permits the interested citizen or the diplomat to take stock of what is happening under his own eyes, whose significance he may have missed under the pressure of daily tasks or, as will be seen, was misconstrued because of frequently inaccurate or misleading news stories.

What makes the Laos crisis so particularly remarkable is that it was as totally avoidable from the Communist bloc's viewpoint as the Berlin crisis was from ours. It is likely that an effectively neutral Laotian government would have satisfied erstwhile Communist objectives, just as the maintenance of the occupation *status quo* in Berlin would certainly have satisfied ours. But in both cases, the "activists" decided to upset the *status quo* for reasons that had little to do with the local situation as such: The United States felt that elimination of an active Laotian left wing would bring about a consolidation of the Laotian state regardless of its inherent social, economic and political defects; similarly, the Soviets seemed to believe that the liquidation of a free West Berlin would solve the basic problems of the East German dictatorship.

In both instances, the radicalization of the problem merely increased the internal pressures: In Laos the pro-Communist Pathet Lao resorted to foreign-supported civil war rather than go under completely; and in the case of Berlin the Ulbricht regime had already had in June 1953 a foretaste of what pressure without a safety valve can do. The process almost invariably culminates in an escalation of diplomatic and military activities in which backing down becomes the less graceful as it has been delayed longer—unless a fresh approach is found (or at least considered) in time which leaves room for a new alternative.

In the Laotian crisis, the escalation process was almost left to run its full course, and the bulk of the pages that follow will deal with the diplomatic, political and military events that contributed to the making as well as to the dénouement of the crisis.

The documentation used is the result of extensive research in the files of the world press, various libraries and some unclassified government archives in the United States, France, and Cambodia. It was supplemented by interviews with various diplomats and specialists from the above countries, the United Nations, and Laos, including some of the principal actors.

Part of the field research for this book was carried out under the terms of a research grant of the Rockefeller Foundation which, however, is not in any way responsible for the views or opinions expressed therein.

BERNARD B. FALL

Washington–Paris–Phnom Penh
April–November 1961

CHINA

BURMA

Phong Saly

Dien Bien Phu

BLACK RIVER

RED RIVER

CLEAR RIVER

HANOI

Nam Tha

Sam Neua

SONG MA R.

SONG CHU R.

Luang Prabang

PLAINE DES. JARRES

Xieng-Khouang

SONG CA R.

Sayaboury

Tha-Thom

Vinh

Borikhane

Kam Kheut

VIENTIANE

MEKONG RIVER

Nongkhai

Muong Nhommarat

Thakhek

Séno

Tchépone

Hué

Savannakhet

Dong-Hene

THAILAND

Saravane

Danang

Ubon

Pakseng

BOLOVENS PLATEAU

Khorat

Champassac

Attopeu

Kontum

BANGKOK

Siem Reap

CAMBODIA

Stung-Treng

Battambang

Kompong-Thom

Kratié

Ban Me Thuot

Pursat

Kompong-Cham

PHNOM-PENH

Sihanoukville

Kampot

SAIGON

Gulf of Siam

South China Sea

Laos

IN INDO-CHINA

Part One:

THE BACKGROUND

I

Prelude at Sop-Nao

———◆———

This was the rainy season in Laos, a time of the year when no one travels unless he has to. In fact, traveling even in the dry season can be somewhat of an ordeal, since there is only a total of 924 miles of so-called "all-weather" roads in all of the 91,000 square miles of the country and only a half dozen airports capable of accommodating a twin-engine transport aircraft. This leaves the rivers as probably the best means of traveling within the country all year around. The largest of those rivers is the mighty Mekong and its many tributaries; to travel throughout Laos in one of the large native dugouts or the heavier European-built motor barges known as *piromoteurs* is still perhaps the most comfortable and reliable way of seeing much of the country. Although the Mekong constitutes most of the western boundary of Laos—separating it from Thailand and Burma—many of its tributaries probe deeply into the country itself, in the direction of the Vietnamese border. The most important of those tributaries is the Nam-Hou which stops only a few miles short of the North Vietnamese border.

The Nam-Hou, in turn, has a little offshoot of its own called the Nam-Houa. The Nam-Houa is a tiny rivulet as far as rivers go; in fact, it is barely more than a creek, but during the rainy season it can carry a native dugout. Flowing through a deeply cut valley, almost entirely shrouded in high trees, broadening here and there into a somewhat wider valley basin where diligent Méo tribeswomen plant irrigated rice in a few small paddies, it winds its way into North Viet-Nam. There, the Nam-Houa ends in a small river fork known as the Nam-Yum. The Nam-Yum is really nothing more than a creek a few miles in length which quickly runs its course in the surrounding hills.

But once upon a time, not too long ago, the Nam-Yum witnessed the agony and death of thousands of men whose decaying bodies nearly choked its brown waters—for the Nam-Yum flows through the town and valley of Dien Bien Phu.

The Nam-Hou had always been one of the traditional invasion routes into northern Laos. For hundreds of years, Chinese pirates and raiders, fierce Méo tribesmen on small ponies, and Black T'ai feudal lords and their retainers have traveled down the valley of the Nam-Hou to Laos, destroying peaceful villages in their passage.

When the French gained control of Laos in the 1890s, they sought to protect it from further invasions from the north and east. They brought the Black T'ai overlords of the powerful Déo family under their control by signing a special treaty with them and by establishing a small border post at a village overlooking the Nam-Hou. The name of the village was Sop-Nao.

Sop-Nao, inhabited by rice-farming lowland Laotians, was never meant to be more than just a border control point. Under the French colonial administration the whitewashed brick and adobe structure had contained two European gendarmes and perhaps a dozen or so native rifle-men—just enough to show the flag and to keep an eye on the dugout river traffic.

When the Indo-China war broke out, Sop-Nao's role was hardly more exalted. To be sure, the gendarmes had been replaced by a regular French army officer and a rifle platoon, but the role of even the platoon was merely to act as an "alarm bell" for the larger garrison down river at Muong Khoua, whose job it was to block any enemy advance along the Nam-Hou to the royal capital of Luang Prabang. Both Sop-Nao and Muong Khoua had performed this role once before and performed it rather well. When Communist Viet-Minh forces for the first time stabbed deeply into Laos in the spring of 1953, Sop-Nao held out long enough to forewarn Muong Khoua where a Laotian army battalion under the command of a French captain was given the order to delay a Viet-Minh division for fourteen days. When Muong Khoua finally succumbed after a siege of thirty-six days, it had virtually fought to the last man. There were only three known survivors. Sop-Nao had fulfilled its role and had saved Luang Prabang.

When peace returned to the Nam-Hou valley in July 1954 Sop-Nao, after a brief reoccupation by the French, returned into Communist hands. This time its occupiers were Laotian rebel forces working with the Viet-Minh, known as the Pathet Lao. For the Pathet Lao, Sop-Nao was little more than a temporary staging area and the border post was soon overgrown with bushes and weeds. This situation changed in November 1957, when, after reaching an accord with the Pathet Lao, Royal Laotian forces were authorized to reoccupy Sop-Nao. Now the red flag with the three-headed white elephant of Laos was again fluttering over the post, and for all intents and purposes Sop-Nao had become a peacetime garrison, again mainly concerned with the activities of Méo opium smugglers. For all one knew, the Viet-Minh had returned to their North Vietnamese lairs and their Pathet Lao allies were safely bottled up in two Lao garrisons while their leaders were negotiating peace terms with the Laotian government in Vientiane.

The commander of the little garrison was Lieutenant Déo Van Khoun, a scion of the famous Déo family of feudal Black T'ai chieftains who, until a few years ago, had been ruling the mountain provinces of northwest Viet-Nam with an iron hand. Since 1954, the North Vietnamese Communists had driven out all the chieftains of the Déo family and some of them had migrated across the border to join their kinsmen in northern Laos. Déo Van Khoun, now a lieutenant in the Royal Laotian Army, was, therefore, "at home" in the area to which he had been assigned. Since his own people roamed the hills on both sides of the border, he had few worries. In fact, he was so confident that he would be warned of any untoward event that, instead of sleeping in the post with his men, he had taken up quarters in the village, where he lived with his wife in a Laotian-style house built on stilts.

July 1959 had been a very warm month in northern Laos. The young rice was growing well in the narrow valleys, and the rain had been abundant. For weeks Sop-Nao had been completely quiet. Rains had washed out most of the footpaths in the areas and swelled the rivers until their waters flowed with treacherous swiftness. For many days Lieutenant Déo Van Khoun had not sent out patrols deep into the surrounding jungle.

Not that the rainy season makes patrolling as such impossible; it merely makes it uncomfortable, but nothing in the present situation made long-range patrolling seem particularly urgent. And in any case, his tribal kins-men across the border would surely let him know if any trouble was brew-ing. Sop-Nao was a good post as border posts go; what it lacked in excitement it made up in scenery, in the friendliness of its inhabitants, and in the absence of inspections from higher headquarters. And opium was both plentiful and cheap.

On the night of July 29–30, 1959, Déo Van Khoun and his wife had retired early. He had eaten a hearty meal of gluey brown rice served in woven wicker baskets along with a fish his men had caught in the nearby river by stunning it with hand grenades; sweetish rice cakes and cool bitter tea completed the repast. By nine o'clock all of Sop-Nao was blanketed by complete darkness; the thrifty villagers were not wasting scarce kero-sene for nothing.

In the early morning hours of July 30, 1959, dark shadows emerged from the whitish ground fog shrouding the hills. One or two of the shaggy Méo dogs roaming through the village attempted to yelp, but were quickly disposed of by well-directed thrusts of long mountaineer daggers. Without hesitation, the small group of black-clad men went directly to Déo Van Khoun's house. A few men covered the exits while four others entered the six-foot-high storage area under the house where the proprietor's cattle are usually quartered. At the very same moment, a larger group of men, armed with rifles and submachine guns, carefully picked its way to the border post of Sop-Nao on its hillock above the village. Its approach was undetected, for not only was it completely silent but it also benefited from the fact that the Laotian soldiers had allowed the shubbery to grow back again along the sides of the hill, thus obstructing the view from the post. The shadows quickly encircled the small post in total silence and then simply settled down to wait for the signal.

The deep silence was suddenly broken by the husky chatter of sub-machine guns fired in a confined space and was almost immediately fol-lowed by screams of pain; the four men under Déo Van Khoun's house had fired through the plank ceiling into the bodies of the lieutenant and his wife lying, Laotian-fashion, on rice straw mats on the floor. The very first burst hit Déo Van Khoun in the chest and groin, while his wife sus-tained a lighter wound in one of her thighs. A servant who tried to come to the help of his master was quickly disposed of by the assailants as they now hastily retreated to rejoin the group attacking Sop-Nao itself. The successful attack on Déo Van Khoun's house was the signal for which the other group had been waiting. With automatic rifle bursts reverberating from the surrounding mountains, the attackers now threw themselves against the completely surprised soldiers of the post.

The very unpreparedness of the Laotians probably saved them from total annihilation, for they simply abandoned the post and ran for their lives, and the same bushes which had prevented the sleepy sentry from noticing the attackers now prevented the latter from shooting at the fleeing soldiers. In Sop-Nao itself, the dying Déo Van Khoun and his wife were able, with the help of the now awake villagers and fleeing soldiers, to head for their dugouts lying on the shore of the Nam-Hou. Paddling frantically downstream toward Muong Khoua, they escaped the attackers who were still in the captured post, sorting out the spoils—American weapons, GI clothing, rice and rations, and, most valuable of all, a precious field radio set.

Lieutenant Déo Van Khoun died during the boat trip to Muong Khoua, which the stunned survivors of Sop-Nao reached the following day. In the ensuing panic, the garrison of Muong Khoua, believing that the survivors of Sop-Nao were being pursued by large Viet-Minh forces, in turn pulled out from its fort (a position which previously had withstood a Communist attack for thirty-six days) and withdrew into the surrounding hills. In Sop-Nao, in the meantime, the attackers had regrouped. They turned out to be T'ai tribesmen themselves, who spoke the tribal dialect of the area and apparently were thoroughly familiar with the terrain. They might as well have been from Sop-Nao itself, for many of their relatives lived in the area. In any case, in those remote mountain areas where national boundaries cut across ethnic groups it is very hard to tell whether a given tribesman is "Laotian" or "Vietnamese." Having collected all their booty in dugouts, they simply paddled off in the direction of the border.

Forty-odd hours later, after a reconnaissance flight by a small plane had shown no unusual activities around Sop-Nao, Laotian troops from Muong Sai and Phong Saly reoccupied Sop-Nao. In Vientiane in the meantime, the general staff of the Lao Armed Forces announced that Sop-Nao had been retaken on August 2, 1959, "after a battle which lasted about three hours."

It will be remembered [the communiqué added] that the post of Sop-Nao was evacuated for technical reasons during the night of July 29–30, 1959. Reinforcements were able, with the co-operation of the local population, to drive the enemy from this advanced post. In the rest of the country the situation is calm.

Yet, the shots fired at Sop-Nao were but the beginning of the final chapter of a struggle which had begun in 1946 and which was to witness yet another Western defeat in Southeast Asia before it was over.

II

Some Glimpses from the Past

The Country and Its People

Laos is neither a geographical nor an ethnic or social entity, but merely a political convenience. Its 91,000 square miles (about the size of Oregon in the United States) is a geographer's nightmare of small deep valleys surrounded by saw-toothed mountains covered with jungle almost to the tips. Its one good avenue of navigation, the Mekong, is cut by rapids near its entry into Cambodia. With its mountain villages inhabited by semi-nomads who displace their whole habitat lock, stock and barrel every four or five years, taking the name of the village along with them (and thus making a mockery of all previously made maps), Laos, seen from the air, gives one the impression of a lunar landscape that had suddenly developed a luxuriant carpet of vegetation. In the words of Norman Cousins, a recent American traveler to the area, ". . . indeed, if you want to get a sense of the universe unraveling, come to Laos. Complexities such as this have to be respected."

This physical chaos alone accounts for much of Laos' present trouble. It accounts for the paucity of overland communications; the inaccessibility to the orderly processes of government of many of the small villages, almost completely isolated in their narrow valleys; the absence of a feeling of national unity, and the fierce family loyalties. What really counts in Laotian life is what happens to one's own clan in one's own valley. What happens elsewhere might just as well happen on the moon for all that it matters in the values of the local villagers. If the Laotian appears self-centered and uninterested in world events, it is certainly not of his own choosing; his country made him that way. Thus, "patriotism" in Laos is at best a furious regionalism.

Geographically, Laos falls into five distinct regions: the Mekong and the rice-growing lowlands through which its tributaries flow; two plateau areas—the Plaine des Jarres in the north and the Bolovens Plateau in the south, whose grassy plains jut out from the surrounding jungle like two natural fortresses; the Annam Cordillera whose formidable spine separates Laos from Viet-Nam for over 500 miles; and finally the high ridges of the northern part of the country which, like waves on a beach, flow away from China's Yunnan province. While none of the Laotian mountains reach Himalayan proportions, some of them tower almost as high as 10,000 feet and the plateau areas reach an altitude of 4500 feet. The Annam Cordillera itself is composed of an almost continuous line of peaks in the 8000 feet range and is readily passable only at three points, all of them in its southern portion.

The people of Laos are about as variegated as its terrain is chaotic. No one knows precisely where the term "Lao" comes from. According to local legend[1] "Lao" comes from the words *Lwa* or *La-Wa,* which was the name of the tribes which inhabited Laos prior to the Thai invasions of the fourteenth century. It is the latter who assertedly transformed the term Lwa into Lao. Another legend has it that the entire Lao people came out of two large gourds, the Pali term for "gourd" being *Lawu.* But barely one-half of the population of Laos can qualify as "Lao"; there are at least forty-two different tribal clusters in Laos which can be grouped into at least five major linguistic families: the Proto-Indochinese, the Thai, the Méo (Miao), the Sino-Tibetans, and lastly, the Khmer.

However, as if tribal distribution alone were not sufficiently chaotic, some of those groups like to live literally "on top of each other," with the latecoming Méo and Man groups preferring the mountaintops above 3000 feet as their natural habitat, and the Sino-Tibetans and tribal T'ai electing to live below 3000 feet. The Lao themselves are strictly valley dwellers and live as far down in the flatlands as possible. Thus, it is not impossible —in fact it happens all the time—that in a very small area one first traverses a belt of Laotian villages followed by a higher lying belt of Kha Mou villages, which might give way to White or Black T'ai villages. As one climbs higher, these will in turn yield to the Lolo Kha Kho, and finally, to the mountaintop settlements of the Méo, some of which will be perched dizzyingly on the edge of abrupt cliffs and limestone hills, where their inhabitants will eke out a meager living growing opium poppies and corn.

The lowland Lao, however, represent the politically and economically dominant group in the country. Like all the other present-day occupants of the Indochinese peninsula, they came from the country to the north, China. Little is thus far known about the aboriginal population of the peninsula; remains found at various places point to a Negrito-type population such as still inhabits the islands in the western Pacific and Australia, along with men belonging to the Malaya-Polynesian racial group. The Mongoloids begin to appear only at the beginning of the Christian era when Laos was in the Bronze Age.

The first outside civilization to penetrate into the peninsula was that of India. Buddhism and Brahmanism developed rapidly throughout the peninsula during the first century A.D., working their way not only into the religious life of the inhabitants but also into their social organization and political structure. Out of the assimilation and modification of these influences—especially the ideas on the organization of the state and the religious justification of kingly rule—were born four kingdoms which at one time or another included large parts of Laos: Fu-Nan, Chen-La, Champa, and Kambuja. The latter survives today in Cambodia, on Laos' southern border.

Early History

From the eighth to the thirteenth century, much of what is now known as Laos was part of the Khmer Empire centered in present-day Cambodia. Mongol pressure in China caused the T'ai tribes, which heretofore had resided there, to push south into the valleys of the Irrawaddy, Salween, Chao Phraya, Mekong, and Red rivers, the traditional invasion routes into Southeast Asia. Slowly but surely, the Hinduistic kingdoms began to degenerate and collapse under the growing strength of the T'ai invaders. Around the end of the thirteenth century, the Khmer lost control of all of northern Laos, including the areas around present-day Luang Prabang and Vientiane. With the capture by the Mongols of Tali, the Lao capital in Yunnan, the flight southward of its inhabitants reached full force.

Unfortunately for the Lao, the Mekong did not prove to be an easy avenue of access to the land lying south. Neighboring Burma's and Siam's (Thailand) broad rivers and plains soon favored extensive colonization by the new owners; in Laos, on the contrary, the narrow valleys, cloud-shrouded peaks, favored "balkanization" into small clans and tribes—a physical handicap that was to dog the Laotians throughout their history and to the present day.

The early part of Laos' history is shrouded in legends in which truth and fancy mingle freely. In spite of their long cohabitation with the literate Chinese, the Lao apparently developed a writing system only after their flight from their Yunnanese kingdom of Nan-Chao. According to the legends, the first king of Laos was the fabled Khun Borom (or Bolom), whose son Khun-Lo conquered the northern part of the kingdom. According to Lao historians, it was the twenty-third king after King Khun-Lo, Fa Ngum, who after having received his education at the court of the Khmer king returned to Laos in 1349 at the head of a small army. By 1351, the young Prince had humbled the Thai kingdom of Sukhothai to the west and the Vietnamese to the east.

Having thus defeated his two major enemies, Fa Ngum now proceeded in a series of rapid campaigns to subdue the various feudal rulers. He conquered Luang Prabang, held by his own grandfather, and he took Vientiane by a ruse: The city being heavily defended by a T'ai Prince, Fa Ngum feigned a retreat and had his archers shoot gold and silver pieces at the ramparts. This led the greedy defenders to open their gates and rush out in search of the precious metal, whereupon Fa Ngum's forces fell upon them, penetrated into the city and conquered it. In 1353—having made Laos a powerful kingdom dominating much of the Indochinese peninsula—Fa Ngum was crowned King of the Lan-Xang ("Land of the Million Elephants"). He encouraged the development of the arts and sciences and the spread of Buddhism in the new kingdom, but like so many successful war leaders before and after him, he became the victim of his own success. As Fa Ngum grew older he became more and more tyrannical. He was overthrown in 1373 and died in exile five years later.

The next two hundred years brought the kingdom of Laos to the peak of its power. A succession of wise kings—Pothisarath, Setthathirat, and Suliyavongsa (or Suryavongsa)—succeeded in staving off several invasions from Burma, Siam, and Viet-Nam. Only Cambodia, Laos' southern neighbor, maintained its traditional friendship and almost never was involved in warlike action against the Lao kingdom. Vientiane, which had become the capital of the kingdom in the 1560s, was from all accounts a beautiful city then—very different from the chaotic assemblage of tin-roofed shacks, decaying colonial bungalows, and ostentatious concrete-and-glass villas that it is today. It contained magnificent temples, including that of the famous Emerald Buddha. Travelers who visited the city in the 1640s brought back tales of the magnificence of its buildings and the friendliness of its inhabitants.

The death of King Suliyavongsa initiated the gradual decline of Laos. In order to secure the throne for himself, one of his grandsons accepted military aid from the neighboring Vietnamese kingdom in return for which he promised political and economic concessions. But while this grandson succeeded in winning control of the area around Vientiane, a half brother fled to Luang Prabang where he established a separate kingdom in 1707, while another prince of the royal house created yet a third kingdom, Champassak, in the deep south of Laos. With the division of Laos into three separate states between 1707 and 1713, all hopes of withstanding Thai pressures from the west and Vietnamese threats from the east were now lost. Repeatedly the Lao in general and in particular the kingdom of Vientiane attempted to wrest themselves from control by foreign over-lords and "protectors," but to little avail. In a bitter war which began in 1826, King Anou, in alliance with the king of Champassak, attempted once more to shake off the Siamese yoke. After a series of victories over the Siamese, the Laotian forces were finally defeated after they had come to within three days' march of the Siamese capital. The king of Champassak was taken prisoner by the Siamese and Anou himself was forced to retreat. With the help of Vietnamese troops put at his disposal, Anou once more attempted in 1827 to liberate Vientiane but was betrayed by a minor feudal chieftain; he was captured and brought to Bangkok where he died a few months later. This time the Siamese decided to end once and for all attempts on the part of the Lao to revolt. In less than one year, nearly one-third of the population of the kingdom of Vientiane was deported to Siam into slavery; the city itself was razed, the temples destroyed, and the precious Emerald Buddha taken as booty to Bangkok where it is still to be seen today. Both Champassak and Vientiane now were simply Siamese provinces. The kingdom of Luang Prabang continued to survive, although barely, for its eastern provinces were progressively amputated in confrontations with the Vietnamese.

In the 1870s, a new threat was to add itself to all the others which the sorely tried Laotians had to endure: strongly organized and armed Ho pirates began to descend into the Lao valleys from China. Within a few years they became so strong that they were able to overrun the kingdom of Luang Prabang almost completely, while the Vietnamese increased their holdings on eastern portions of the Plaine des Jarres. The same process took place in Vientiane which, under Siamese tutelage, had become hardly more than a backwater village. A renewed Siamese push toward the north, probably motivated as much by British attempts to reach the Mekong from Burma as by French activities in Viet-Nam, resulted in several Siamese military expeditions into the kingdom of Luang Prabang between 1883 and 1885. This renewed Siamese intervention finally brought about a French reaction.

The French Arrive

The French intervention in Laos was pretty much the work of a single man, Auguste Pavie. He was one of a long line of travelers, explorers, administrators of many nationalities who in the nineteenth century were the *bâtisseurs d'empire*—"empire builders"—who almost single-handedly carved out vast colonial possessions for their homelands. Pavie was an extraordinary little man. Physically, he was just a little over five feet tall and extremely frail. He had first come to Indo-China as a postal employee and had spent long years as head of the telegraph office in a small town in Cambodia. It was there that he discovered his avocation as a student of Khmer history. His enthusiasm for the mores and cultures of the area in which he lived was so contagious that he finally convinced the French Governor-General at the time, Le Myre de Villers, to authorize him to go as far north as he could.

For the next fifteen years, Pavie and a tiny group of officers and soldiers traveled on foot over much of what is today northern Laos and the mountain areas of northern Viet-Nam, eating local food, often walking barefoot after their shoes had worn out,[2] clad in ragged clothes hardly better than those of the Laotian farmers whom they encountered. Five of the members of his group died while on the march and another six died soon thereafter, but Pavie, having been transferred to the diplomatic service in 1886 with the lowly rank of vice-consul, rightfully deserves the title of "Father of Modern Laos." It was Pavie, who, in a series of treaties negotiated with the Siamese and the British, stabilized the western borders of Laos. After having been nearly killed, along with the King of Luang Prabang, when Chinese "Black Flag" (Ho) pirates captured and pillaged the royal capital in June 1897, Pavie personally negotiated the peace treaty with the T'ai tribal overlord, Déo Van Tri, who ruled much of the northern Vietnamese uplands from Lai Chau to Dien Bien Phu. Laos then began to take on its present-day shape in a succession of negotiated treaties between France and Siam (1893, 1902, 1907), and between France and China (1895) and Britain (1896).

The French colonial administration maintained a dual relationship with Laos. The kingdom of Luang Prabang remained a distinct political entity as a French protectorate under King Sisavang Vong, who reigned until his death in 1959. The remainder of Laos was in fact, if not in law, administered as a French colony; that is, the French administrators did not act through Laotian authorities but directly administered the areas under their control. In Vientiane this was due mainly to the fact that the ruling elite had been completely exterminated during the Lao-Thai war of 1828. In the southern principality of Champassak, on the other hand, the local rulers retained nominal authority over the provinces of the principality, but were subject to French control. It was only during World War II, on September 29, 1941, that King Sisavang Vong was recognized by France as sovereign over all Laos.[3] Thus Laos was reborn as a unified state after 250 years of chaos, war, and internal strife.

III

From War to War

---◄◆►---

"Pax Gallica"

If ever the burden of foreign domination rested lightly on a people's shoulders, it was that of the French on the people of Laos. From the French viewpoint, Laos was merely a buffer designed to preserve the areas of economically important northern Viet-Nam from British or Siamese influence. With the disappearance of those influences at the beginning of the twentieth century, Laos lost its importance to France either as a political bastion or as an avenue of approach for French penetration into Yunnan. And within the over-all administrative and political context of the Indochinese Union, there was little reason for France to consider Laos as anything more than a delightful backwater suitable for administrators and officers who wanted to "get away from it all."

All sources available on the subject—including the most recent books and articles written by Laotians[1]—agree that French influence (what there was of it) was largely beneficial. In Luang Prabang, the traditional form of government was largely maintained along with Laotian legal codes brought up-to-date where necessary; in the Laotian areas outside Luang Prabang the French colonial administration also made extensive use of the existing traditional structure, intervening in such fields as education, health, and public works only where new Western methods were definitely superior to those traditionally available. Perhaps the only major mistake made by the French in their sixty years of tutelage in Laos was the extensive use they made at subordinate echelons of Vietnamese civil servants. As in the case of the Indian civil servant used by the British in Burma and Malaya, the result was that too few capable native administrators were trained to hold positions of responsibility in their own country. This deficiency was to make itself felt after full independence was gained and is likely to be felt for decades to come.

Militarily and politically also, Laos was considered as the *enfant sage* (the "well-behaved child") of the Indochinese Union. From 1893 until 1945, exactly three uprisings took place, all of them staged not by plains-dwelling Lao but by the mountaineers, particularly the warlike tribes living near the Chinese border. However, a very serious rebellion took place in 1934 among the Alakh, Phouthai, and Lové tribes of the southern Bolovens Plateau, which, initially caused by intertribal warfare involving kidnaping and human sacrifices, degenerated into a bloody, no-quarters-given jungle war. Although the French succeeded in restoring order in the Bolovens after almost two years of fighting, the extremely primitive tribes of the area have never really reconciled themselves to outside control. This fact, suitably exploited by the Communists, accounts for much of the insecurity which still prevails in the mountainous areas of southern Laos.

The outbreak of World War II in Europe did not change the placid course of life in Laos—at least not immediately. The defeat of mainland France at the hands of the Germans in June 1940 nevertheless had its repercussions in the Far East where Japan and its lone Asian ally, Thailand, were getting ready to follow in the footsteps of their European Axis allies. In true Axis fashion, Thailand first signed a non-aggression pact with France on June 12, 1940, and proceeded to attack French Indo-China without warning on January 9, 1941, hoping to regain two Laotian provinces on the right bank of the Mekong which they had lost in 1904 and 1907. While the Thai forces were militarily beaten to a standstill by the French, their Japanese protectors soon stepped in and "mediated" the dispute in their own particular way. The French were summoned to Tokyo and on March 11, 1941, were forced to sign an agreement which gave Thailand two Cambodian provinces and the provinces of Sayaboury and Bassac in Laos.

Moreover—and this may come as a surprise to the American reader—
the French already had fought a short but bloody war with the Japanese
in September 1940—a full year before Pearl Harbor. Shortly before
France's agony in Europe, the Japanese had asked the French to let their
troops pass through North Viet-Nam in order to attack the Chinese Nationalist forces from the rear. The French having at first refused to comply
with this request, the Japanese attacked French garrisons along the Chinese border on September 22, 1940, without warning, while two days
later, their bombers attacked the open port of Haiphong. More than 800
Frenchmen were killed in less than two days' fighting while pleas addressed by French Indo-China to France's allies in the Pacific remained
unheeded. The Japanese then asked their German partners to exercise
pressure upon the French government at home, and an order for cease-
fire was given. Soon the Japanese occupied all of Indo-China. French
hegemony in Laos, Cambodia, and Viet-Nam had suffered a blow from
which it would never recover.

Yet those war years were not a total loss to Laos. First of all, the
French surrender of two Laotian provinces to Thailand brought about
French concessions to the Laotian King in the form of the already mentioned Treaty of Sovereignty of 1941. It also brought about the creation
of a Laotian cabinet under the King which, though at first only endowed
with formal powers, at least gave Laotians some experience in the administration of senior government positions. Also, the Axis-inspired emphasis in France as well as in French possessions of youth movements
and physical fitness stimulated a surprisingly rapid development of the
Boy Scout movement in Laos. Many of the later political leaders of
Laos and Viet-Nam were graduates of those wartime youth movements.
Another entirely unexpected consequence of the wartime isolation of
Indo-China was a sudden upsurge in the number of schools and in the
number of students attending them. This was mainly due to the fact that
with the Japanese occupation of the country, the only field of activity
left open to the remaining French colonial administration was that of
education and public works. Thus, while the total number of students
in all three Indochinese countries was 525,000 in 1940, the number had
increased to 666,000 in 1943 and to 960,000 in 1944.[2] In another do-
main, the French, unable to receive new recruits from France, now began
to train Laotian troops in addition to Vietnamese and Cambodian forces.
Until 1942 Laotians had served on an individual basis in French units;

in 1943 the French created the first battalion of *Chasseurs Laotiens* (Laotian light infantry).

The Japanese Coup

But Laos could not remain an island of peace in a continent engulfed by war. As it became clear to the Japanese that they were to be brought to their knees by the Allies, they, like their German partners in Europe, lashed out in a destructive rage in all directions. A handy target for them was the remaining French administrators and underarmed units in Indo-China. On March 9, 1945, Japanese troops once more attacked without warning, wantonly killing French soldiers and civilians. French pleas for American help were ignored.[3] Within a short time, all Frenchmen in Indo-China—women, children as well as men—were interned in Japanese camps; all, that is, except those in Laos.

In Laos, as well as in neighboring Cambodia and Viet-Nam, the Japanese struck their *coup de force* on March 9, 1945, but the terrain made it more difficult for them to execute their plans in lightning fashion. In a spontaneous movement of generosity and courage equaled only by the attitude of the Filipinos toward the Americans, the Laotian people came to the help of the French. Literally hundreds of Frenchmen were hidden from their Japanese pursuers by Laotian friends, humble as well as of high station. In Champassak, Prince Boun Oum—the hereditary ruler who was to become prime minister of Laos in 1960–61—decided to keep on fighting against the Japanese with all means at his disposal. Aided by a handful of French officers and soldiers, Prince Boun Oum set up guerrilla bases in southern Laos which soon harassed Japanese communication lines in the area. The officers and soldiers of the Laotian First Battalion also took to the hills and began to fight against the hated invaders. Some of the Laotian lieutenants of that heroic era are now the Laotian Army's generals; this is the case, for example, of General Amkha Soukhavong. This Laotian-French resistance movement was, in fact, so successful that Britain soon began to parachute weapons and equipment to the jungle fighters, followed in May and June 1945 by French and British liaison teams of the famous "Force 136." A special medal was struck after the war by grateful France to commemorate the heroic deeds of the Laotian-French resistance movement. As in the Philippines, many of Laos' political leaders in the difficult years of the 1960s, both of the Right and of the Left, are "graduates" of the anti-Japanese underground.

"Free Laos"

As in all the other colonial areas of Southeast Asia, the Japanese now pressed Laos to declare its "independence" from its former colonial master and to accept Japanese overlordship instead. While all the other Asian rulers complied with the Japanese demand—some with alacrity, others out of opportunism—the King of Laos alone stood up to his captors. He simply stated that independence given under such conditions of duress would be meaningless and that he, for one, preferred to wait until a more stable situation permitted the full renegotiation of the international status of Laos.

The Japanese were understandably angered by this unheard-of show of resistance on the part of men from so tiny and powerless a country. Having in the meantime found in Vientiane a group of Laotian nationalists, the *Lao-Issara* ("Free Laos") under Laotian viceroy Phetsarath willing to collaborate with them, the Japanese now resorted to direct pressure to bring the Laotian monarch into line. When the Japanese took Crown Prince Savang Vathana—since 1959 the King of Laos—into custody and transported him to Saigon, it became obvious that further resistance on the part of the Laotian monarch would be useless and would only lead to bloodshed. On April 8, 1945, King Sisavang Vong formally proclaimed the "independence" of Laos under Japanese control. But the doom of the Empire of the Rising Sun was not far away; with its once-mighty fleet pounded to bits by American aircraft carriers and its arrogant armies cornered in hundreds of cut-off islands and jungle hideouts under the relentless pressure of Allied ground forces, Japan's occupation of Laos was at best symbolical. A Japanese "Supreme Adviser" installed himself with a small staff at the Laotian royal court of Luang Prabang while another Japanese staff, apparently unmindful of the theoretical independence of the Lao kingdom, took over the duties of the former French colonial administration in Vientiane. The only change that occurred was that the Japanese, feeling perhaps that Vientiane was too far removed from a good evacuation route, soon transferred the administration to the southern city of Thakhek.

When VJ-Day came on August 15, 1945, the Japanese "Supreme Adviser" and the occupation staff at Thakhek lost no time in retreating into Thailand as fast as they could, pursued and harassed by the Lao-French guerrillas now supported by joint British-French special operations teams of "Force 136." The fact that, according to the agreements made between the major allies at Potsdam, all of Laos and Viet-Nam north of the 16th parallel was to be occupied by the Chinese Nationalists while the areas to the south were to be occupied by the British might have had something to do with the hasty departure of the Japanese: After all, it was likely that the Britons of the 20th Indian Division were more conversant with the terms of the Geneva Convention on Prisoners of War than the Chinese troops of the 93rd Division who now began to wind their way slowly into the valleys and towns of northern Laos.

The Struggle for Control

In the meantime, the fate of Laos had taken another turn eight thousand miles from Vientiane. On March 24, 1945, General Charles de Gaulle, then first President of the provisional government of the French Republic, issued a declaration on the future of French relations with her colonies. He expressly laid down a policy of self-government, which, unfortunately, he was able to implement only when he was called again to power in 1958, after eight years of fighting in Indo-China and four years of fighting in Algeria. The declaration of March 24 offered Indo-China a federation of states of which Laos was to be one component member out of five (the others being Cambodia, and the three regions of Viet-Nam). While the De Gaulle declaration certainly represented a step forward over the old colonial regime, it fell far short of the "full independence" which the Japanese had granted those states—at least on paper.

What happened next in Laos was a scene of utter political confusion of the kind that was to become peculiar to the mores of this unfortunate country during its stormy history since World War II. On August 18, 1945, the viceroy, Prince Phetsarath, acting as Prime Minister of the royal government, announced that the independence granted under Japanese rule would be considered as legal regardless of the Japanese defeat, and that it applied to the provinces of Laos which heretofore had been under direct French control as well as to the kingdom of Luang Prabang. He also announced at the same time the creation of a committee of Lao-Issara as the initial nucleus of a Laotian political party. Among the key members of that committee were his brother Prince Souvannaphouma and his half brother Prince Souphanouvong, as well as other Lao politicians and members of the civil service. While this was going on in Vientiane, the King himself issued a declaration on August 30, 1945, addressed to General de Gaulle in which he reaffirmed the fidelity of Laos to its earlier engagements, thus in fact disavowing all changes made under Japanese pressure. The Lao-Issara in Vientiane also was of a divided mind: Some of its members were resolutely anti-French; others felt that the best chance for Laos' survival under the circumstances lay in gradual evolution toward independence; still others, in the face of Chinese depredations and the prospect of indefinite Chinese presence, felt that the rapid return of French control was the least harmful solution—at least for the time being. The provisional government in Vientiane also confirmed the merger between the kingdom of Luang Prabang and the remaining provinces in the south to form the unified kingdom of Laos as of September 15, 1945.

In the meantime, the clash of wills between Prince Phetsarath and the King of Laos came to a head. As French troops began to land in some force in Saigon and small but well armed and highly trained French paratroop teams were dropped on many points in Laos, the King felt that his policy of maintaining good relations with the French was more justified than that of the provisional government in Vientiane which, as turned out to be the case, would involve the country in armed clashes. But the enthusiasm of the young Laotian elite in Vientiane was not to be dimmed by such practical considerations; when the King as a last resort dismissed Phetsarath on October 10, 1945, from his position as both viceroy and Prime Minister, a "People's Committee" in Vientiane formed a provisional constituent assembly and, having installed a new government on October 12, pronounced Sisavang Vong's dismissal from the throne on October 20, 1945. In fact, the King was imprisoned in his own palace for a few days.

The new provisional Laotian government, headed by an old civil servant, Khammao, as Prime Minister, represented a sweeping coalition from the left to the right. However, the key posts of foreign affairs, defense, and the command of the armed forces were in the hands of young Prince Souphanouvong, already known for his left-wing views. The other brother of Prince Phetsarath, Prince Souvannaphouma, became minister of public works in the new revolutionary government. The minister of finance was a man of humble origins who seemed quite out of place among all these aristocratic northern Laotian revolutionaries; his father had owned a "bistro" in Paksé in southern Laos and his mother in fact was a member of one of the mountain tribes whom the lowland Laotians so greatly despise. His name was Katay Don Sasorith and he was to play an important role in Laotian politics until his death in 1959 at the age of fifty-five. Finally, the post of minister of education went to a man who was then Laos' only bachelor of letters, Thao Nhouy Abhay.

The King was now faced with the *fait accompli* of a new government in Vientiane. Although he was backed by a small French paratroop force under Major Fabre and Colonel Imfeld, it was obvious, however, that a civil war between the King and his partisans and the Vientiane authorities would be to the advantage of no one. Here, as fifteen years later, we find the makings of a typical Laotian crisis: The King neutralized in his own northern capital; a government in Vientiane claiming popular support but with no effective authority beyond the immediate surroundings of the town; and finally a foreign-backed force slowly marching up the Mekong valley from the south. In 1945, those forces were French and Laotian; in 1960 they were to be Laotian, but with American support.

The solution that was finally hit upon by the Laotians also was typical in its spirit of seeking to reconcile the almost implacable extremes. The King signed a declaration in which he accepted the authority of the newly constituted government in Vientiane and in which he affirmed not to have made any diplomatic agreements with French representatives invalidating the declaration of independence of April 8, 1945. The Laotian government in Vientiane professed to be satisfied with this declaration and, uncomfortable about having deposed the King, petitioned him to reascend to the throne of Laos. The negotiations that went on to achieve this were as drawn-out and laborious as those which were designed to achieve a neutral Laos in 1961–62. Personal emissaries and couriers traveled to and fro between Luang Prabang and Vientiane; politicians changed their opinions from day to day on the basis of rumors and tempting counteroffers; while at the same time the news of the progressing French and Laotian troops added an element of panic to the whole proceedings. Finally, Sisavang Vong was crowned once more King of Laos on April 23, 1946.

While the coronation ceremonies were going on with pomp and circumstance at Luang Prabang, some of Prince Souphanouvong's ill-trained guerrilla forces were making their last stand against the battle-hardened French paratroops in the Mekong valley. The tide had turned in favor of the French this time, for on March 6, 1946, Ho Chi Minh's rebel government in neighboring Viet-Nam had signed a preliminary accord with the French which now enabled them to throw more troops into the reconquest of Laos. Thus when Prince Souphanouvong's Laotians attempted to block the French advance at Thakhek, they were soon swept away by the superiority of French fire power. According to Communist sources,[4] Souphanouvong personally commanded his troops and was severely wounded during the battle. Another brief last-ditch fight took place at the outskirts of Vientiane itself—again a prefiguration of events to come in 1960—but the French entered Vientiane exactly one day after the coronation of King Sisavang Vong in Luang Prabang, on April 24, 1946. The Lao-Issara government of Premier Khammao hastily withdrew across the Mekong River into neighboring Thailand and set up shop as a government-in-exile in Bangkok. On May 13, 1946, the French forces from Vientiane linked up with the small paratroop forces in the north and within a few months, France was again in full control of all of Laos.

However, the clocks of time had not stopped. Although the King, by an ordinance of May 13, immediately declared as null and void all documents he had been made to sign under duress, he did not intend to assume once more the role of figurehead monarch of merely one province of Laos. In a letter addressed on May 15 to the French High Commissioner in Saigon, the King stated that it was the desire of the people of Laos that the country become a constitutional monarchy as soon as possible. Furthermore, the King requested that his country be given effective economic and administrative aid so that Laotians could be rapidly trained to take over responsible positions in the affairs of their own country.[5] The French High Commissioner, Admiral d'Argenlieu, agreed with surprising alacrity, and a joint commission of French and Laotian experts soon began to meet in order to draft an agreement defining the new relationships between Laos and her former colonial protector. Here again with surprising speed (and contrary to what was happening at the same time in Viet-Nam, where parallel negotiations had become bogged down in mutual refusals to compromise) the joint commission produced on August 27, 1946, a provisional *modus vivendi* which substantially confirmed all the demands made by the King. One thorny issue in the *modus vivendi* negotiation proved to be the status of Prince Boun Oum of Champassak. As will be recalled, Boun Oum had loyally and bravely fought with the French against the Japanese during the last months of World War II, and he was the rightful heir to the crown of this southernmost of Laos' three former kingdoms. At first the French sought to leave open a possibility for the kingdom of Champassak to maintain its own national identity with a Lao state, while the Laotian delegates maintained that nothing less than full unification of Laos would be satisfactory under the circumstances and would be likely to match the program of the Lao-Issara government-in-exile.

The matter was finally settled in a compromise: in a secret protocol to the *modus vivendi*, Prince Boun Oum permanently renounced the throne of the kingdom of Champassak and merged the latter permanently with the Lao state. In exchange for the sacrifice, Boun Oum was fully confirmed in his rank as a prince (*tiao*), and made Inspector General of the kingdom for life, and his heirs were in fact assured of continuing rule over the southernmost provinces. Thanks to the sacrifice of Boun Oum, the unity of Laos was saved—or, at least, some real differences were temporarily plastered over, although they were to come to the fore again later, in 1960–61, when Boun Oum was Prime Minister of Laos.

Constitutional Government

The first elections in Laotian history took place on December 15, 1946. All male Laotians over eighteen went to the polls and elected a Constituent Assembly which, with the help of some French legal advisers, now faced the job of having to draft a Laotian constitution. Yet even this first faltering step on the road to democracy was not to take place without sacrifices. While they journeyed to the opening meeting of the Constituent Assembly which took place on March 15, 1947, three of the legislators from the southern provinces and a French adviser traveling with them were ambushed by Lao-Issara rebels north of Thakhek. Captured alive by the rebels, two of the Laotians and the Frenchman were later found murdered, but the third Laotian representative, left for dead, later recovered from his wounds. It is under those somber auspices that the remaining thirty-five legislators began their job at Vientiane.

Many members of the Constituent Assembly were new to politics, although most of them, in order to be eligible at all for their job, had either worked in the Laotian civil service or had been school teachers. The work proceeded swiftly and on May 6, 1947, the Assembly could report that it had terminated its duties and that the new constitution was ready to be submitted to the King for approval. In their enthusiasm over a job well done, the young Laotian legislators sent a telegram to the French National Assembly in Paris which contained the following passage:

> Proud of the association of their country with the great French nation but conscious of their inexperience, the elected Representatives of the Lao people expect in confidence that the French National Assembly will show them the way toward a future of prosperity, order, and peace.

Considering the fact that this same French National Assembly, dominated by the largest Communist parliamentary faction in the Western world, had barely managed to ratify its own constitution a few months before and had precipitated a first-class government crisis over the Indo-China budget on May 4, 1947, the telegram contained an unintended irony. On May 10, the government and the Constituent Assembly met in solemn session in which the constitution was officially presented to the world. Here also, words were said which, in view of later events, were to have an ironic twist. Congratulating the Laotians for their new constitution, the French Commissioner of the Republic in Laos, Monsieur de Reymond (who was later murdered in neighboring Cambodia by the Communists), said to the assembled Laotian dignitaries, "We love Laos like a French province, like another Algeria. . . ."[6]

When on the following day, May 11, 1947, the King officially promulgated the document, Laos, at the stroke of a pen, became a constitutional monarchy. The constitution itself was fairly brief, providing for the essential democratic freedoms and a bicameral legislature, and for a cabinet and prime minister chosen from among the legislators and responsible to the National Assembly. It was to be amended several times in the course of the following years, as the international status of Laos changed. While, for example, the 1947 constitution referred to Laos as an "autonomous state within the French Union," a later amendment substituted the word "independent" for "autonomous"; and yet a later amendment eliminated altogether any reference to special ties with France. Universal suffrage was introduced in 1955, and in July 1961, a section dealing with the powers of the King was amended to allow him to assume the reins of government in case of an emergency situation.

The Exiles

In the meantime, however, the Lao-Issara exiled in Bangkok started squabbling among themselves. Prince Khammao, the erstwhile Prime Minister, relinquished his powers again to the ambitious Prince Phetsarath, who now liked to refer to himself as the "Regent" of the kingdom. Nhouy Abhay, the able minister of education, had not even waited that long and already had returned to Vientiane as early as August 1946. Phetsarath's brothers, the Princes Souvannaphouma and Souphanouvong, remained with him in Bangkok but politically drifted farther and farther apart. Already endowed with strong left-wing leanings, Souphanouvong had made a trip to Hanoi in July 1946 and had been impressed with what he saw. In a meeting with the Viet-Minh leader Ho Chi Minh, Souphanou-vong was said to have asked for advice as to what to do next. Ho Chi Minh's answer had been simple and to the point: "Seize power from the colonialists."

Souphanouvong meant to do precisely that. He and his aides now began to make a thorough analysis of the situation in Laos and quickly came to a decision which was to ensure their eventual success, just as it had ensured success of their Viet-Minh neighbors in Viet-Nam: They began to make fullest possible use of the warlike tendencies of the minority moun-tain tribes. Within a short time there were Lao-Issara bases among the primitive Alakh tribes of the Bolovens Plateau, followed by other bases in Khammouane province, and particularly among the T'ai and Méo of northeastern Laos. A decision apparently was made by the Communist leadership in both Laos and Viet-Nam that the revolution, in order to be successful, had to be based *not* on the fence-sitting intellectuals of the cities or the corrupt bureaucracy, regardless of the fact that both groups contained the largest number of educated leaders of the mountain areas in which the rebels had to take refuge in order to escape the attacks of the French. At first, Souphanouvong's attempt to set up strong anti-French fighting forces did not meet with particular success. This was due to the fact that, as a Laotian lowlander and a prince, he inspired little if any confidence in the mountaineers. Also, no outside aid whatever was avail-able except what few weapons could be bought for extremely high prices in Bangkok; and, moreover, the policies undertaken by the new royal government in Vientiane truly met with the aspirations of the large major-ity of the people. The policy of "gentle firmness" which was to become the hallmark of Laotian foreign relations (particularly those with the former colonial power) began to pay off and the French, heavily engaged in fighting in Viet-Nam, were willing to meet Laos at least halfway in its demands for a larger measure of self-government. The fact that the French had also been able, in their peace treaty with Thailand, to regain for Laos the two provinces which the Thai had grabbed in 1941, also contributed to their relative popularity. In other words, for once, time was on the side of the non-Communists, and Souphanouvong knew it.

A brief offensive launched by Lao-Issara partisans under his command against French posts in Laos met with complete failure. This further de-moralized the Lao-Issara in Bangkok because it seemed to prove to them that they were now losing whatever popular following they may have had before. Again like a tragic prefiguration of things to come, the Lao leadership broke into three factions, each headed by one of the three princely brothers. Phetsarath still held to his idea of a Laotian "Royal" government under his rule, but was now willing to consider a Laotian republic, if necessary. Souphanouvong, after the failure of his own go-it-alone military action became patent, was willing to merge his own partisans with those of the Communist Viet-Minh across the mountains in Viet-Nam; while the moderate Souvannaphouma believed, now more than ever, that Laos could become a fully independent state only by continuing negotiations with the French. Souphanouvong decided to bring the dissensions within the Lao-Issara out into the open since he alone among the three brothers could count upon a certain following beyond that of the small clique of Laotian politicians in Bangkok, for between 1946 and 1947 close to 60,000 Communist-led Vietnamese refugees from the Mekong valley had settled down in northeastern Thailand in order to escape from the advancing French. Those refugees, settled in compact villages from Nongkhai opposite Vientiane in the north to Ubon in the south, constituted a real force to be reckoned with—as the Thai were to find out later on when, tired of being the unwilling hosts to a Communist subversive movement, they tried to get rid of them.[7]

Soon leaflets began to circulate among the Laotian exiles in Thailand intimating that Prince Phetsarath had made a deal with the French. While this, of course, was not true, it had happened sufficiently often in Bangkok among other Laotian exiles to be considered at least possible. The result was that the split between the moderates and extremists widened ever more. For the time being, however, Phetsarath and Khammao prevailed, and Souphanouvong, not yet expelled from the Lao-Issara regime, was gradually frozen out. When it became apparent that the Laotian government in Vientiane was heading toward a meaningful independence, the bulk of the émigrés in Bangkok decided to return to Vientiane to share in the proceeds as well as in the glory of effectively governing a country instead of weaving petty intrigues in the teahouses of Bangkok. Time now was short, for events moved swiftly in Vientiane. King Sisavang Vong and Vincent Auriol, the President of the French Republic, exchanged letters on November 25, 1947, and on January 14, 1948, which in the United States would be tantamount to executive agreements. Those letters provided for the establishment of a Laotian-French convention in which Laos' full independence would be confirmed by the French in exchange for which Laos would agree to remain within the French Union.

On July 19, 1949, the "General Franco-Laotian Convention" was signed in Paris. Its first paragraph contains these fateful words: "The French Republic recognizes the Kingdom of Laos as an independent state." The great moment had come at last.

"Pathet Lao"—Round One

With this new state of events,[8] most of the Lao-Issara in Bangkok were now rebels without a cause; it but remained for them to find a face-saving way of disappearing into history. This way was finally found through a great deal of wisdom—a quality that seems to be found more abundantly among the Lao than among their non-Asian advisers. On September 30, 1949, the Royal Laotian Government in Vientiane sent a letter to Prince Souvannaphouma (whose destiny, as will be seen, seems to be that of being an intermediary between irreconcilable extremes) in which it promised full amnesty to the exiled leaders whose return would take place in "friendship, honor, confidence, and total security." The French authorities in Indo-China addressed a similar letter to the Bangkok exiles on October 6, 1949.

On October 24, 1949, the "Provisional Government of Free Laos" held its last meeting in Bangkok. In a document almost unique in its formality, considering the fact that the Lao-Issara "government" had never represented much more than its own membership, the Lao-Issara group declared its dissolution to be effective as of October 25, 1949. It also dissolved all its armed forces and other paramilitary organizations, whose members were now left free to join the Royal Laotian Army, the French Army, or the Laotian gendarmery. All this, of course, did not apply to Prince Souphanouvong who already had been expelled from the Lao-Issara on May 16, 1949, and who in the meantime had succeeded in crossing all of Laos and much of North Viet-Nam in order to join Ho Chi Minh in his struggle against the French.[9] From now on, shorn of its nationalist pretenses, the pro-Communist rebel movement had to "go it alone."

On August 13, 1950, Souphanouvong convened a congress of hardcore rebel leaders—not in Laos or in his former host country, Thailand, but at Ho Chi Minh's own mountain hideout of Tuyên-Quang in North Viet-Nam. Among the leaders present were Phai-Dang (Faydang), a leader of the Méo tribesmen; Sithone Komadone, representing the Kha tribes, and Nouhak Phoumsavan. The new congress, with the obvious encouragement of Ho Chi Minh, proceeded to "elect" a new "resistance

government" of the Pathet Lao (State of Laos). Souphanouvong was, of
course, chosen as "prime minister" of the new regime. At the same time
it was agreed to create a new political arm to supplement the propaganda
effort of the new movement; this new movement took the name of the
Neo Lao Issala ("Free Laos Front") which was created at a special meeting in November 1950. The program of the new regime was exceptionally
simple: equality of all races in Laos; a united fight against the French;
abolition of all unjust taxes.

With the formation of the Pathet Lao regime, all pretenses of loyalty
to the King of Laos were swept away. The Pathet Lao adopted its own
flag—red-blue-red horizontal bars with a white disk in the blue field, curiously resembling the North Korean Communist flag—and soon the Pathet
Lao received from their Communist Vietnamese masters their first issue
of quilted jackets and dark green uniforms, along with modern rifles and
submachine guns. Thus far, nevertheless, Souphanouvong's rebellion still
qualified, in spite of its outside Vietnamese support, as an indigenous
Laotian movement, but this was not to be for long.

A few months later, the Viet-Minh convened a meeting at a secret place
in North Viet-Nam between the leader of the "Vietnamese United Front"
[*Liên-Viêt*] and the leaders of similar Communist front movements in
Cambodia and Laos. Communist sources[10] have left us with a photograph
of this solemn occasion: Ton Duc Thang (a Vietnamese old-line Communist ever since he tried to stage a mutiny aboard a French cruiser in
1919 in order to turn it over to the Soviet revolutionaries in the Black Sea,
and since 1960 Vice President of the North Vietnamese Republic) sat in
the presiding chair, flanked on his left by Sieu Heng, the head of the "Cambodian National Liberation Committee," and on his right by Souphanouvong. The purpose of the meeting was clear from the beginning; it was to
provide for an ideologically justifiable basis for the invasion of the two
small countries by the Vietnamese, their historical enemies. After one
week of negotiation, the common strategy had been developed.

Here again, it is a Communist source[11] which gives the best picture of
what was to come:

> It was decided to set up a Vietnam-Khmer-Lao alliance which called
> on the people of the three countries to coordinate their fight to defeat the
> colonialists. It was on the basis of these decisions, published on March 11,
> 1951, that the Vietnamese volunteers later entered Cambodia and Laos to
> fight side by side with the Khmer Issarak forces and the Pathet Lao. . . .
>   As it had done in Cambodia, the creation of the Viet-Khmer-Lao alliance

in March 1951, paved the way for Vietnamese volunteers to help in the struggle. The latter were greatly reinforced by local Vietnamese. . . .

The March 11, 1951, agreement between the Pathet Lao and the North Vietnamese Communists must be regarded as a vital step in the recent history of Laos, for it paved the way for the initial invasion of that peaceful country by North Vietnamese Communist forces. For a whole year following the adoption of the agreement, the Viet-Minh and its Pathet Lao allies concentrated upon organizing guerrilla bases throughout the country. There is a great deal of evidence, in fact, that the Viet-Minh did not overly trust their new-found ally for much of the organization work was done by Vietnamese residing in Laos. Also, the newly created Pathet Lao fighting units were heavily interspersed with Vietnamese "advisers"— a practice which seems to have remained in effect to this day. In terms of administrative organization, the Viet-Minh treated Pathet Lao territory merely as an extension of its own; Laos was divided into three operational zones (North, Center, and South), each of which was subordinate to its neighboring Viet-Minh "Inter-zone" [Liên-Khu], thus ensuring full coordination of all operations between the two countries.

The Communist onslaught was not too long in coming. On October 11, 1952, Communist General Vo Nguyên Giap smashed with three battle-hardened infantry divisions the ill-defended French outposts of the T'ai hill country covering the Laotian border, bypassing the hastily thrown-up French fortress at Na-San and continuing his victorious and almost unchecked sweep across the wide empty spaces of the mountainous north. On November 30, 1952, Dien Bien Phu, then defended by a small Royal Laotian Army unit, fell for the first time into Communist hands. On Christmas Day, 1952, Vietnamese Communist forces supported by the Pathet Lao were poised at the Laotian border. After but the briefest spell of both peace and freedom, the small kingdom now had to face the realities of invasion and war.

IV

The Road to Geneva

━━━━━━━◄◆►━━━━━━━

The Invasion

What happened then in Laos is something which no historian, with the
exception of a few French military specialists,[1] has thus far openly acknowledged:* What the small Laotian and French forces in Laos faced at
the beginning of 1953 was not simply a rabble of unorganized local guerrillas but a full-fledged, well-organized and well-armed *invading army*
barely smaller than the Japanese forces which in 1942 invaded Burma! Lest
anyone think this to be a figment of journalistic imagination, he would
do well to refer to the United States Army's official history of "Merrill's
Marauders:"

> Before the conquest of Burma the Japanese had concentrated two divisions
> in southern Thailand. . . . Rangoon, the capital and principal port, was
> taken on 8 March [1942]. The Japanese then turned north in two columns.
> . . . A third enemy column of two divisions . . . landed on Rangoon on
> 12 April 1942. . . . When the monsoon rains came in June the Japanese
> held all of Burma except for fringes of mountain, jungle and swamp on
> the north and west.[2]

* *Editor's Note:* The appearance in 1964 of Arthur Dommen's *Conflict in Laos, The
Politics of Neutralization* (New York: Praeger) filled this lacuna. See pp. 40 *et sqq.*

The same thing exactly now happened to the Franco-Laotian forces. Since its modest beginnings in 1943, the Royal Laotian Army had grown into a military force of about 10,000 men. The Laotian Military Academy had been set up by the French at Dong-Hene, and Laotian officers who had served in other French units were transferred to the young but as yet untried army. French troops in Laos under Colonel Boucher de Crèvecoeur numbered perhaps 3000 and consisted mostly of such specialized units as transport and signal companies, artillery, and armor. There also existed a small Laotian river patrol squadron equipped with armored reconnaissance craft to "show the flag" on Laos' main rivers.

This small force, at best geared to maintain law and order in peacetime or at most capable of keeping a few rebel bands or pirates in check, now was faced with the full might of General Vo Nguyên Giap's 304th, 308th, 312th, and 316th Infantry Divisions, reinforced by at least 2000 Pathet Lao rebels under Prince Souphanouvong. Each division of the "Viet-Nam People's Army" numbered 10,000 combatants and carried with itself a strong complement of heavy mortars and recoilless cannon. In order to make this force completely jungle-going and almost totally impervious to French air attacks, each division was followed—and in many cases, preceded—by a 15,000-man force of civilian porters who carried its ammunition and supplies.

The Viet-Minh had devised a very ingenious system of having combat troops preceded by porter columns which would infiltrate stealthily into villages along the main invasion route and would force the population to prepare food and supply caches for the troops. The villagers then would be threatened into complete silence (very often the Viet-Minh or their local sympathizers would stay behind to see the secret would be kept) so that the advancing Communist troops could push forward at full speed without being hampered by a sudden interruption of their supply lines. This daring method of supplying combat troops proved eminently successful many times and accounted for the lightninglike speed with which Communist troops could advance or retreat. As will be seen later, however, this method could on occasion also backfire on the Communists.

General Giap's battle plan was deceptively simple: While the bulk of the 316th Division advanced on a wide arc over the top of northern Indo-China into the Nam-Hou valley in order to strike against the royal capital of Luang Prabang, the main force composed of the 308th and 312th Divisions was to strike directly against the main French and Laotian positions and attempt to conquer the vital Plaine des Jarres with its airfields and

Laos
1953-54

⟹ Viet-Minh offensives
▶ Franco-Lao offensives
░ Viet-Minh held territory, 1954
∴ Major Viet-Minh guerrilla
  territory

CHINA

BURMA

Phong Saly

Dien Bien Phu

1953

Nam
Tha

B. Houei Sai

1954

1954

Sam-Neua

1953

Luang
Prabang

1953

1954

1953

Xieng-
Khouang

Vang Vieng

Tha-Thom

Paksane

Kam Kheut

MEKONG

R.N.13

VIENTIANE

RIVER

M. Nhommarat

1953

Thakhek

1953-54

1953

Séno

M.Phalane Tchépone

Savannakhet

Dong-
Hene

M.Phine

VIET-NAM

Saravane

1954

Pakseng Attopeu

THAILAND

CAMBODIA

crossroads, thus directly threatening Vientiane, while the 304th Division would penetrate deeply into central Laos and seek to reach the Mekong.

The French, although forewarned of the impending offensive, simply could not spare any additional troops for the defense of northern Laos. Fortunately for them, however, the Méo mountain tribes, led by Touby Lyfoung, were largely favorable to the French and could be counted on to warn them of the advance of Communist forces. By the beginning of April 1953, the French High Command decided to withdraw the most exposed border posts in the hope of being able to save the bulk of its troops from piecemeal annihilation until additional reinforcements could be airlifted in from the quieter sectors of Viet-Nam and Cambodia. It is under such trying circumstances that the young Royal Laotian Army had to meet its first trial by fire.

Much was said in 1960–61 about the "lack of combativity" of the Laotian soldier—at least of those on the non-Communist side—and many easy explanations were forthcoming on the subject, such as the moral principles of non-violence of their Buddhist religion, and other fairy tales. The hard fact is that throughout history, the Buddhist countries fought just as many and as bloody wars as the non-Buddhist countries, and that Buddhist troops will fight as well as any other, providing that they are well led. The Laotian troops who were engaged in heavy and desperate fighting against great odds during the 1953 campaign proved this in full. In the northern sector, the post of Muong-Khoua was given on April 13, 1953, the mission to delay the advance of the Communist 316th Division for at least fourteen days. The post was held by a regular Laotian infantry battalion under a French captain. Not only did the battalion fulfill its mission, but instead of the fourteen days it was expected to hold out in order to buy time for a French defensive build-up further down in the valley around Luang Prabang, it held out *thirty-six* days and literally fought to the last man. When the post was finally pounded to bits by Communist artillery, there were exactly three known survivors.[3]

In the central sector, the city of Sam-Neua, capital of Laos' easternmost province jutting deeply into North Vietnamese territory, was garrisoned by three battalions largely composed of Laotian troops. One has to have landed (as this writer repeatedly has) on the short dog-leg-shaped airstrip of that post, surrounded by steep hills on all sides, to realize how indefensible it is against any determined attack. This was equally obvious to the French, who on April 12, at 1600, ordered the garrison of Sam-Neua to pull out in a forced march after having abandoned and destroyed all its heavy equipment. The operation involved a 110-mile dash across territory that already was largely held by Communist advance units, using secondary trails and crossing a mountain chain whose passes reached altitudes of 6600 feet. Also involved was the fording of at least thirty rivers, many of which were already swelling under the impact of the beginning monsoon season. Furthermore, the column was slowed down by the many casualties from previous engagements which it carried on stretchers and muleback. Here again, a comparison exists between the Viet-Minh offensive in Laos and the Japanese conquest of Burma: While the former involved less troops, the conditions which the retreating Lao-French column from Sam-Neua faced were in every way similar to those encountered by General Stilwell as he withdrew from Burma into India with the battered survivors of his Sino-American forces.

After marching all night of April 12 with 5th Company of the First Lao Infantry Battalion in the lead, the column fell into the first Communist ambush, laid at Muong-Peun, about twenty miles to the southwest of Sam-Neua. The attack came with the usual ferocity and suddenness that was the hallmark of the well-laid Viet-Minh trap and within a few minutes the whole column of 2400 men was engulfed in a desperate hand-to-hand battle with the 3000 regulars of Regiment 98 of the 316th Viet-Nam People's Army Division, supported by renegade Méo tribesmen and some Pathet Lao elements. In spite of heavy losses, the Laotians held on grimly, charging repeatedly into the nearby hills to clear out machine-gun nests covering the path, and finally fought their way out at bayonet's point.

The following night, they bivouacked at Hua-Muong, an almost mesa-like high plateau (which, after it had later been provided with an airstrip, was promptly dubbed "the Aircraft Carrier" by the French pilots who had to attempt the perilous landings and take-offs from it) fifteen miles down the road. The trek started anew at 0400 of April 15, 1953, and again the Viet-Minh, unburdened by supplies and wounded, were ready for the Sam-Neua force. As it entered the village of Muong Lap, it was literally blanketed by withering machine gun and mortar fire—and this time there was no way out except straight into the muzzles of the enemy guns. Although French "Bearcat" fighter-bombers were on hand to keep the Viet-Minh down with their rockets and guns (whose effect in a thick canopy of jungle was, of course, minimal), only battered remnants of the Lao-French force succeeded in breaking out of the trap. On April 26, exactly fourteen days after the column's departure from Sam-Neua, a company of about one hundred eighty Laotians and one French and two Laotian officers entered the French defense perimeter of the Plaine des Jarres. Many of them no longer had any shoes and their uniforms were torn to tatters, but they still had their weapons, their radio sets, and their pack animals. They, along with a few scattered survivors picked up later by Méo guerrillas in the jungle, were what was left of the garrison of Sam-Neua.

The desperate rearguard fights of the border garrisons had nevertheless accomplished their purpose. The advance of the Communist forces had been sufficiently slowed down to permit a vast airlift to converge on the Plaine des Jarres. The Plaine des Jarres, as its name indicates,[4] is a magnificent plateau covered with grass and small hills spread out over almost 500 square miles—"a sort of giant-sized golf course," as a wag once put it. For a long time it had been the center of the small, autonomous kingdom of Xieng-Khouang whose capital was the present-day seat of the provincial government at Xieng-Khouang. In normal times, the Plaine des Jarres was a quiet place, sought after because of its better climate, and supported a modest amount of tea planting and cattle raising.

It also was the major center of activity of the Méo tribes in northern Laos, and every year fairs would take place at Xieng-Khouang at which the hardy mountaineers would sell the opium crop which they had harvested from the poppies whose colorful blossoms dot much of the countryside. (During the more peaceful postwar years, European smugglers came directly from various Southeast Asian cities in their own little planes to buy up the opium produced by the mountaineers, thus cutting out the Chinese middlemen and increasing their already scandalous profits). At the beginning of April 1953, no fortifications whatever existed on the Plaine des Jarres and the existing airfields at Xieng-Khouang and Phong-Savane were little more than two pieces of turf outlined by old gasoline drums. One month later, nine infantry battalions and one artillery battalion had been flown in via an improvised airlift; a completely new airfield covered with pierced steel mats had been hastily laid out amid the huge stone burial jars that had given the Plaine des Jarres its name, and even disassembled tanks and armored cars had been flown in and had been reassembled on the open field by French army mechanics. On the night of April 21 at 2200, the forward elements of two Communist divisions, having overrun the city of Xieng-Khouang twenty miles to the southeast of the fortified camp, began their attack against the Plaine des Jarres.

This time, the French and Laotians were ready. They were facing the enemy on an open field, where the French aircraft and heavy weapons could play at their full advantage. Also, the open field was far too wide to be simply bypassed by the Communists in their intended advance against

Vientiane, and the Franco-Laotian forces were now far too big and aggressive to be left behind without constituting a constant danger to Viet-Minh supply lines. Thus, on May 9, the French were able to launch their counteroffensive against the leading Communist elements. After bitter fighting involving three French paratroop battalions and the 5th Battalion of Laotian *chasseurs,* the French and Laotian forces reoccupied Xieng-Khouang on May 18.

A few days later, the 6th Battalion of the Laotian chasseurs, starting its way north from the Mekong River city of Paksane, succeeded in doing in two weeks what stronger and better-equipped royal Laotian forces could not do in 1961 in four months: It clawed its way north along rain-swept footpaths in the Nam Sane River valley to Tha-Thom in the face of strong Communist resistance and pushed north, in a coordinated pincer movement with French paratroops descending along Road 4 from Xieng-Khouang, just on time to capture an important Communist ammunition and supply depot at Muong Ngam. Thus, on May 31, the Communist thrust against Vientiane had been definitely blunted.

The Communist attack against the royal capital of Luang Prabang was more of a "photo finish." There, the bulk of the 316th Viet-Minh Division, now reinforced by Regiment 98, had successfully destroyed the retreating garrison from Sam-Neua and swept away one by one the string of small Laotian posts covering the Nam-Hou valley in the direction of Luang Prabang. On April 23, 1953, General Salan, then the commander in chief of all French forces in Indo-China, personally came to Luang Prabang to inform the King of Laos that the city would have to be evacuated. The old King looked straight at the French general and said: "The *Phou-Kéo* [Vietnamese] did not succeed in taking Luang Prabang when they attacked us in 1479. Neither will they succeed this time."

In firmly deciding to stand and die in his capital, the old King committed the French to the defense of northern Laos. To be sure, they could have abandoned Luang Prabang and Vientiane and withdrawn to the apparently easier-to-defend narrow waist of the country; this, however, would have made short shrift of the disastrous moral impact the loss of the two capitals would have had upon not only the Laotian population but also upon neighboring Thailand and Cambodia—not to speak of the capture, dead or alive, of the King by the Communists.[5] This *political* decision to defend northern Laos against a Communist invasion was to have far-reaching military consequences: In 1953, it compelled the French to withdraw seven battalions of elite troops from other vital areas in order to provide for an adequate garrison to defend Luang Prabang, and in 1954, it committed the French High Command to the battle of Dien Bien Phu in order to save northern Laos once more. These hard facts were to influence events in Laos for probably decades to come. It is certain that they at least motivated in part the American decision not to fight for Laos in 1960–61.

In Luang Prabang, in the meantime, the arrival of three Foreign Legion battalions, followed by Moroccans and paratroopers, had completely revolutionized the tranquil atmosphere of the sleepy little city. Bulldozers were busy lengthening the airfield while the surrounding hills resounded with the noise of explosions as the Legionnaires dynamited century-old trees to clear the hilltops for blockhouses and bunkers. Even the usually quiescent Laotians pitched in and were seen digging trenches and stringing out barbed wire around the hastily thrown up field fortifications to the northeast of the city. That is, they did so until April 25. On that day, most of the Laotians simply disappeared and soon were seen making purchases usually associated with a Laotian *boun* [holiday]. When the bewildered French sector commander, Major Marlic, questioned the Laotian governor of Luang Prabang why none of the Laotians had shown up for defense work, he received the smiling reply:

"But *mon commandant,* there isn't any further need for fortification. After all, the Blind Bonze already has told us that the Phou-Kéo [Vietnamese] shall not come to take our city. So we are preparing a festivity to thank Buddha for having saved our city once more from invasion."

Indeed, Pho Sathou, the blind bonze who resided at the That Sen pagoda, was known throughout Laos for his supernatural powers and uncanny accuracy of his prophecies. That his prophecies were true down to the smallest detail had been verified by French anthropologists[6] and no Laotian government official in Luang Prabang or Vientiane would have even dreamed of challenging his authority at so critical a time. The hard fact is that Pho Sathou had correctly predicted on April 24, 1953, that the Viet-Minh forces of the 304th Division and of Regiment 98 would be halted and would retreat northward. It was Pho Sathou who again on April 30, after a trance, stated that no Communist troops were on the road to Vientiane, having bypassed the Plaine des Jarres—a fact which French Army intelligence was to confirm a few days later.

Some of the French intelligence officers and American journalists who were familiar with Laos tended to ascribe the supernatural powers of the Blind Bonze (who never left his pagoda) to "subversive" connections with the Communists. That glib explanation, however, fell to pieces one day when he was telling a French anthropologist in front of several witnesses about a French military countermove *while it was being planned in French military headquarters several miles away!* Those are some of the facts of life with which a military planner has to reckon in Laos, even if they do not square with such Western gimmicks as electronic computers and supersonic aircraft.

The Winter Offensive

As the French were to find out much later, the Communist retreat from Luang Prabang in 1953 had been prompted by the accidental destruction of a Communist supply depot by a French unit in the jungle behind the main thrust of the Communist advance. This missing link in the Communist supply train, particularly now that the rainy season had set in for good, compelled the Communists to withdraw. On May 9, the Communist northern pincer was broken and Laos saved from invasion for the first time. The unsuccessful Communist offensive against northern Laos was to be but the prelude to two more onslaughts which were to take place in the winter of 1953–54. The second Communist offensive was led by an artillery battalion which, under the cover of the impenetrable jungle, crossed the Annamite mountain chain from Viet-Nam into Laos, made contact with local Pathet Lao elements and, reinforced by the latter, moved swiftly across the narrow waist of Laos in the direction of the Thai border.

On Christmas Day 1953, avenging their defeat of 1946, Pathet Lao elements aided by Viet-Minh regulars and by Communist Vietnamese from the refugee villages across the river in Thailand, briefly reoccupied Thakhek. Indo-China now indeed was cut in two. Within less than a week, by a series of deep penetrations, the Communists had widened their wedge into a broad belt ranging up to fifty miles to the south of Road 12, the main east-west artery, and were directly threatening Séno, France's major air base in Laos. Again, the sorely tried French had to face several dangers at once: While the defense of Dien Bien Phu was absorbing more and more French troops and that of the Red River Delta required more than 80,000 men, the "second front" created by the Communists in south-central Laos—coupled with the new invasion of northern Laos which was to follow—simply swallowed up whatever French reserves were left in the Indo-China theater.

Within less than a week, General Henri Navarre (who had taken over the command of Indo-China in May 1953 with the promise that he would regain and hold the initiative over the enemy) was compelled to organize yet another airlift. The air base of Séno now became a veritable fortress bristling with tanks and artillery; three motorized French regimental combat teams, Mobile Groups 1, 2, and 51, reinforced by Laotian infantry and the young Laotian cadets from the nearby Royal Laotian Military Academy at Dong-Hene, succeeded in establishing a defensive line along the strategic Road No. 9 leading from Savannakhet to the Vietnamese coast. In a seesaw battle which lasted until February 6, 1954, and in which the French suffered extremely heavy losses, the Communists were finally pushed back to the Vietnamese border only to disappear in the jungle and to reappear one week later 120 miles further south, again sweeping ahead of themselves a string of small Laotian posts, conquering the perpetually rebellious Bolovens Plateau (the home area of the Pathet Lao leader Sithone Komadone) and stabbing deep into the northeastern corner of Cambodia where they laid siege to the town of Voeunesai.

While the Franco-Laotian forces were reeling under the Communist blows in southern Laos, the Laotian northern front had not remained inactive. With three Communist infantry divisions and the famous 351st "Heavy Division" blocking the already-doomed Dien Bien Phu, the Communists decided to disperse the French effort further by throwing a feint against Luang Prabang, leaving two infantry divisions and the heavy mortars and artillery of the 351st Division at Dien Bien Phu. General Giap, on January 27, 1954, threw the three infantry regiments of Division 308, reinforced by units from the 316th Division and Independent Regiment 148, against the weak covering forces of French and Laotian troops which had reoccupied the Nam-Hou valley. Once more the French and Laotian forces of Muong-Khoua had to pay a heavy price: Acting as a rear-guard for the garrisons along the Nam-Hou which were now rapidly falling back toward Muong Sai and Nam Bac, the 2d Battalion of Laotian chasseurs and the 2d Battalion of the 3rd Foreign Legion Regiment were completely destroyed. Their doom, however, once more bought time for Luang Prabang; but once again, northern Laos had been saved at far too heavy a price as yet another French airlift began to ferry four infantry battalions and one paratroop battalion into the threatened Muong Sai sector. By February 20, the Communist high command and its Pathet Lao allies had achieved exactly what they wanted; with the same lightning speed and excellent concealment with which they had come the Communist troops now began to disappear northward again.

But as the Communist regulars disappeared in the direction of the Lao-Vietnamese border, they left behind not only a string of Vietnamese instructors but also a cadre of well-trained Pathet Lao administrators. The conquest of the city of Sam-Neua had, by the way, given the Pathet Lao a "capital" on Laotian soil and the opportunity to set up the beginnings of a regular administrative system. With the exception of a brief interval in 1957–58, that system was to control much of northern Laos and large stretches of the southern Laotian hinterland.

Thus, as the year 1954 dawned, Laos already had suffered two Communist invasions and the Laotian troops had fought, and fought well, side-by-side with their comrades of the French Union Forces on all the battlefronts of their country. What was more important, the French had been able to induce the lowland Laotians to fight in many of the upland areas which they traditionally shunned. In addition, the French had succeeded in creating commando groups of T'ai and Méo mountaineers who gave an excellent account of themselves. Such a Méo stronghold as Ban Pa-Thi in Sam-Neua province—an eagle's nest almost grazing the clouds—defied all Communist assaults until the cease-fire of July 1954, and was finally taken by the Communists only during the fighting in 1959. And then it was taken by renegade Méos fighting for the Pathet Lao.

The last grim task of the Royal Laotian forces during the Indo-China war was to rescue the few survivors of the Dien Bien Phu disaster. When it became obvious that Dien Bien Phu was doomed, the French high command hastily organized a rescue column under Colonel Boucher de Crèvecoeur, an "old Laos hand" who had first been parachuted into the country in 1944 with Britain's "Force 136." Theoretically, the objective of that column was to break through to the embattled garrison itself but it soon became apparent that to do so with the 8000 men which the French high command could spare for this operation (dubbed "Condor") was sheer folly; this was the rainy season and in the valley of Dien Bien Phu there were 50,000 Communist troops. Yet, doggedly, the Laotians and French of Operation Condor clawed their way forward through the mist and rain of the mountain passes of the Nam-Hou with the forlorn hope of at least diverting upon themselves part of the enemy's effort. Fighting off repeated attacks by Pathet Lao and Viet-Minh advance elements, they had come to within thirty miles of the doomed fortress when it fell on May 8,

1954. They were able to rescue seventy-six men of the 16,000 who had fought at Dien Bien Phu.

Thus, contrary to popular belief, the Laotians had not "sat out" the Indo-China war on the sidelines. Of the almost 20,000 men of the Laotian Armed Forces (including those who had enlisted in French Units), almost 3000 died on the battlefield. Uncounted civilians were killed in the seesaw battles of northeastern and southern Laos, and hundreds of Méo partisans were murdered by the Viet-Minh and Pathet Lao because they refused to surrender. This is a war record of which Laos can be rightfully proud. The French, too, had real reason to feel pride: They had kept their word to a small ally.

The royal government had signed a treaty of friendship and association with France on October 22, 1953, in which France promised to come to the help of the small kingdom. The Viet-Minh invasion was the acid test of whether France would be willing to stand by her word when the safety of even a small ally was threatened. The preoccupation with the safety of northern Laos was clearly visible in the telegram sent by General Navarre, the French commander in chief, to the French government after the first landing of French paratroops at Dien Bien Phu on November 20, 1953:

> I have decided a thrust upon Dien Bien Phu, whose reoccupation will cover the approach to Luang Prabang which, without it, would be in grave danger within a few weeks. The operation began this morning at 1030 by the drop of a first wave of two paratroop battalions. . . .

To be sure, the French National Defense Committee had addressed to Navarre on November 13, 1953, a directive in which he had been "invited . . . to adjust his operations to his needs," but the fact remains, however, that Navarre had clearly realized that a total evacuation of northern Laos, including the two capitals, would have had such a demoralizing effect on both Viet-Nam and Cambodia as to make the continuation of the war fairly hopeless. The battle for Laos was, therefore, part of an over-all strategy which could not be readily divorced from the physical and psychological environment of the war. A great part of the disasters in Laos and South Viet-Nam in 1960 and 1961 must be ascribed to the fact that this elemental truth was forgotten.

V

Phony Peace

Showdown at Geneva

The cease-fire negotiations began at Geneva on May 8, 1954, under the worst possible conditions for the West, for on that morning at one o'clock the last remaining French position at Dien Bien Phu had been overrun by the Viet-Minh. Yet it was precisely at Geneva that Laos had its first "coming out" in international politics, as the smallest (in terms of population) interested party. The Laotian delegation, led by Phoui Sananikone (who was to become prime minister of the country during another tragic period) stayed, according to a recent French historian, "most of the time in the shadow of the French delegation for reasons of tactical modesty rather than nonchalance."[1] This tactical modesty did not stop the Laotian delegation from proudly defending its positions when it felt that its essential interests were threatened by the Viet-Minh, which, spurred on by its victories on the battlefield, now sought to have the conference accept delegates from the "Khmer Resistance Government" and the Pathet Lao as legal delegates fully equal to those of the Royal Governments of Cambodia and Laos. In behalf of the Soviet delegation, Foreign Minister Molotov supported the Viet-Minh stand by citing a United States Congressional Report to the effect that Cambodia and Laos were not yet truly independent states.[2]

Finally, however, the Cambodian and Laotian delegations won their point. Phoui Sananikone was particularly forceful in driving home his arguments:

> . . . the situation in Laos and Cambodia cannot be compared with the situation in Viet-Nam; and it is quite simple.
>
> It is different because there is no civil war in Laos and Cambodia; and it is simple because withdrawal of the foreign invading troops would mean *de facto* the cessation of hostilities there. . . .
>
> There are three fundamental points we can make without fear of contradiction even by the most exacting observers if they would agree to go and seek enlightenment on the spot. . . .
>
> First Point. Laos is independent. On October 22, 1953, it signed with France a treaty of independence and association of which M. Molotov and Mr. Dong (Head of the Viet-Minh delegation) appear to be ignorant. . . . We do not think that countries which pride themselves on achieving federal unity amidst a variety of nationalities can fail to recognize that our membership in the French Union merely safeguards and strengthens our independence in a world where absolute autonomy can only lead to the worst forms of enslavement.
>
> Second Point. We maintain that in Laos national sentiment, centered in His Majesty Sisavang Vong, is unanimous to a degree which many countries might envy us. . . .
>
> Third Point. We have said, and we repeat, that the military operations in Laos are the work of Viet-Minh troops, that is to say of troops foreign to the country in race, tradition, and ideology. We maintain that the so-called "free government," which by a gross abuse of language they misterm "the Laos Resistance Government," has been fabricated lock, stock, and barrel by the foreign invaders.[3]

Both Laos and Cambodia were likewise adamant in their refusal to allow "foreign enemy forces" (i.e., Vietnamese Communists) to be permanently regrouped on their soil. While Cambodia was entirely successful, Laos had to pay the price of the deteriorated military situation prevailing at the time of the cease-fire: The two northernmost provinces of Phong Saly and Sam-Neua and a connecting corridor between them remained under Pathet Lao control until a political settlement was reached by the two parties.

Laos still fared considerably better than Viet-Nam with regard to its political and military situation. While the cease-fire agreement for Viet-

Nam specifically prohibited the introduction of certain types of armament (jet aircraft, etc.) and the maintenance of foreign bases, Laos was authorized to retain a 1500-man French training mission along with two French air and land bases and 3500 French troops. One of the bases, Séno in southern Laos, is an all-weather bomber base which was modernized after the cease-fire and reinforced by French armor withdrawn from Viet-Nam in April 1956.

Other articles of the Lao cease-fire agreement included convenient escape clauses. Article 9, for example, prohibited the introduction of "armaments . . . of all kinds" into Laos but exempted from this prohibition a "specified quantity of armament (*not* specified elsewhere) deemed necessary for the defense of Laos."[4] Likewise, the promise made by Laos and Cambodia in the Final Declaration of the conference not to join military alliances was conveniently qualified by the proviso "so long as their security is not threatened."[5] Lastly, an International Commission for Supervision and Control (better known as "ICC"), composed of Polish, Canadian, and Indian members and chaired by the Indian, was to supervise the execution of the cease-fire provisions.

Interestingly enough, some of the "break-throughs" which permitted a settlement of the Pathet Lao problem at the conference were made by none other than the Communist Chinese Foreign Minister, Chou En-lai. The Vietnamese agreements had, of course, been those which had been given absolute priority over all the others. Thus, when July 19, 1954, dawned—July 20 was the deadline which French Prime Minister Pierre Mendès-France had set to negotiate an accord or to break off the conference and resume the war—the first draft of the Laotian and Cambodian cease-fire agreements had not even been put on paper. It was then that Chou En-lai succeeded in persuading the Viet-Minh to yield on its demand that Laos, like Viet-Nam, abandon a permanent occupation zone to the Pathet Lao forces.[6] When the Vietnamese accords were finally hammered out on July 20, at 5:15 P.M., only the first draft of the Laotian and Cambodian agreements had been written and not even their preliminary approval had been secured from the interested parties.

It is then that there occurred an incident which will for the present remain almost unique in the annals of East-West diplomacy: A small country stood up to the Soviet Union. With the Vietnamese treaty already duly signed, Cambodia was presented in turn with its treaty whose terms had been hammered out by diplomats representing the Big Powers.

To everyone's surprise the Cambodian delegate simply rebelled at the terms which made his country a helpless pawn in the hands of the Big Powers: Total neutralization without any explicit rights to request outside military help in the case of aggression. These terms, while negotiated politically, were part of the *military* aspects of the cease-fire; thus, in the case of Laos and Viet-Nam where the French still held over-all military command, the signature of France alone was required. In the case of Cambodia, which had obtained control over its own armed forces from the French in October 1953, the signature of the Cambodian delegate was absolutely necessary.[7] And the Cambodians refused to be budged.

It was way past midnight in the Palais des Nations and, theoretically, the French Prime Minister already had lost his "bet"—had it not been for a small parliamentary trick which the French legislature uses regularly when it must, according to statute, pass the budget before the clock strikes midnight on December 31 preceding the new fiscal year: The engineer of the Palais des Nations in Geneva had simply stopped all the electric clocks one minute before midnight. Finally, at 3:43 A.M. of July 21, 1954, the man who next to the late Vishinski best personified the Soviet Union's negative approach in international affairs, relented and allowed Cambodia, in a magnificent piece of diplomatic double-talk, to appeal for outside aid or even have foreign bases, "should its security be threatened."

Having made this, by Soviet standards, momentous concession, Molotov looked questioningly at his Western counterparts and said:

"Well, I hope that everybody is satisfied now?"

But the French Prime Minister apparently was not entirely satisfied, for, in the manner of a polite student in an advanced seminar, he raised his hand:

"I would like to add something, if I may."

"Well? What now?" (It was very obvious that Molotov was getting both tired and irritated).

"Well, don't you think that what has been granted to Cambodia could also be granted to Laos? This would be a matter of simple equity—"

With a loud bang, Molotov's fist crashed down on the table. His little eyes glinted behind the steel-rimmed *pince-nez*. The Frenchmen and Cambodians present shuddered at the thought that Premier Mendès-France's last phrase, uttered as an afterthought and almost in jest, had been the "straw that broke the camel's back." Molotov was going to sulk or explode in one of his feared cold rages and stomp out. The conference would be wrecked at the last moment when all the major issues had already been settled and when the whole world was waiting to hear the good news that

—for a very short time, at least—there would be no hostilities anywhere in the world.

But Molotov suddenly relaxed. A frown of exasperation replaced the scowl of annoyance on his face as he conceded:

"Khorosho, i dlya Laosa tozhe." ["All right, for Laos also."]

Laos was saved from partition and authorized to retain two French bases. The Laotian delegation did not know it until the next morning; having considered the whole matter as settled, it had simply gone to bed at a somewhat more orthodox hour than 3:43 A.M.

Yet the valiant Cambodian stand in the matter of national defense and the providential intervention of the French Prime Minister in July 1954 were to prove of vital importance when another conference, convened at Geneva by the Big Powers, was to devote itself exclusively to settling the fate of Laos in 1961.

The cease-fire agreement had not been a total loss for the Pathet Lao either. Although not recognized as a "resistance government," it had nevertheless received official stature as the "Pathet Lao Fighting Units," better known henceforth by their French initials of UCPL (*Unités Combattantes Pathet-Lao*). Under Article 14 of the Laotian cease-fire agreement, the UCPL was given 120 days to regroup its forces within the provinces of Phong Saly and Sam-Neua, and in joint final declaration of the Geneva Conference, it was noted under Point 3 that:

> The conference takes note of the declarations made by the Governments of Cambodia and of Laos of their intention to adopt measures permitting all citizens to take their place in the national community, in particular by participation in the next general election, which, in conformity with the constitution of each of these countries, shall take place in the course of the year 1955, by secret ballot and in conditions of respect for fundamental freedom.[8]

In a later comment by Prince Souvannaphouma, who was Prime Minister of Laos at the time of the signature of the agreement, he noted "the dangerous lack of precision of the Geneva agreements," for they left several gaps which subsequent Laotian administrations had to try to fill in bilateral negotiations with the Pathet Lao over the next five years. For example, while the agreement explicitly provided for the withdrawal of Vietnamese Communist forces from northern Laos and likewise prohibited the latter from introducing new weapons into the country, there was nothing in the agreement which prevented the Viet-Minh from taking with them into North Viet-Nam thousands of young Laotians, training them in North Viet-Nam and reinfiltrating them into Laos once their training had been completed. According to French intelligence sources of the time, no less than 10,000 young Laotians were transferred into the Communist areas of North Viet-Nam in 1953–54, a great many of them against their own will.

This training effort in North Viet-Nam was further expanded when, in violation of the cease-fire agreements, the Pathet Lao not only regrouped in the two northeastern provinces of Laos but also set up a *de facto* civil administration in the two provinces from which all royal government representatives were excluded. Two politico-military training centers were set up in the UCPL areas, one at Ban Tian Kha in Phong Saly province and the other at Muong Sone in Sam-Neua province. In Sam-Neua itself, the UCPL, with the help of Viet-Minh instructors, set up the Komadone Military Academy for the training of officers and guerrilla leaders, the school being named in honor of Komadone, a southern tribal leader killed during the Bolovens uprisings of the 1930s. In addition to the military academy, there existed "School 44," a training center for administrators and political officers of the UCPL; and lastly, there was a special school for leaders from the various tribal minorities in which they were indoctrinated in their own tribal tongue. In addition, several hundred carefully selected Laotians were sent for advanced training to Hanoi, Peking, and even the Soviet Union. As early as August 1952, Pathet Lao delegations had shown up at various Communist or Communist-inspired conferences, such as the Asian and Pacific Peace Conference in August 1952, the World Congress for the Defense of Peace in Vienna, Austria, in December 1952, the World Youth Congresses in Bucharest and Warsaw, etc. These delegations were often made up in part by Lao trainees in Soviet bloc countries.

In other words, if peace and unity for Laos had been gained at the international conference table in Geneva, its actual implementation in Laos was still largely open to question. Prince Souvannaphouma, faced with the staggering task of having to govern a country ravaged by war and as yet assured of little, if any, outside help (United States aid to Laos was to make itself felt only as of 1956) fully realized that his country's salvation lay in obtaining an effective implementation of the cease-fire agreement with the Pathet Lao.

"In order to attain this objective," he was to say later, "the usual [diplomatic] weapons were going to be used—untiring patience, a gradual wearing down of the nerves and the morale of the adversary, and, if necessary, the recourse to force."[9]

The Lao as a Negotiator

In view of the fact that many of the events in Laos' recent past (and in all likelihood in Laos' future) hinged upon diplomatic negotiations, it is of interest to examine how the Laotians performed as negotiators. One of the best examples by which Laotian diplomatic performance can be judged is that of Lao negotiations with the French, because their records can be compared with those of the Vietnamese and Cambodians who, at the same time, were also facing the French.

In the case of the Vietnamese, negotiations usually bogged down in a hopeless quagmire of mutual recriminations complicated by legal infighting over diplomatic minutiae. This was partly due to the fact that the Vietnamese nationalists, faced with Communist Vietnamese competitors, felt that they had to be more intransigent in their dealings with the former colonial power than the Viet-Minh. After all, the latter being in a state of open war with France, did not have to "prove" their non-subservience to the colonialists, while the Vietnamese nationalists were always open to charges of being "puppets of the imperialists." This inferiority complex, coupled with the high caliber of legal training of the Vietnamese negotiators, resulted in the fact that literally none of the Franco-Vietnamese agreements drawn up between 1946 and 1956 ever saw final legislative ratification on either side—and that includes even the final Franco-Vietnamese independence agreement signed in April 1954 in the shadow of the impending Dien Bien Phu disaster. In every case, the equally legalistic turn of mind of the French negotiators did the rest.

In the case of Cambodia, unyielding determination to pay the ultimate price—hostilities—at a cost which would make the operation unpalatable for a stronger nation, became the hallmark of Prince Norodom Sihanouk's diplomacy. It worked equally well on the French who, in October 1953 were practically compelled to evacuate Cambodia while still in the midst of the Indo-China war; and, as we have seen, it worked on Mr. Molotov. This fierce stubbornness, balanced with a certain quiet modesty in the presentation of its case, has served Cambodia well in international affairs. Another constant in Cambodian foreign relations seems to be a sincere concern for the welfare of the Laotian brother-state to the north, due without a doubt to experiences suffered in common at the hands of the two countries' larger neighbors to the east and west: Viet-Nam and Thailand.

Laotian diplomacy differs from that of its two neighbors on two important points. First, the Laotians seem never as much concerned by abstract principles as they are with coming to grips with the smaller but well-defined issues that often hide behind those larger principles. Thus, it was Laos which led the other two Indo-China states when it came to establishing constitutional governments in 1947; it was Laos which was the first in taking advantage of the July 3, 1953, declaration of the French Premier, Joseph Laniel, promising to "perfect the independence of the Associated States." While the other two countries still were studying the implications of the French declarations, the Lao government promptly sent a note to France on August 24, asking for the transfer of all residual French powers in Laos; and with negotiations with the other two states completely bogged down over questions of form, the Laotians, on October 22, 1953, signed the two treaties which made Laos a fully independent state.

This Laotian ability to break down a complex issue into a series of separate smaller problems which can be tackled one by one was never shown up more brilliantly than in the Lao government's dealings with the Pathet Lao between 1954 and 1957 when, in a series of moves which will be discussed in greater detail, it succeeded for a time in isolating the latter from its Communist outside supporters while gaining simultaneously the approval of the hitherto-aloof "Bandung bloc" nations.

At the same time, unfortunately, this particular ability at negotiating has been marred by a constant spilling over of personality conflicts into the field of foreign affairs. With much of the actual business of governing in the hands of an exceedingly small—less than three dozen people on both the Communist and non-Communist sides—elite, the "who" of the negotiations seems to overshadow completely the "what" and "how" of the process. While this idiosyncracy is not unique to the Laotians (personal foreign policy-making has also been the apanage of such men as John Foster Dulles, Konrad Adenauer, and Charles de Gaulle), it has, nevertheless, in the precise case of the Laos crisis of 1960–61, repeatedly brought close to ruin the delicate diplomatic handiwork of the other powers involved. Yet, in the period of uneasy truce which was to follow the Geneva cease-fire of 1954 and was to end with the outbreak of hostilities in July 1959, Laotian politicians of all factions (with the obvious exception of the Communists) seemed to have at least agreed upon a common policy course, regardless of various flamboyant statements to the contrary made by individual politicians—statements which were most of the time directed to the foreign observer rather than their fellow-Laotians.

Much of what was to happen later must be attributed to a failure on the part of the outside observers to understand the psychological background of Laotian negotiation processes, thus confusing the "signals" by which the game was played.

Grinding Down the Pathet Lao

The methods now adopted by the Royal Laotian government to come to terms with the Pathet Lao involved a struggle on several diplomatic fronts: Firstly, to make the International Control Commission (ICC) as effective as possible; secondly, by diplomatic overtures to the Communist bloc and India (the latter in its quality as leader for the uncommitted nations), to bring about sufficient moral and political pressure on the Pathet Lao to make the latter amenable to bargaining in good faith; thirdly, to receive sufficient moral and physical backing from Laos' major Western allies, particularly the United States and France, so as to be certain of friendly support in the case of a serious crisis. The Souvannaphouma government and the succeeding government of Premier Katay D. Sasorith went about accomplishing those tasks with a determination and vigor which received very little appreciation outside and certainly no publicity in the world press.

The first task—that of making the ICC fully operative—was far harder than would have been imagined. Composed of Indian, Canadian, and Polish diplomats and military personnel under the chairmanship of the senior Indian delegate (first Dr. J. N. Khosla and later Mr. Samar Sen), its members at first seemed appalled by the physical conditions under which they had to operate: The country was devoid of decent roads and airfields, lacked adequate electricity, water, and refrigeration, and was endowed with a climate that can be mildly described as debilitating. As in the other two countries under its jurisdiction, the ICC for Laos operated with an administrative headquarters located in the national capital, Vientiane, and with a series of fixed and mobile teams. The purpose of the fixed teams was mainly to supervise the inflow of military equipment on both sides; the purpose of the mobile teams was to verify as speedily as possible all allegations of violations of the cease-fire provisions. However, on the side of the Laotian government at least, disappointments were soon to be felt, for the very ponderousness of the supervisory machinery made it not the best tool for the enforcement of a cease-fire in a roadless, jungle-covered country. In a recent book on the subject, Sisouk na Champassak, Laotian delegate to the United Nations and during the first tenure of the ICC in Laos the royal government's liaison official with that body, expressed his feelings about the ICC in the following passage:

> . . . The ICC was . . . practically a tool and a spokesman for the policy of the opposition, even before it arrived in Laos.
>
> When the Commission did arrive, the three delegations settled in Vientiane, although there was nothing there to supervise or control. It soon became evident that the Commission's concern for the proper implementation of the cease-fire agreement was giving way to personal comfort and easy living. . . . The few night clubs in Vientiane, which the delegates attended assiduously, seemed to be virtually the only subject they could discuss with competence. The monthly expenditures of the ICC amounted to some $200,000. . . .[10]

That feeling of exasperation with not only the slowness of the operation of the ICC but also with its ostentatious living standards was also shared by the French, who, for the time being, had to foot the bill for the ICC and had to provide aircraft as well as ground transportation for its trips. Every transport pilot in Laos has his own store of tales about the ICC's operation: How a helicopter was requested on an emergency basis to ferry blocks of ice from Vientiane over 350 miles of jungle to cool the drinks of the ICC fixed team in Phong Saly; or, the story of the non-Western delegate who insisted upon taking his tub bath in soda water because he felt the brown waters of the Mekong, which everyone else used for their ablutions, were too muddy for his tender skin. Thus, when the rainy season started in the spring of 1955, the ICC requested that the French stock supplies for three months for the northern fixed teams on the assumption that they would be fully cut off from the outside world—an occurrence that had not happened in the French-occupied territories since the 1890s.[11] Mobile teams in particular—and those were the teams upon whose success the enforcement of the cease-fire largely depended—proved so slow and unwieldy that they almost always came too late to discover the allegations of violence. (That the Polish Communist delegate was, for obvious reasons, not particularly eager to increase the swiftness of the ICC's operation did not help matters further). On April 14, 1955, the ICC decided to withdraw all its mobile teams from Laos with the exception of that which was installed in the royal capital of Luang Prabang and whose "mobility," therefore, did not suffer from an undue lack of comfort.

This voluntary limitation of the ICC's work to the control of military equipment at points of entry unfortunately had little if any effect upon the major violations of the cease-fire provisions which took place *inside* the boundaries of Laos, such as the arrest and deportation to North Viet-Nam of Lao elements known to be hostile to the Communists, the non-restitution of military prisoners held by the Pathet Lao, the organization of a Pathet Lao administrative structure which in many areas paralleled that of the Royal Administration, and the maintenance on Laotian soil of at least a cadre force of North Vietnamese Communist military and political instructors. This led the royal government to the publication in May 1955 of a "White Book" on the *Implementation of the Geneva Agreements in Laos,* in which it charged that the Commission had "failed to exercise the role of arbitrator" and that with regard to the two northern provinces, "no effective control whatsoever is being exercised over these provinces, not even by the International Commission whose reserved attitude on this question is most disappointing."

While it was without a doubt true that on certain occasions it should have been possible for the ICC to intervene more actively, it must be realized that it was, after all, composed of representatives of three nations whose views and interests in the Laos question were worlds apart. In fact, that is the main reason they were chosen to be on that commission. Yet, to those observers who had been members of other such international commissions, the apparent placidity with which the ICC in Laos handled its job must have been particularly galling. This is apparently what had crossed the mind of the French colonel who headed the Franco-Laotian military delegation to the ICC. Colonel Sorre had been a member of the United Nations Truce Supervisory Organization which controlled the cease-fire in Palestine and had witnessed not only excruciating discomfort by members of that commission operating in the murderous heat of the desert but had also witnessed the death of Prince Bernadotte—the Swede who first headed the Commission and was murdered by Israeli terrorists—and also that of several American, Belgian, and French representatives caught in Arab-Israeli cross fire while doing their duty. In an address to the International Commission, Colonel Sorre remarked:

> From personal experience I am fully aware of the difficulties of travel and life in the mountains and in the jungle of Laos. It is nevertheless a fact

that it is precisely in this jungle that the truth which I beseech you to un-cover lies hidden. This will demand of you great exertions and discomfort to which you are not accustomed. This will very often lead you to have to forego the Sabbath, which to many of you is sacred.

The peace mission which is incumbent upon us is even more sacred, and no sacrifice is too great when such a mission is to be accomplished, whether one be a soldier of war as myself or of peace as you gentlemen of the International Commission.

Since at the same time there was an increase of incidents between Royal troops and Pathet Lao forces—substantiated, contrary to what was to be the case in 1959–60, by solid physical and documentary evidence in the form of North Vietnamese identification papers and signed orders, in addition to arms and ammunition—the Laotian government by late spring of 1955 felt that its first avenue to the re-establishment of peace in the country, the ICC, had about reached the maximum extent of its useful-ness. The time now had come for the exploration of the second avenue of approach: Pressure on both the Pathet Lao and its Communist partners by other Asian countries. The Asian-African Conference held at Bandung, Indonesia, from April 18 to April 24, 1955, was to provide the Laotians with a suitable opportunity to make such a direct approach.

At Bandung the Lao delegation sided with Prince Norodom Sihanouk when he expressed Cambodia's willingness to steer an "independent and neutral" course providing that "more powerful nations (i.e., North Viet-Nam and Communist China) were willing to give proofs and guarantees to smaller nations."[12] Here again, without raising larger philosophical and moral issues, the Lao diplomats concentrated on getting their oppo-nents down to cases. Having clearly documented Viet-Minh illegal activi-ties in Laos in the White Book addressed to the ICC, whose publication was timed to make it appear on the eve of the Bandung Conference (em-barrassing greatly, no doubt, both the Viet-Minh and Red Chinese dele-gations, which were having their first "coming out" at Bandung among the non-committed Afro-Asian nations) they were now in an excellent posi-tion to exact non-interference pledges from Chou En-lai and Pham Van Dong, the Prime Minister of the North Vietnamese government who had been head of the Viet-Minh delegation the year before at Geneva.

Chou En-lai seemed particularly eager to repeat the assurances which he had made to Nehru and U Nu the year before to the effect that China had no intentions whatever of intervening in the internal affairs of Laos, and there is little doubt that, as in Geneva the year before, the more obstreperous North Vietnamese leaders apparently acted out of deference to China's desires than out of their own volition. The agreement signed at Bandung between the Viet-Minh and the Laotian delegation was short and to the point:

> First, the government of the Democratic Republic of Vietnam considered that the settlement which is due to take place between the royal government of Laos and the Pathet Lao, by virtue of the Geneva agreement, is a question of internal order which the royal government of Laos and the Pathet Lao are entirely free to solve in the best way possible in the higher interest of the country and people of Laos.
>
> Second, the government of the Democratic Republic of Viet-Nam and the royal government of Laos will develop and harmonize the good neighborly relations which should tie these countries to each other within the framework of the Five Principles defined in the Sino-Indian Agreement of April 29, 1954.

This was a solid victory for the royal Laotian government and one which it was not slow in exploiting. With a skill worthy of old-line diplomatists, the Laotians now prepared themselves for the second round. While the Laotians already had explained their views to Prime Minister Nehru during his visit in Vientiane on October 17, 1954, they took advantage of a return invitation extended to the Laotian Prime Minister and to Crown Prince Savang Vathana by the Indian government in September 1955 to further increase their favorable position among the non-committed nations. Repeating once more their Bandung gambit, the Laotians issued a supplementary handbook of correspondence between the government and the ICC on the eve of the government delegation's departure to New Delhi. While there, the Lao delegation made full use of the opportunity to stress the bonds of common "spiritual origin" as well as the unity of views with India in seeking peaceful solutions to outstanding political problems and reaped in turn solid Indian assurances of support in its forthcoming negotiations with the Pathet Lao. The diplomatic position of the Sasorith government was now considerably reinforced: Both Red China and Communist North Viet-Nam had been nailed down in writing to a position of formal non-interference in accordance with the Geneva Agreements and India, then still the unchallenged leader of the neutralist bloc and chairman of the ICC, was now willing to lend the kingdom the prestige of its open support.

Sasorith was thus prepared for a direct approach to the rebel prince, Souphanouvong. A meeting between Laotian and Pathet Lao emissaries in neutral Rangoon, Burma, resulted in the signature of a joint declaration on October 11, 1955. This document again shunned the larger issues and simply concentrated on avoiding further clashes between the two parties. A buffer zone was agreed upon and a joint commission to deal with other outstanding problems was appointed. However, the important issue of the participation of the Pathet Lao in the forthcoming national elections of December 25, 1955, remained unsettled as its delegate argued for an extension of the filing deadline beyond the date authorized under the Laotian constitution, a demand which the royal government felt compelled to refuse under the circumstances. The elections took place at the appointed date in all the provinces of Laos except in those which were occupied by the Pathet Lao.

Travels to the East

The December 1955 election, far from clarifying the Laotian political situation, further muddled it. In spite of the fact that the only whole-hearted opponent, the Pathet Lao, did not participate in the electoral race and that all the other parties were more or less agreed on the kind of program that Laos needed in order to be saved from disaster, the various political factions (or rather, the small cliques around various ambitious politicians) refused to cooperate with each other. The result was a government crisis which lasted a full six weeks—beating almost anything that the Laotians could have learned from their acquaintance with French political mores. In final desperation, the Laotian legislature again turned to Prince Souvannaphouma who once more assumed the post of prime minister in January 1956.

His return to power coincided with one of the few positive moves of the ICC. On January 7, 1956, that body issued a resolution addressed to both sides in which it urged the early conclusion of political accord as prescribed under the Geneva Agreement and the return of the provinces of Sam-Neua and Phong Saly to the authority of the royal government. The Pathet Lao, probably overestimating the strength of its position or perhaps unaware of a subtle change of line in Hanoi and Peking, committed one of the few tactical errors of its stormy history: It rejected flatly the ICC resolution on January 25 and, to its surprise, was faced with a fairly scathing report by the ICC to the two co-chairmen of the Geneva Conference, the governments of the United Kingdom and of the USSR.[13]

For once, the royal government could afford to play a comparatively safe card in simply standing pat on the January 7 resolution of the ICC. This, in turn, gave Britain an opening gambit with which to persuade the Soviet Union to press for a *détente* on the part of the Pathet Lao. The preliminary agreement which was reached between Souvannaphouma and the Pathet Lao on August 7, 1956, was beyond a doubt due at least in part to Soviet influence. This preliminary agreement provided for the integration of the two northeastern provinces into the administration of the royal government, the integration of Pathet Lao forces and civilian officials into the royal army and government, cessation of hostilities, and supplementary elections. In addition, the Pathet Lao submitted to the royal government a five-point program which embodied all those points and which also, as Point 4, provided for the "adoption of the five principles of peaceful co-existence."

Prince Souvannaphouma again was ready to operate along the three fronts of Laotian foreign policy: Having turned the ICC in his favor and having the preliminary approval of the Pathet Lao in his pocket (Britain and France already had approved the policy of the Laotian government) the Prince now was ready to nail down the Pathet Lao to a hard and fast commitment by securing the benevolent neutrality of Hanoi and Peking, if not their outright approval.

This was the reason for Souvannaphouma's trip to Red China which began on August 19, 1956, and which was to brand him as a "left-winger" in Washington, Bangkok, and Saigon. That disapproval was not only implicit but clearly explicit; when the Royal Laotian delegation took off for Peking from Vattay airfield near Vientiane, the ambassadors of the United States and of Thailand were conspicuous by their absence from among the official well-wishers.[14] The trip was officially advertised as a *visite de bon voisinage* ("a visit of good neighborliness") and as such included the usual official banquets, "spontaneous" demonstrations and visits to public works. But on August 21, the Laotians—Souvannaphouma, Vice Premier Katay Sasorith, and Finance Minister Leuam Insisiengmay settled down to some hard bargaining with Mao Tse-tung, Chu-Teh, and Chou En-lai. According to those present, there was a considerable amount of give and take on both sides.

Again faithful to their tactics of attacking large issues by splitting them into smaller, manageable problems, the Laotians insisted that the Chinese and North Vietnamese honor certain promises they had made in writing the year before at Bandung, in exchange for which the royal government promised to adhere strictly to the five principles of peaceful co-existence as defined in June 1954 by Prime Minister Nehru and Chou En-lai.

The list of Chinese counterdemands was somewhat more extensive. The Chinese demanded (and their demands were later matched by those of Hanoi) that the Laotians forbid the installation on their soil of any "American bases," that they also forbid entry to American military advisers, and that they accept the installation in Vientiane of a Red Chinese consulate-general. On the other hand—and the fact that this was never clearly reported in the American press is indicative of the built-in bias on the subject—Peking stated that it had no objection to the continued existence in Laos of "any bases permitted under the Geneva Agreements." Those, it will be recalled, included the French bomber base at Séno and a second French base at the Plaine des Jarres, as well as the stationing in Laos of 3500 French troops and of a French training mission of 1500. And since France is a member of the Southeast Asian Treaty Organization (SEATO), this in effect meant that Red China was not as much against the existence of a Western "trip-wire" in Laos as it was against the existence of American bases close to its own borders. This retrospective view of the situation appears to be borne out by American specialists who made a particular study of Communist reactions to the Laos crisis. Commenting upon Red Chinese intentions regarding Laos prior to the 1959 crisis, such specialists stated that:

> It is our general impression that the over-all design of CPR [Chinese People's Republic] foreign policy that developed during 1958, in the wake of the Russian sputnik, considered East Asia its first priority target and Southeast Asia quite secondary. . . . The implications of this strategy, executed as a cold-war operation, are beyond our present scope. In Southeast Asia, we believe that what they most wanted was a quiet rear.[15]

We arrive here at one of the crucial points in the Laotian tangle, to wit, that much that happened in the ensuing year was due mainly to a complete misreading of each other's intentions on the part of the two major protagonists in the area, the United States and Red China. And in the twentieth century, it is of those misreadings that world wars are made.

The Laotians were quite willing—in fact they were eager—to accede to Red China's first two demands. On the other hand, they remained adamant on the issue of the Red Chinese consulate-general. Souvannaphouma explained that Laos had thus far abstained from accepting a Nationalist Chinese consulate-general and, under those circumstances, the acceptance of the Red Chinese consulate-general would be an initiative at variance with Laos' avowed policy of neutrality. The Chinese contented themselves with that explanation and the subject was dropped.[16]

With Peking apparently assuaged, the Laotian negotiators felt on much more solid ground when they arrived in Hanoi on August 29, 1956. Hanoi, in fact, was to prove even easier to deal with than Peking because many of the Laotian and Vietnamese leaders knew each other from their high school and college days under the French colonial regime. The issues raised by the Viet-Minh were of a less general nature than those raised by the Chinese and so were those posed by the Laotians: On the side of the Viet-Minh the major concern seemed to be that the Pathet Lao would be given a voice in Laotian affairs commensurate with its political and military importance. Hanoi also was disquieted by what it considered to be preferential treatment extended by Laos to the South Vietnamese government: In the eyes of the Viet-Minh, the fact that the Laotians maintained a diplomatic mission in Saigon (although it was not given the name of an embassy) but maintained no such mission in Hanoi seemed to be an indication of special preference.

Here again the Laotians fared remarkably well: In regard to the treatment of the Pathet Lao, the Laotian delegation was able to point to the agreement signed with the latter on August 7 and 10, 1956; and, in regard to the Laotian representation in Saigon, it was observed that this representation had already existed when the French High Commissioners were still in Saigon and this merely constituted a continuance of the *status quo*. This argument was accepted by the Viet-Minh, and a communiqué resembling that signed earlier in Peking was issued. Both statements were, at the very best, a sign of the good intentions of Red China and North Viet-Nam and could not be taken literally; the Laotian negotiators were very well aware of that. As one of them, Sisouk na Champassak—in 1960–61 the representative of Laos to the UN and by no means a close friend of Souvannaphouma's—was to say in his book on the subject:

> Our journey, however, was not a complete failure. Prince Souvannaphouma had not gone to China and Viet-Nam naïvely expecting the Communists to sign with him a definitive agreement permanently solving the Pathet Lao problem. The visit had one purpose: to create a favorable climate pending negotiations with the Pathet Lao.[17]

There can be, in all fairness, no doubt that this objective was achieved in full by the Laotian mission to Hanoi and Peking.

The 1957 Accords

As far as the Pathet Lao was concerned, there was not the slightest doubt about the fact that it now felt outflanked. In fact, not only did the Pathet Lao feel outflanked diplomatically, but it also felt outmaneuvered politically and isolated morally. Many of its fighters who had held the jungle since 1952 began to yearn for home; others merely yearned for the bright lights, well-stocked shops and air-conditioned wide-screen movie houses of Vientiane. But now that the Pathet Lao was willing to discuss terms, a further obstacle to progress was put up by the anti-Communists in Vientiane who, no doubt influenced by suggestions that the introduction of Pathet Lao elements into the fabric of the state might lead to a *coup de Prague* (i.e., a Communist peaceable take-over similar to that which occurred in Czechoslovakia in 1948), balked at the idea of integration of the Pathet Lao. The debate raged to and fro for almost a whole year. In defense of Souphanouvong, the more and more exasperated Souvannaphouma made a series of statements attesting to the non-Communism or non-Marxism of his half-brother,[18] which provided further fuel for the arguments of those Laotians and Americans who believed that out of naïveté or overambition, Souvannaphouma was ready to sell his country to the Communists. Ominous, "non-attributed" pronouncements were issued about a change of American policy toward Laos and mention even was made of the possibility that the integration of the Pathet Lao into the national community might bring about the cessation of American aid.[19]

The Pathet Lao, on its side, did nothing to improve its international standing, either. It now began to demand that the royal government, in addition to implementing the August 1956 agreements, exchange embassies with various Communist countries and accept Soviet bloc economic and technical aid—the latter in spite of the fact that, as Prince Souvannaphouma wryly noted, it had *never* been offered by any of the Communist powers. It is not entirely clear at this time whether the obstreperousness of the Pathet Lao was due to secret orders from the outside or to an ideological struggle between various factions within the rebel organization itself. The consensus of the specialists is that both were possible; Souvannaphouma himself at one time was persuaded that his half brother Souphanouvong was far less extreme in his views than some of his aides such as Phoumi Vongvichit and Nouhak Phoumsavan.

Souphanouvong's Vietnamese wife was also reputed to be an orthodox Communist exercising a great deal of influence over her husband.

Thus, as the spring session of the Laotian National Assembly drew to a close late in March 1957, total turmoil engulfed Vientiane which, in Laotian politics, is the preface to a large-scale crisis. The simultaneous return after ten years of exile in Bangkok of the former Viceroy, Phetsarath—the older brother, it will be recalled, of Princes Souvannaphouma and Souphanouvong—added further fuel to the fire. For Phetsarath, though much aged, had not mellowed and, after ten years of banishment, had many scores to settle.

He immediately disconcerted his Western supporters by stating in a press interview on March 29 that Laos' only chance for survival lay in complete neutrality, that he did not believe the Pathet Lao were Communists (remarking in an aside that he did not believe in Communism by association), and lastly, he completely soured the American Embassy on him by declaring that "the greatest danger of Communist subversion came not from the Pathet Lao but from the bad use being made of foreign aid."[20] This was to be the first open outcry against the misuse of American aid in Laos and its nefarious consequences on Laotian political life. There were more to come in the future.

All this certainly added much fire to the issue but shed little additional light. Thus, when the Assembly reopened its session on May 11, there still was no clear majority for either the adoption or the rejection of the integration proposal. In a long policy speech that was remarkable for its statesmanlike approach and for its strong stand against the excessive demands of the Pathet Lao—another fact that was conveniently ignored in news dispatches because it did not fit the theme of the "politically naïve" Souvannaphouma—the Prime Minister stood absolutely firm against making any concessions to the Pathet Lao with regard to the acceptance of foreign aid from anyone. The Prime Minister also considered as significant the violent reactions of the Pathet Lao against policy statements made by the governments of the United States, Britain, and France on April 24 which, in fact, were rather mild and merely expressed support for the unification and national independence policy of the Souvannaphouma administration.

Souvannaphouma's address was probably the most important statement of policy ever made before the Laotian National Assembly, and when the problem of negotiations with the Pathet Lao was put to a vote, the results were as follows: (a) The National Assembly approved the

August accords with the Pathet Lao by a vote of 24–0; (b) the Assembly defeated by 16 votes a motion that these accords should be used as the basis for the reunification of the country; (c) and finally, the Assembly also defeated the government by 13 votes on the issue of whether the government should continue to negotiate with the Pathet Lao along the line presented in the Prime Minister's declaration.[21]

The vote, in its very confusion, pointed up the political chaos reigning in the National Assembly, for it simultaneously approved the agreements made with the Pathet Lao while disapproving all negotiations based on them. In spite of the fact that the government had not been defeated on a vote of confidence or by a constitutional majority, Souvannaphouma nevertheless handed in the resignation of his cabinet on May 31. The outgoing Vice Premier, Katay Sasorith—whose views opposed those of Souvannaphouma—was entrusted by the Crown Prince with the task of forming a new government. When the Prime Minister-designate was finally ready to present his new cabinet to the National Assembly for approval on June 19, it turned out that the indispensable Souvannaphouma was the Foreign Minister-designate in the new cabinet.

The program presented by Katay differed from that of Souvannaphouma merely on method, not on principle. He promised a policy of firmness toward the Pathet Lao whom he called "Laotian units of the Viet-Minh party," at the same time expressing willingness to pursue negotiations with the Pathet Lao and to make every concession that would be compatible with the Laotian constitution and Laotian honor. Katay failed to muster the necessary two-thirds majority and the initial game of political musical chairs went on, as the Crown Prince asked one political leader after another to try his hand at forming a government, including the then neutralist leader Bong Souvannavong (who only three years earlier had been directly implicated in the murder of Laotian Defense Minister Kou Voravong). Katay Sasorith again tried to form a government on July 9, but again failed to obtain the requisite majority.

Laos thus drifted without a government for a full two months until in desperation the Crown Prince appealed to Souvannaphouma. On August 9, Souvannaphouma presented himself before the National Assembly with substantially the same program for which he had failed to muster support almost three months earlier. This time, the Laotian legislators were aware of the fact that time was once more running against them and that the spectacle they were offering to the world and to their own people was more to the advantage of the Pathet Lao than to anyone else's. This time,

Souvannaphouma's program passed without more than a token opposition from the neutralists who felt that it did not go far enough. As one looks over the record of those six months, it can fairly be said that the only person in Laos who apparently seemed to know what he was doing and was trying to do it, for better or for worse, was Souvannaphouma. Yet, commenting upon the new Laotian administration (which included again such solidly pro-Western elements as Katay Sasorith and Phoui Sananikone) the New York *Times* of August 26, 1957, opined that the new government constituted a "setback for the West."

At last, the road was clear for the integration of the Pathet Lao into the national community, but the non-Communist Laotians had wasted almost a whole year in futile discussions and had lost much of the momentum gained during the 1956 negotiations in Hanoi and Peking. Now, the Pathet Lao had had time to recover from its period of disarray, and the last round was to be by no means easy. But, after a year of sterile discussion, the Laotian parliament was eager to come to terms with the opposition. On October 13, 1957, the Laotian cabinet approved the negotiation of a political agreement between Souvannaphouma and the Pathet Lao, and on November 1, Souvannaphouma signed a joint communiqué with Souphanouvong which, in substance, covered the same ground as the agreements reached in August 1956.

Both sides agreed on the formation of a coalition government which would include Pathet Lao members; the program of that coalition government would be that presented by Souvannaphouma on August 8, 1957. But prior to the formation of a new coalition government, the Pathet Lao and its recently formed political arm, the *Neo Lao Hak Xat* [NLHX, or "Laotian Patriotic Front"] was officially to return to Royal control the administration of the provinces of Sam-Neua and Phong Saly as well as the command of the UCPL armed units. While this agreement was being reached at the highest level, military and civilian delegations of the royal government and of the Pathet Lao were simultaneously meeting in Vientiane and working out the details of the military and political integration of the Pathet Lao.

The military agreements were completed on November 2 and included fourteen articles. Among the most important points in the agreement was the provision for the integration of 1500 men of the UCPL into the Royal Laotian Army and for the discharge of members in excess of that number. The latter would be treated as discharged veterans of the regular Laotian armed forces, with all the privileges and rights of army veterans.

Article 3 of the integration agreement proved to be the rock on which the whole fragile edifice of these agreements was to founder in 1959; it provided for the reorganization of the UCPL units "according to the norms prevailing in the National Army," and it also provided that after a transitional period during which the UCPL members would remain in their own separate units, the General Staff of the Laotian Army could transfer such men "so as to attain more flexibility in the field of administration and command." According to Article 7 of the agreement, integration was to begin within sixty days after the formation of a government of national union (including Pathet Lao members). Article 9 provided for details of the integration process of the various units, including transmission to the Laotian High Command of exact personnel lists and statistics on armament and equipment to be placed under Laotian Army control by the UCPL. The royal goverment in turn promised full safety to the discharged UCPL members and their families and all facilities on the part of the royal administration for their transport home.

With the military accords signed—they were not to be made public until the political accords were signed on November 12—all major road-blocks toward harmonious integration seemed to have finally been removed and Souvannaphouma, in his final speech before the National Assembly as it ended its session on November 3, felt sufficiently optimistic to state that it was now "possible to hope for a general reconciliation followed by a rallying to the national community of all the Laotians in all the provinces of the kingdom."

The political accord proceeded apace, being negotiated on the Pathet Lao side by some of the most powerful members of the NLHX: Phoumi Vongvichit, Nouhak, and Singkapo, among others. The preamble to the accord mentioned that the negotiations had taken place "in an atmosphere of reciprocal cordiality and understanding" and that both delegations felt that the "national reconciliation constitutes the basis for peace, safeguarding of democracy, and of independence and progress."

In brief, the political agreements provided for the integration of the administration of the two northern provinces and of the civil servants stationed in those provinces, and the transfer to the royal government of properties held by the Pathet Lao in those provinces. All this was to take place after the creation of a government of national unity. The integration of the provincial administration was to be organized on the basis of a typically Laotian compromise: The key province of Sam-Neua would receive a royal Laotian governor seconded by a Pathet Lao deputy governor, while the less important province of Phong Saly would be endowed with a Pathet Lao governor seconded by a deputy from the royal Laotian administration. Later on, a special joint commission was to apportion equally the positions of district officers and town mayors between pro-Pathet Lao elements and pro-royal elements throughout the two provinces.

The second section of the political accords, Article 8 particularly, provided that the head of the UCPL, (Souphanouvong) would make a declaration of transfer to the royal authority of the two provinces and the military units and civilian administrators, while the Prime Minister of the royal government would give his accord (Article 9) to the exercise of free democratic rights by the *Neo Lao Hak Xat* throughout the country.

On November 18, Prince Souphanouvong, after eleven years in rebellion, formally returned to the authority of the King the provinces of Sam-Neua and Phong Saly and the Pathet Lao personnel under his command. One day later, on November 19, 1957, the Laotian National Assembly, recalled into special session, gave its unanimous vote of approval to the new government which now included two Pathet Lao members. The whole Assembly and the spectators broke out in spontaneous applause as the vote was announced. Laos was finally at peace for the first time since World War II.

The new agreements were received with unmitigated approval in Paris and London. The Soviet bloc, while not overly enthusiastic, nevertheless felt the agreements constituted "a step forward toward stabilization and peace." As far as the International Control Commission was concerned, its Indian chairman sent a letter to Prime Minister Souvannaphouma on November 26, 1957, in which he noted on his own initiative that the agreements signed with the UCPL and the inclusion of two Pathet Lao members in the Laotian cabinet constituted "the preliminary political settlement as stipulated in Article 14 of the Geneva Agreement" and that "by this fact, the activities of the International Commission are near reaching their normal end." In his letter, the Indian Chairman also noted that the only remaining task of the ICC would be to supervise the supplementary elections that were to be held according to the agreements, on May 4, 1958.

In Washington, the Department of State released an official statement commenting upon the integration of the Pathet Lao which contained the following passage:

The United States feels, however, that a coalition with the Communists is a dangerous line of conduct, for the history of similar coalitions elsewhere in the world reveals that they end tragically in penetration and seizure of the country by the Communists. Consequently, the evolution of the situation in Laos is a source of serious concern to the United States, which is observing very closely the situation in that country.

In his own study, Sisouk na Champassak, a known friend of the United States and a member of the many anti-Communist government coalitions that held power in Laos between 1958 and 1961, commented in the following terms on the United States position:

> This pessimistic statement was the only discordant note in the general praise and congratulations that followed the agreements. Reaching Vientiane in the midst of her rejoicing, it created the worst possible effect for the U.S., one of selfish ill temper.[22]

Yet even in Washington, that pessimistic estimate of the situation was not shared by everyone; in fact, the Pentagon which all along, as will be seen later, had been less sanguine about Laos than the civilian branches of the government, estimated that on the whole the situation had developed favorably for the West because the integration of the two northeastern Laotian provinces with the rest of the country under royal control was one of the few instances (Austria and the tiny republic of San Marino being the others) where territory was peacefully recovered from the Communist bloc. In the words of Charles H. Shuff, Deputy Assistant Secretary of Defense for International Security Affairs in testimony before the House Appropriations Committee in June 1958:

> The fact of the matter is [that] the test out there is on the real estate. . . . Whatever we have given [the Laotian government in terms of aid] must have done some good. Otherwise, the whole piece of real estate would have gone to the Communists prior to this time.

The 1958 Elections

The implementation of the agreement at first proceeded fairly smoothly. Souphanouvong took over his new job as Minister of Planning, Reconstruction, and Urbanism, while Phoumi Vongvichit, became Minister of Religious Affairs and Fine Arts. Many reproaches were addressed to Souvannaphouma with regard to the posts assigned to the two Pathet Lao members of his cabinet. To be sure, to have a pro-Communist handle foreign aid—for that was in fact the major business of the Ministry of Planning—would obviously not sit well with the United States, since it was the latter which contributed the overwhelming bulk of the foreign aid funds allocated to Laos, with the French providing the rest. There were some justified fears that such aid would be directed toward projects likely to further increase the popularity of the Pathet Lao rather than to benefit the majority of the Laotian population.

The obvious reply made in Vientiane to this argument was that the United States was giving aid to other countries whose regimes were neutralist or whose economic planners were in fact Communists, such as in the case of Yugoslavia and Poland; and that, in any case, aid could not be any more misdirected or squandered under Souphanouvong than it had been in previous years under non-Communist aid administrators. It was pointed out also that the appointment of a pro-Communist or Communist to the post of religious affairs would probably have a more far-reaching negative effect than in the field of foreign aid because the bonzes, if indoctrinated with Communist propaganda, could spread it among large masses of the population with all the authority their religious calling could convey. As it turned out, in fact, neither Souphanouvong nor Phoumi Vongvichit stayed long enough in his post to make his subversive influence felt to any great extent.[23]

In the field of military and administrative integration, matters also seemed to proceed smoothly. By January 19, 1958, at the very same moment when Prince Souvannaphouma and a party of his ministers arrived in Washington in the hope of convincing the United States of the correctness of the integration solution, Laotian armed forces occupied both the provinces of Phong Saly and Sam-Neua in accordance with the November 1957 agreement, and at a special ceremony held on February 18, 1958, at the Plaine des Jarres, attended by the military committee of the ICC, 1501 members of the UCPL were integrated into the Royal Army. Another 4284 Pathet Lao military personnel were processed for discharge along with 1479 dependents, civilian officials, and sick and disabled UCPL personnel. According to the members of the International Commission who were present at the ceremony, the Pathet Lao forces "looked happy and healthy and showed no sign of underfeeding."

The Pathet Lao also surrendered to the royal government a total of 4773 weapons including 23 machine guns, 65 mortars and 10 automatic rifles. A later report by the Department of State implies that this total of 4773 weapons surrendered for an accounted total of 6199 UCPL members was somewhat inadequate and was probably due to the fact that not all weapons in the hands of the Pathet Lao had been turned in.[24] In view of subsequent events in Laos, this implication was not altogether incorrect.

The reception accorded Souvannaphouma and his party in Washington ranged from dubious to cool. In the words of the New York *Times:*

> Prince Souvanna Phouma, Premier of Laos, is a man of whom Washington has officially disapproved for sometime. His determination to negotiate with the Communist-controlled Pathet-Lao . . . seemed suspect.
>
> Now Prince Souvanna Phouma not only has come to terms with the Communists but has visited Washington to defend the way he did it.
>
> Prince Souvanna Phouma is enthusiastically confident that the elections will sweep the Communists out of the political picture.
>
> But Walter S. Robertson, Assistant Secretary for Far Eastern Affairs in the State Department is dubious. He fears that the legalized Communist party will prove dangerously contagious in Laos.
>
> However, Secretary of State Dulles' attitude is: just watch it. It might work.[25]

In the United States, Souvannaphouma admitted that he was perfectly aware of the fact that subversive efforts by the Pathet Lao were feasible, and he emphasized the point that "His Majesty's Government would not hesitate to take very strong steps against those who would endeavor to make the country Communist."[26] He made that point time and again in his talks with American leaders and expressed hopes that he had been understood as he left the country to return to Laos.

Souvannaphouma anticipated that the forthcoming elections of May 4, 1958, were going to be won by a large majority of non-Communist or even anti-Communist candidates. With his prediction the then American Ambassador to Laos, J. Graham Parsons, one of Souvannaphouma's severest critics, concurred. As Ambassador Parsons, in the meantime appointed Deputy Assistant Secretary of State for Far Eastern Affairs, was to explain to a House subcommittee on May 7, 1958, i.e., *after* the election had taken place but *before* the results were known:

> We can hope, therefore, if this information is accurate, that the results of the election will be such that only three or four Communists out of the fifty-nine seats in the full legislature will be held by former Pathet-Lao. . . . We therefore have some basis for hoping that when the present government resigns, as it is committed to do after the elections, a government may be formed which does not include Communists. When that comes

about, the situation in Laos will have arrived at a point where the fighting has been ended, the Communists have been rolled back in the two provinces, the Communists will have been eliminated from the government, and Laos will be united and independent. It is also a country which has no Soviet, Communist Chinese, or other Communist bloc diplomatic representation, and a country which has not as yet accepted any aid from the Communists.[27]

That optimistic picture, painted by an American official who, in the words of another House report, had "fought the [1957] settlement as long as he could," constitutes at the same time a clear-cut tribute to the achievements of the Souvannaphouma regime. Two things, however, remained to be done before the royal Laotian government could consider its most urgent political tasks to be accomplished: Winning the May 1958 elections and, in consequence, liquidating the control of the ICC over Laotian affairs.

At issue in the elections were twenty-one new seats in the Laotian National Assembly, which would boost its membership from thirty-eight to fifty-nine members. Additional seats had not only been created to take into account the return of the two northeastern provinces to the kingdom but also the underrepresentation of other areas. Thus, while not all the seats in the Assembly were at stake, the election nevertheless had a sufficiently countrywide character to provide a fairly good picture of the national mood. Already in the months prior to the election, demoralization was apparent. The inability of Vientiane to provide for effective leadership had become clear in the protracted game of political musical chairs, which terminated in the acceptance by the National Assembly of essentially the same program that it had spurned one-and-a-half years earlier. Furthermore, the corruption engendered by the misuse of American aid had reached such scandalous proportions that its gradual unraveling was to provide ammunition for both the Communist internal enemies of the royal government in Vientiane and the extremely conservative legislators in the United States who opposed foreign aid to any country. The usual division of the anti-Communist candidates in the running did the rest.

On the non-Communist side, there were the Independent Party of Phoui Sananikone, the Nationalists of Katay Sasorith and the Progressives of Souvannaphouma, each further split by personal factions and rivalries by men trying to double-cross each other. In spite of a pre-election agreement among the senior party leaders that only one candidate for each party would run in each contested district, many districts had to contend with up to eight or nine candidates from the same party vying for the favors of the electorate. And since election to the parliament then was a sure way to riches in the form of dollar import licenses, those of the candidates who were finally persuaded to desist from running demanded "abstention bounties" of up to $10,000—in a country where per capita gross revenue runs around $100 a year![28]

Among the left wing, the problem was somewhat simpler. First of all, there were only two parties in the running, the *Neo Lao Hak Xat* and the "neutralists" (*Santiphab*) party of Bong Souvannavong. The NLHX and its neutralist allies ran on a brutally simple platform: A vote for them was a vote for Lao unity and peace as well as against government corruption and inertia in Vientiane. It is here, perhaps, that Prince Souphanouvong's strategic position in the Laotian foreign aid administration paid its most handsome dividends, for it gave him access to an enormous amount of concrete evidence not only of corruption within the Laotian government it-self, but also among some of the American personnel of the United States Operations Mission (USOM) in Laos. In short, this was likely to be the only election in many a year in which Communist candidates were run-ning on a platform which promised a better and more equitable distribu-tion of American aid to the population at large. They also promised the population that, should they win, they would make efforts to obtain more aid from the United States.[29]

Both the Laotian government and the United States Embassy in Vientiane were aware of the changed nature of the left-wing campaign strategy and in the fall of 1957, Ambassador Parsons, in an effort to spread the benefits of American aid down to the villages where the voters were, conceived what was later known as "Operation Booster Shot." That operation was a crash program involving more than ninety small work projects selected more for their psychological impact than for their long-range beneficial effect: Repairs of schools and Buddhist temples, con-struction of some first-aid stations and dispensaries, and the dropping by chartered aircraft of some 1300 tons of food and medical supplies as well as other commodities to remote villages. In addition, many of the pro-government candidates were extended credit lines in cash or merchandise from which they could draw in order to make appropriate gifts to village heads or the villagers themselves.

In some areas, the enchanted villagers were suddenly provided with leather shoes (whose use in a roadless, rainsodden country is highly prob-lematical) or were provided with food, clothing, or farming implements which previously they had not received in spite of numerous pleas which they had addressed to their government in Vientiane. While the idea of "Operation Booster Shot" was not unsound as such—in fact, the U. S. Ambassador Horace Smith who in 1958 succeeded Parsons in Vientiane described "Operation Booster Shot" as having had "a greater impact on Laos than any other aid program which the United States has undertaken"—it nevertheless backfired badly during the elections. In those villages which had benefited from "Operation Booster Shot," the Communist candidates used the following arguments: "You see, little villagers? Now that your votes are precious to the government, you are being showered with gifts. Those gifts are very expensive. If the government is so rich that it now can give away those things to you, you can imagine how much the government has put away in its coffers for the past years, depriving you of your rightful share of American aid!"

In spite of the $3,000,000 spent on "Operation Booster Shot," it simply came too late and with too little impact to reverse a general trend. When the results of the May 4 election became known around mid-May, it was obvious that the government candidates had suffered a bad defeat. Nine of the twenty-one contested seats had been won by the NLHX itself —and, remarkably enough, their candidates included two princes, one woman legislator, and a mountaineer of the Kha minority—while the fellow-traveling neutralist Santiphab party had won another four seats. While those results certainly were nothing to cheer about from the royalist point of view, they did not represent an immediate menace to the Laotian legislative balance, because, after all, the Pathet Lao and its allies held only thirteen seats out of a total of fifty-nine; in other words, a lesser proportion of Communist or pro-Communist seats in relation to the majority than, say, the Italian and French parliaments at that very same moment. In fact, it is no exaggeration to say that the Pathet Lao was about as surprised by its strong showing as the Western candidates themselves were. In an interview granted on May 6 (that is, before the results of the elections were known) by Prince Souphanouvong to Tillman Durdin of the New York *Times*, Souphanouvong declared that he favored the participation of the NLHX in a coalition government regardless of the outcome of the elections and that he would accept the verdict at the polls even "if the majority parties were unwilling to take in *Neo Lao Hak Xat* representatives," provided that the new government pursued a policy of peace and neutrality.[30] All professions of peacefulness notwithstanding, the electoral defeat proved a bad jolt to the Laotian politicians to the right of

Prince Souvannaphouma; for that matter, even Souvannaphouma had not expected such a bad showing on the part of the non-Communist candidates.

Now began a much overdue "agonizing reappraisal" of the internal situation by the various political leaders. The conclusion of this self-evaluation briefly ran as follows: Firstly, the Souvannaphouma administration had grossly neglected internal reform in its single-minded preoccupation with the problem of re-integration of the Pathet Lao; secondly, foreign aid had indeed been squandered and misused to an incredible degree which, in turn, had given rise to corruption on a scale that left almost no one in governing circles (from the vice prime minister to the lowliest army officer) guiltless; and thirdly, the continuous bickering and squabbling among the non-Communist party leaders had prevented the anti-Pathet Lao elements from making a sufficiently united stand to defeat pro-Communist elements at the polls. While the first two points of the appraisal were largely beyond immediate remedy, the third presented some more hopeful aspects, and at the beginning of June, the Independent Party of Phoui Sananikone and the Nationalist Party of Katay Sasorith merged to form the Rally of the Laotian People, known by its French initials of RPL (*Rassemblement du Peuple Laotien*)—a name obviously inspired from the Rally of the French People, which in 1948 sought to return General de Gaulle to power. Again, and this is worthy of note in view of later developments, both Sananikone and Sasorith agreed that Souvannaphouma was the indispensable man to lead the new movement, whose avowed aim it was to "unite the national forces for a resolute fight against Communism and subversion."

With the election out of the way—and the extent of the Pathet Lao victory seemed a good indicator of its fairness—Laos had entirely complied with every stipulation of the Geneva Cease-Fire Agreement of July 1954. In his capacity as caretaker Prime Minister until a new government was formed, Souvannaphouma addressed a letter to the chairman of the ICC on May 22, 1958, in which he informed the Commission that:

> The royal government considers as fully accomplished the implementation of the agreement of the cessation of hostilities in Laos as well as the fulfillment of the obligations undertaken by this government at the Geneva Conference. . . .
>
> The International Commission for Supervision and Control in Laos thus sees the mission which had been entrusted to it by the Geneva Conference drawing successfully to a close. . . .

The royal government shall be grateful to the International Commission
if it could kindly inform it about the arrangements which it has been able
to make regarding its impending departure from Laos. . . .

To be sure, the Soviet bloc was not particularly pleased by the attitude
of the Laotian government in the matter, and the Polish delegate to the
ICC vigorously objected to the suggestion that the Commission should
adjourn. The thesis of the Soviet bloc was that while Laos had fulfilled
the conditions of the cease-fire agreement with regard to the *internal*
policies of Laos, it still devolved upon the International Commission to
supervise the fulfillment of such *external* obligations as the banning of
unauthorized foreign military personnel and the limitations imposed upon
the importation of additional war matériel. In order to clarify that issue
and to deprive the Soviet bloc and its Polish representative on the ICC
of any further pretext for delaying the withdrawal of the Commission,
Souvannaphouma sent a second letter to the Commission on May 31,
1958, in which he clearly stated "that the royal government intends to
continue to observe the obligations contained in its declarations made at
Geneva."

With that categorical assurance on the record, even the punctilious
Indians could find no further reason to delay the withdrawal of the ICC
from Laos. On July 19, 1958, the Canadian delegate and the Indian chairman outvoted the Polish member of the Commission and adjourned the
Commission *sine die*.

As co-president with Great Britain of the Geneva Conference of 1954,
the Soviet Union attempted a last diplomatic rear-guard action in London
on August 26, 1957; Great Britain—supported in its stand by the United
States and France—successfully fought off the usual Soviet references to
"SEATO aggression" and the matter was held in abeyance until the Soviet
Union finally acquiesced to the indefinite adjournment of the ICC in a
joint Soviet-British statement issued on February 4, 1959.[31]

On July 22, 1958, the Laotian National Assembly confirmed the election
results of May 4, 1958, and on the same day Prime Minister Souvannaphouma submitted the resignation of his cabinet to the Crown Prince
in the absence of the ailing King. In accepting his resignation, Crown
Prince Savang Vathana noted that the Souvannaphouma administration, entrusted with the problem of integrating the Pathet Lao in the national community, had fulfilled its responsibility with the holding of the
recent election. And this, in brief, indeed summed up the record of Souvan-

naphouma's work since 1954: Laos was at peace for the first time since 1945; it was reunified and the royal government exercised control over the whole country; foreign Communist forces had evacuated Laotian territory with the exception of perhaps a few Vietnamese Communists who had been longtime residents of Laos; the native pro-Communist Pathet Lao had surrendered in large part, if not in totality, its armament and had begun to operate as a legal party; and if the country had not become prosperous, a generous measure of American and French aid had permitted the opening of additional schools, hospitals, and of a few modest semi-industrial enterprises such as sawmills and cigarette plants.

None of this had come easily because the anti-Communist Laotians were divided among themselves and Western policies in Laos were hardly more united in their approach to the problem. Thus, the diplomatic successes scored by the Laotians between 1954 and 1958 were almost entirely due to the political acumen and perseverance of such men as Katay Sasorith and Souvannaphouma. This hard fact did not, to be sure, square with the stereotyped view of the situation which became accredited in Washington, with the benefit of poor hindsight, in 1960–61. It nevertheless remains true that for a fleeting moment in 1958 the situation in Laos had all the makings of a viable compromise and with but a modicum of intelligent economic aid and political support from the outside, Laos had a fighting chance of becoming a truly (if precariously) non-committed country on the rim of the Soviet orbit, after the model of Finland or Austria in Europe, and of Afghanistan, Nepal, or Burma in Asia.

But, as will be seen, this was not to be.

Part Two:

THE CRISIS

VI

The Pendulum

Swing to the Right

While Souvannaphouma was winding up the affairs of his government after the May 1958 elections, the reappraisal that had taken place among Lao non-Communist politicians had gone one step further. The newly created Rally of the Laotian People (RPL) while certainly a step forward under the circumstances, nevertheless failed to satisfy some of the younger and more politically conscious elements of the Laotian elite in Vientiane. This younger elite group (most of its members were below forty) had, on the whole, received a far broader education than its elders, had traveled abroad more often and more extensively—i.e., while their seniors had only traveled to France, many of the younger generation had been to many countries of Asia and some also to the United States—and they were frustrated by what they felt to be the stagnation of politics in Vientiane. They also saw that, in the words of one of them, "certain families continued to divide titles and prerogatives among themselves" and "ministerial posts either cloaked the most disgraceful trafficking or were traded about like currency."[1]

After meetings on June 15 and June 17, 1958, this group of young diplomats, civil servants, and army officers formed the "Committee for the Defense of National Interests" (CDIN, after its French title, Comité pour la Défense des Intérêts Nationaux). Although backing the RPL program, the group of "young Turks" presented a reform program which ran from elimination of graft and corruption to anti-Communism and the advocation of greater discipline among the Buddhist clergy. It later expanded its program to include reforms in the judicial system, elimination of nepotism, and elimination of discrimination on the basis of social class. It was open knowledge that the CDIN had American backing and that, for a time at least, many other Western observers placed great hopes in the "new brooms" in Vientiane.

The "young Turks" of the CDIN were soon given ample opportunity to prove their mettle, since four of their principal members occupied key posts in the new government formed by Phoui Sananikone on August 18, 1958. CDIN members received the portfolios of foreign affairs, finance and economic affairs, justice, and that of information, youth, and sports. A military member of the CDIN, a colonel who was later to become a general and emerge as the "strong man" of Laos for a short while, Phoumi Nosavan, later received the post of Secretary of Defense.

The program of the new government was clearly exposed in the first issue of the bi-weekly newspaper of the CDIN, *Lao Hakxa Sat*. In his initial declaration to the National Assembly which had voted him into power by a fairly narrow margin of twenty-nine votes against twenty-one, Phoui Sananikone declared that "my government shall not depart from the main aim which it has assigned itself: The struggle without fail against the implantation of the Communist ideology in Laos," while his new Vice-Premier, Minister of the Interior and of National Defense, Katay Sasorith, declared at the same moment that "our number one enemy is Communism."[2]

It was obvious from the beginning that the combination of the RPL and the CDIN was at best a marriage of convenience, with both sides simply trying to buy time until its position was strong enough to dispose of the other group. The CDIN had considerable strength among the junior members of the administration and some of the army officers, strength which was further heightened by the fact that it enjoyed American support. The RPL, on the other hand, had all the tactical advantages that age, entrenched position, and connections with the traditional leadership in the Royal House could confer.

At first, there were high hopes that the "new brooms" would be sweeping in at least some of the overdue reforms: In October 1958, the Laotian *kip* was devalued from thirty-five to the United States dollar to eighty to a dollar, which at least eliminated the most blatant currency black-market transactions; and, mindful of the temporary success of "Operation Booster Shot," a Department of Rural Affairs was established whose job it was to be to bring the benefits of the aid programs down to the village level. But it was to be in the field of foreign relations that the most drastic changes were to occur.

Prince Souvannaphouma himself was eased out and given the post of Laotian ambassador to France. Laos at the same time began to establish closer relations with the pro-Western regimes of South Viet-Nam and Thailand and completely reversed her earlier stand of noncommitment on the China issue by establishing official relations with Taiwan and allowing the installation of a Chinese Nationalist Consulate General in Vientiane. On this point, all existing interpretations seemed to agree: These steps were taken unilaterally by Laos and without prior provocation by the Communist regimes to the north and east. In the words of Sisouk na Champassak, "these significant overtures toward the West must have exasperated the Chinese and North Vietnamese Communists . . . but much had changed since the country's November [1957] blindness. The Phoui government's anti-Communism was vigilant, active, determined." In the eyes of Souvannaphouma, "the policy of strict neutrality was abandoned under pressure by the United States and replaced by an openly pro-American position." He added:

> Three fundamental errors were committed: The authorization to install a Consulate-General from Formosa in Vientiane; the raising to the rank of Embassy of the Laotian representation in Saigon; and the authorization to admit to Laos American military instructors.[3]

The Rand Corporation study on the same subject prepared for the United States Air Force gave the following explanation of the now-developing situation:

> . . . Communist anguish at the prospect of Laos being converted into an "American base" served to embolden the Sananikone government to view the trickle of [United States] military aid as the prelude to a huge flood of equipment and an adequate military training mission—to the eventual development of the Royal Army into a force that could accommodate any internal threat and act at the same time with confidence on the frontiers . . . and it closed the gaps that had existed in the concert of Laos-American coordination.[4]

It is very likely that neither Vientiane nor Washington fully realized the implications of those gestures—for they were essentially gestures and did not materially alter the situation—as far as Laos' Communist neighbors were concerned.

Within a few days of those Laotian initiatives, incidents began to break out on the Lao-Vietnamese border close to the 17th parallel, with North Viet-Nam all of a sudden accusing Laos of having violated the North Vietnamese border. After almost a year of relative quiet, the North Vietnamese radio began to assail Vientiane, accusing the Sananikone government of having encouraged Laotian troops to cross into Vietnamese territory and of "spying" with Laotian Air Force planes on North Vietnamese territory in the Huong-Lap area. On January 9, 1959, it was the turn of Laos to complain that North Vietnamese troops had penetrated nine miles into Laotian territory and occupied several villages in the Tchépone and Nong-Het area.[5]

In a pattern that was to repeat itself from Berlin to Saigon, Hanoi now began a propaganda barrage against the Sananikone government supported from the inside by the nine Pathet Lao legislators led by Prince Souphanouvong. The latter backed the charges made by North Viet-Nam and began an intensive letter-writing campaign aimed at both the Indian government and the co-chairmen of the Geneva Conference, asking for the reactivation of the International Control Commission. The situation was further complicated by the fact that the Sananikone government on January 14, 1959, requested and received plenary powers for one year. Sananikone now was a complete prisoner of the "young Turks." In the cabinet reshuffle resulting from the vote of plenary powers, the remaining older ministers were eliminated and replaced by army colonels and Sananikone became more or less a figurehead in his own government.

Vientiane now faced two sets of problems: The increasing pressure on its borders, complicated on the Laotian border with Red China by a refugee influx from Yunnan which brought no less than 14,000 Yao, Méo, and T'ai-Lü tribesmen into the Muong-Sing valley, and on the other hand the still unresolved internal problem of the Pathet Lao elements who continued to cling to their government jobs and army ranks by virtue of the November 1957 agreements. The key problem in the field of relations with the Pathet Lao was that of the integration of the 1501 members of UCPL Battalions No. 1 and 2, who, more than a year after the signature of the agreements, were still far from integrated in the Royal Laotian

Army. It was over the integration of those troops that the crisis was finally to reach its breaking point.

On the external plane, another Laotian gesture designed mainly to impress American public opinion added more fuel to an already explosive situation. On February 11, 1959, Premier Sananikone issued a statement at a press conference to the effect that he considered "the application of the Geneva Agreements as fully accomplished and that, therefore, Laos was no longer bound by its provisions." The statement made, like many that were to follow in the next two years, was at best one of general intentions, best shown by the fact that after many long paragraphs following a strong pro-Western line, the declaration ended in a reaffirmation on the part of the Sananikone government that it would adhere to the "peaceful co-existence policy" of the *Panch Shila*.

Unfortunately—and this was not to be the first time that the whole political climate of Laos was to be altered simply by the slanted reporting of events in the world press—the statement was sufficiently ambiguous to leave it open to widely varying interpretations, and a pro-Western press in Asia and the American press in general interpreted it to mean that Laos had fully renounced its obligations under the 1954 Geneva Agreements. For example, the New York *Times* of February 13, 1959, headlined its story on the Sananikone statement as follows: "Laos Clears Way for More U.S. Aid—Geneva Pact Renunciation to Let Americans Help Train Armed Forces;" and an editorial on the same subject in the New York *Times* of February 23, 1959, presented the situation in such inane terms as to give the Communist press ample material for verbatim quotation:

> The denunciation of the Geneva Agreements of 1954 by the tiny and beleaguered kingdom of Laos is realistic. As the first of the hitherto agreeing countries to make a formal renunciation of the Geneva actions, the courageous Laotians are putting it on the record that the agreements were never fulfilled and are worthless.
>
> Collateral testimony to the correctness of the Laotian move is given by the wild fulminations that it has evoked from Red China.

Indeed, the Soviet bloc reacted true to form, the more so as the Laotian statement had been followed on February 12 by an official American statement to the effect that the Laotian denunciation of the Geneva Agreements now permitted the United States to increase freely the size of its military aid program in Laos. The Laotians were the first to be appalled (as they were to be many times more later) by the scope and sharpness of world reaction to the February 11 statement. This prompted the Laotian government to issue a new communiqué on February 17, 1959, whose words in effect fairly well negated everything that had been said in the February 11 statement. In fact, going one step further, the statement that was issued put the blame for those exaggerations on South Viet-Nam and Thailand:

> Certain neighboring countries interested in the Southeast Asia Defense Alliance have not hesitated, for the benefit of sympathizers, to assert that the Lao Prime Minister's declaration is the first step taken by Laos toward joining SEATO. . . . The truth is that all these assertions are only presumptions or pretexts for propaganda.[6]

According to the news release, "The Lao people, basically peace-loving, have never nurtured any hostile sentiments against anyone. . . . The Royal Government of Laos sees no reason to establish new military bases" and "finally, it sees no reason at the present time for participating in any military alliance. . . ." The impact of that statement was further strengthened a few days later when Sisouk na Champassak in his capacity of Information Minister, further declared that "Laos has never denounced and has no intentions of denouncing the Geneva accords; it merely considers them as fully accomplished as far as it is concerned." In other words, in theory at least, the situation was exactly back where it had been before the February 11 statement. The sole exception was that the statement had been made, was on the record, and now gave ample ammunition for the Communist bloc to express real or fancied fears that Laos was indeed becoming an "American base." On February 19, 1959, Chinese Foreign Minister Chen-Yi received separately the Soviet and British chargés d'affaires in Peking and handed them a letter to be transmitted to Soviet Foreign Minister Gromyko and to Britain's Selwyn Lloyd, in their capacity of co-chairmen of the Geneva Powers, in which he asked them to "take speedy action in regard to the serious violation of the Geneva Agreements so as to check the U.S. scheme of military intervention in Laos and safeguard peace in Indo-China."[7]

The Communist counteroffensive in Laos was on. It was not to stop again until it had reached all, or nearly all, of its objectives.

The UCPL Integration Crisis

In Vientiane also, the Sananikone government was now caught helplessly in the dynamics of the situation which it itself had created. On March 20,

1959, Vientiane officially informed the President of the ICC in Saigon that aircraft of the International Commission would no longer be authorized to land in Laos while in transit to North Viet-Nam; and a few days later, rumors started—whose validity was later verified—that some of the nationalist Chinese guerrillas operating in the Shan states of neighboring Burma had crossed over into Laotian territory and were being supplied by an airlift of "unknown planes." Laos nevertheless still sought a measure of neutral support in its new situation and a brief visit from the President of India, Rajendra Prasad, in Vientiane late in March 1959 was used successfully by the Laotians to convince the Indians of the dangers that faced Laos from its Communist neighbors. Since the Indians themselves had at that precise moment been able to witness Communist brutality right at their own doorsteps in the invasion of Tibet and were protesting Red Chinese encroachments upon India's own northern frontier, the Laotians found them particularly receptive to their problem. When he left Vientiane, President Prasad assured Laos that India would consider it henceforth "as its spiritual daughter and would not be left indifferent by anything which happened to it."[8]

Fully realizing the increasing seriousness of the situation—brought to his attention by a Laotian complaint to the United Nations on January 18, 1959—United Nations Secretary General Dag Hammarskjöld also visited Vientiane in March 1959; and in their various other diplomatic contacts, notably at the meeting of the Interparliamentary Union in April 1959, the Laotians insisted on their faithfulness to the policy of neutrality which had been pursued prior to August 1958. Closer to home, better relations were again established with neighboring Cambodia, with the newspaper of Prime Minister Sananikone explaining that the temporary coolness existing between the two countries had not been due to the departure of Laos from its policy of neutrality but because "internal problems monopolized a great deal of the attention of our successive governments." But no amount of external sympathy could help Laos meet its major remaining test of internal strength: The integration of the two recalcitrant UCPL battalions.

For the past eighteen months, the problem of the final integration of those 1500 men had been left in abeyance. UCPL Battalion No. 1 had been sheltered in the non-commissioned officers training camp at Xieng-Ngeun near the royal capital of Luang Prabang, while UCPL Battalion No. 2 had been quartered in the former French barracks at the Plaine des Jarres. In Asian fashion, the families of the soldiers had soon congregated in and around the camps of the two battalions, giving them the air of gypsy encampments rather than of military garrisons. If any training at all was going on it was hardly ever visible to the naked eye, and to all intents and purposes, the Pathet Lao units, now better housed and fed than when they were holed up in the jungle hills of Phong Saly and Sam-Neua, seemed to enjoy their quiescent peacetime life.

As the non-Communist Laotian troops were to find out later, that total absence of spit and polish among the Pathet Lao troops did not prevent them from maintaining their jungle-going and jungle-fighting abilities. What also made those two battalions—whose numbers certainly were no numerical match for the 25,000 men of the Royal Laotian Army and its artillery, tanks, and paratroops—such fearful opponents was that the Pathet Lao, in selecting the 1500 men who would retain their arms at the time of integration, had seen to it that both battalions would contain a large number of mountain tribesmen thoroughly familiar with the terrain in which they were likely to operate.

Yet, Sisouk, in his description of those units, reveals the contempt for the mountain minorities that is so typical of every lowland Laotian and was to lead the Royal Laotian Army to grief and disaster in 1960–61. He describes the Pathet Lao units as "a strange mixture of T'ai, Méo, Kha and a minority of Lao," three-fourths of whose officers could not read.[9] The clear-cut national distinction which Sisouk makes between the mountain minorities of his own country and what he calls the "Lao" (meaning the lowland Laotians) unfortunately is typical of the attitude of the lowland Laotians toward the mountaineers and in good part explains the latter's resentment of the former and the ease with which the Communists have been able to exploit that hostility to their own advantage. Similarly, the contempt displayed by him for the UCPL guerrilla leaders, whose lack of formal education was more than made up by their fearsome ability to run circles around lowland Laotian officers who boasted a formal education and advanced military training in France and at American military schools, is symptomatic of the overconfidence of the "young Turks" during that fateful period—overconfidence that was to be rudely shaken when that "strange mixture" of tribesmen and their equally rag, tag, and bobtail officers corps brought the "young Turks" to ruin and shame before the year was over.

But in the late spring of 1959, there still was reason for confidence. With the civilian administration of the country now solidly in the hands of the CDIN, the Sananikone regime felt strong enough to take on the

UCPL integration issue. Immediately at stake was the question of *how* exactly this integration was to proceed, for the agreements of November 2, 1957, had been left conveniently vague about the matter. Even within the Western camp, opinions were divided: American experts believed that the safest way to integrate those 1500 UCPL into the Laotian army (if integration had to take place at all) was to disperse them throughout the whole Laotian army on the assumption that such a distribution would prevent the continuance of a subversive nucleus within the troops. The British and French view, on the other hand, was that each of the 1500 UCPL members would become an ardent propagandist for his cause (and that, in fact, he had been especially picked for that ability) and that their dispersal throughout the Laotian Armed Forces would merely spread the disease to all units throughout the country. The British and French felt, therefore, that the intent of the November 2 agreement could best be served by maintaining the UCPL units intact but suitably boxed in by reliable non-Communist battalions so as to ensure their loyalty to the Royal administration.

On the Pathet Lao side, interest in any integration at all seemed to have completely waned with the political setbacks suffered by the *Neo Lao Hak Xat* during the recent months, and interest appeared to center on a continued maintenance of the ambiguous *status quo*. First of all, the Pathet Lao wished to retain an excessively high number of officers—for example, they wanted to retain one colonel, three lieutenant-colonels and nine majors (for a two-battalion force which, in the Royal Laotian Army would have been commanded by one major each) as a cadre force for a possible future expansion of Pathet Lao elements and also in the hope of their being assigned to other troop units where they could exercise their subversive influences; and secondly, the UCPL now posed political conditions for their integration. Thao Khé, the UCPL commander at the Plaine des Jarres, notified the Laotian general staff that Prince Souphanouvong or Colonel Singkapo, the UCPL over-all commander, should be invited to the integration ceremony that was to take place on May 11 at the Plaine des Jarres. On the following day, the Laotian General Staff replied that there was no reason to invite Souphanouvong (his present position was that of a legislator in the National Assembly) since the integration ceremony was of a military nature.

On May 11, General Ouane Rathikoun, the Lao Chief of General Staff, personally came to the Plaine des Jarres camp to preside over the integration ceremony of UCPL Battalion No. 2. This was Constitution Day,

Laos' national holiday, and flags were flying on all the flag poles, stands had been prepared at the entrance of the camp for the integration ceremony, along with a table covered with the new Laotian Army shoulder boards to be presented to the Pathet Lao officers upon confirmation of their new ranks in the Royal Laotian Army. But when General Ouane arrived at the UCPL Camp with an honor guard, he found the 2d Battalion not in parade formation but with rifles and machine pistols pointing at the visitors. Many contingencies had been foreseen by the Laotian government in the integration crisis but a refusal pure and simple without even the pretense of an explanation and asserted with outright threats apparently was not one of them. After several hours of humiliating haggling with the UCPL, General Ouane left the Plaine des Jarres at 1330.

On May 12, the National Defense Committee of the Laotian Government decided to place the key NLHX leaders in Vientiane under guard and to address an ultimatum to the two UCPL battalions to surrender within twenty-four hours. This decision, made in great secrecy, was communicated to all Laotian Armed Forces units on the thirteenth of May in the morning. In the course of that day, the Laotian Army undertook to encircle the two UCPL units with loyal troops. That afternoon Prince Souphanouvong and his fellow NLHX deputies trooped to the National Assembly and protested vigorously against what they called the "high-handed practices" of the government. Apparently they, too, had been taken by surprise and had underestimated the willingness as well as the ability of the CDIN regime to act decisively.

Indecision, however, seemed to reign in the field, where the two UCPL battalions were cornered. At the Plaine des Jarres, UCPL Battalion No. 2 simply remained in its cantonments, although one officer and one sergeant of the Pathet Lao broke out of the camp and surrendered with their arms to the Royal Forces; at Xieng-Ngeun the Pathet Lao, even more cut off from their political leadership in Vientiane, apparently was somewhat more demoralized and forty officers and non-commissioned officers came forward to the Royal forces to accept integration on an individual basis. On May 14, the Lao General Staff finally issued an order to its forces at Xieng-Khouang and Luang Prabang to present a twenty-four-hour ultimatum to the encircled UCPL units. In order to render this move effective, additional troops were airlifted to both cities. The four battalions of Royal troops which now encircled the Plaines des Jarres were put on alert status but were not given an explicit order to blockade the UCPL units in their position. The latter continued to circulate freely outside their camp and, in the course of the following day, received several couriers from Vientiane.

At the expiration of the twenty-four-hour deadline on May 16, the government still delayed open action against the defiant UCPL units; on the other hand, it executed part of the plan to crack down on the NLHX political leaders in Vientiane, closed down the party's newspaper (which, with a circulation of 40,000, had become the largest paper in the country) and arrested Thao Khé who had voluntarily returned to Vientiane. Once more, Souphanouvong tried to see Phoui Sananikone, but the Prime Minister, on the instructions of his CDIN cabinet members, refused to receive him. The arrest of Thao Khé during his stay in Vientiane finally brought matters to a head. On the one hand, it left the UCPL battalion in the Plaine des Jarres without its senior leader; on the other, it tipped off the Pathet Lao that this time the Laotian government meant business. When he was arrested, Thao Khé steadfastly denied that the NLHX had at its disposal an underground radio network and also maintained that the UCPL had in fact meant to integrate its units, had the Laotian permitted the NLHX leaders to attend the ceremony. More ominously, Thao Khé calmly admitted that a break-through from the Plaine des Jarres to Communist North Viet-Nam was contemplated in case of the failure of the integration talks. In fact, Thao Khé seemed most cooperative and quite willing to do his best to bring about peaceful integration of the two units. That such a peaceful integration was still possible became apparent on May 17 at Xieng-Ngeun. There, UCPL Battalion No. 1 was solidly surrounded by Laotian infantry and, containing a larger proportion of lowland Laotians than UCPL No. 2, was apparently more willing to come to terms. After a brief exchange of messengers, both the UCPL and the local Laotian commander agreed that integration of the battalion would take place on the following day.

The situation was quite different at the Plaine des Jarres. There, at 2320 of May 17, some of the royal Laotian outposts surrounding the UCPL battalion were fired upon by unknown assailants. On May 18, UCPL Battalion No. 1 at Xieng-Ngeun capitulated and, in the presence of General Ouane, Information Secretary Sisouk na Champassak and Thao Khé, the battalion marched out of the camp, surrendered its weapons and accepted their Laotian Army rank insignia. News of the surrender of Xieng-Ngeun was immediately flashed to the Plaine des Jarres where it was received with a sigh of relief by everyone concerned. Word was passed around that UCPL Battalion No. 2 was going to accept integration after a face-saving delay of a few days and the Royal troop cordon around the Pathet Lao position was more or less perfunctory; in any case the wives and children of the UCPL soldiers were seen going to market and returning as if peace had already returned to the Plaine. At 1900 that evening, Cham Nien, an ex-pirate from Thailand who had followed Prince Souphanouvong since 1949 and now was deputy-commander of the battalion, informed the commander of the Royal Laotian troops opposite him that the majority of the lowland Lao and the Méos of the battalion would be ready to accept integration on May 19 but that the Kha minority, i.e., the minority which had usually been treated worst by the Laotians, still was adamant against integration and still had to be persuaded.

The night from the eighteenth to the nineteenth was dark and moonless. In addition, it had rained part of the day and evening and the Laotian Army sentries, wrapped in their rubber ponchos and raincoats, shivered from cold and loneliness as they stood in a vast ring on the open plain watching the fires go out one after another in the UCPL camp a few hundred yards away. Soon the shaggy Méo dogs which usually kept up a steady howl all through the night fell silent until not a sound was heard from the camp. At five A.M., a blanket of milky fog began to settle over the plain announcing the warmth of the rising sun which was soon to make its appearance over the wooded hills to the east of Phongsavan. In the Laotian army camp, a few fires were lit for the preparation of the vegetable broth which often constitutes the breakfast of the simple soldier in Laos. On the Pathet Lao side nothing stirred. To the Laotian sentries peering through the now slowly lifting fog, the Pathet Lao camp seemed absolutely deserted. Prudently the skirmish line of Laotian soldiers and officers began their advance on the camp. When they finally reached it, it became evident that the whole battalion, including its women, children and old people had simply filtered across the surrounding Laotian troops and disappeared. Heaps of American-made "suntan" uniforms, already received in full expectation of eventual integration, had been left behind neatly stacked. The French-made "Pataugas" jungle boots with their thick rubber soles and broad cleats, on the other hand, had been carefully slashed to pieces with machetes so as to be of no use to anyone else.

The news hit Vientiane like a thunderclap. At nine o'clock in the morning General Ouane arrived at the Plaine des Jarres with Thao Khé, and Thao Khé was asked by Ouane to prepare a message for the fleeing UCPL battalion, asking it to surrender.

At eleven o'clock, Thao Khé acquiesced with the demand and wrote out a message which later was parachuted by a Lao Royal Air Force plane on the retreating UCPL battalion whose long drawn-out columns were still marching on the open plain in a southeasterly direction, trying to reach the North Vietnamese border across forty-five miles of saw-toothed high mountains and jungle. The message was not acknowledged. At twelve o'clock, the Laotian High Command ordered the 25th Infantry Battalion and one paratroop company to Ta Viang in order to block the retreat of the UCPL toward the border; but Cham Nien and his Pathet Lao had not been retained among the elite troops for nothing: Just as they were expected to head for the nearest point along the North Vietnamese border, they veered west-southwest deeper into Xieng-Khouang province and established their first night camp at 1700 at Ban Mai, ten miles to the southeast of Xieng-Khouang. In spite of the fact that they were slowed down by women and children, they were still a respectable fighting force armed with 338 rifles, thirty automatic rifles, two machine guns, four 81-mm. mortars and were in possession of one American radio transmitter; in addition, they carried food for at least four days, which was to last them well over a week.

On the Royal Laotian side, this first series of moves had thoroughly confused the High Command; precious hours were wasted before the full intentions of the enemy became clear. More troops were airlifted in and on May 20, the High Command decided to attack the UCPL forces at Ban Mai at dawn on the following day. Again, Cham Nien requested a truce in order to "negotiate the integration of the Pathet Lao forces." Eager to avoid an armed clash, the Laotian army command accepted and called off the attack on Ban Mai. While the Pathet Lao were again coming forward with detailed proposals and requests for guarantees, they broke up their force into platoon-size groups which began to slip through the Royal Laotian Army cordon while the negotiations were still going on. On May 22, some of the Méo soldiers of UCPL Battalion No. 2 suddenly appeared at Muong Ngam, thirty miles southeast of Xieng-Khouang, where the local Lao police post and civilian administrators expected them least and immediately fled in panic. On the same day another detachment was all of a sudden seen on the road back to Xieng-Khouang, which created a panic in that provincial capital administration of the province.

At the same time, Cham Nien again sent emissaries to the Royal Laotian command asking for two uncontrolled itineraries back to the Plaine des Jarres where, he promised, his troops would accept peaceful integration into the Laotian Army. At 1600 on the same day, another UCPL detachment was sighted at Ban Sanoth where it overran a Laotian army unit that was in its path, killing two soldiers and capturing another. It was obvious that the Royal Army attempt at capturing UCPL Battalion No. 2 had completely failed, in spite of the armed forces deployed and the overwhelming material superiority of the Royal troops. On May 24 and 25, a few rearguard detachments of the Pathet Lao troops were sighted both at Ta Viang and at Muong Ngam—only to disappear completely from view. Both sides had now resorted to force and Laos, after only the briefest period of relative peacefulness, was again plunged into war.

VII

"The Laos Fraud"

---◄◆►---

The American government, the American press, and you and I
along with them, swallowed *The Big Deception from Laos,* hook,
line, and sinker; and when the truth appeared at last, we
made scarcely a gulp of protest.

> William J. Lederer
> *A Nation of Sheep*
> Norton, 1961

The Early Phase

What followed the successful escape of UCPL Battalion No. 2 into North
Viet-Nam was probably one of the worst fiascos of Western policy in Laos
or, for that matter, in the Far East. What makes this crisis even worse
than some of the other recent American fiascos, such as the U-2 or Cuba,
is that it has remained largely unreported or erroneously related in the
American press, while the press of most of the other non-Communist
countries—notably that of Great Britain, France, Australia, and Canada—
reported a story that was almost diametrically opposed to that fed the
American public, and, apparently, even to American officialdom. It was
left to a few more enterprising and imaginative American journalists and
to Captain William J. Lederer (USN, Retired), the co-author of *The Ugly
American* and the author of *A Nation of Sheep,* finally to bring out the
truth of the story to the American public as well. Unfortunately, this was
done far too late to do any good for public understanding of what was at
issue in Laos, with the result that for almost two years the American view
of what was happening in that remote part of Asia had a rather curious
quality of "everybody-is-out-of-step-but-me" when compared with what

other responsible Western sources, both official and in the news media, had to say about the situation.

Basically, the two versions of the facts can be boiled down to the following: The official American version, also shared by the Royal Laotian government and in fact based very often on information released by the latter, accused the Pathet Lao of having started the hostilities and of having continued them with the help of not only Communist North Vietnamese equipment but of a North Vietnamese invasion force whose size was variously estimated as ranging from between three to eleven battalions (2000 to 9000 men);[1] the British-French view of the situation was that, politically, the Laotian government and its American supporters had largely themselves to blame for the outbreak of the fighting and that the Royal Laotian Army was so demoralized that the Pathet Lao could defeat it piecemeal without Viet-Minh assistance save for some ammunition and equipment and a few communications and other technicians.

In fact, as calmer counsel began to prevail in the United States, the British-French view of the initial phase of the crisis began to be accepted here even among government specialists—although *nowhere* was a correct version of the facts ever issued publicly for the information of the average citizen and of Congress, as was done later in the case of the U-2 and the Cuban crisis. Americans specializing in Chinese Communist affairs, who studied the 1959 crisis strictly from the technical viewpoint and without any particular axes to grind, summed up the situation as follows:

> In retrospect it is apparent that the Sananikone government precipitated the final crisis that led to war in Laos; it also is apparent that while the Sananikone government knew, at the time, that it was running a serious risk of open conflict with the NLHX and its mentors in Hanoi, the pattern of Communist behavior up through mid-May had not been sufficiently belligerent to deter it. To each of the successive crises the Communist replies had been primarily verbal.[2]

Certainly, there is no reason to believe the Pathet Lao's objective in Laos had ever been anything but a complete take-over. This does not mean, however, that the Pathet Lao, having reverted to the "legal struggle" pattern in November 1957 and having made a good showing in the 1958 election, had any particular reason to resort again to revolutionary warfare in May 1959—the more so as its whole political and military leadership was in the royal capital of Vientiane, a virtual hostage of the royal government. That it indeed was in such an exposed position was amply proven when, in the sole successful operation of the whole Laos crisis of 1959, in July the royal government arrested and jailed all the major Pathet Lao leaders. It is highly unlikely that as experienced and wily a group of guerrilla leaders as Prince Souphanouvong and his aides would have started the rebellion without at least taking adequate measures for their own safety. Thus, it is not difficult to agree with Sisouk na Champassak (certainly no friend of the Pathet Lao as a member of the CDIN and General Phoumi's regime) when he states:

> Although the Neo Lao Hak Xat leaders in Vientiane launched the rebellion, they soon were powerless to stop it, even if they wanted to. They lost all control over it. Not only were they from the beginning under surveillance and completely cut off from their troops, but with the start of guerrilla warfare, the military leaders naturally held the reins. After May 15, it was no longer Souphanouvong who led the rebellion, but men like Kayson and Cham Nien and their lieutenants.[3]

According to Sisouk, Souphanouvong even tried to "reverse the trend," offering to intercede with the rebels in order to induce them to lay down their arms, *but the Lao government rejected his offers.* Curiously, Sisouk avers that the Communists in Peking and Hanoi were probably happy at the removal of Souphanouvong from the scene and the temporary transfer of power to the "young wolves" of the UCPL who were thirsting for battle —for exactly that same picture could now be seen in the Royal Laotian camp, where the "young wolves" of the CDIN and the as yet largely untried military leaders of the Royal Laotian Army now seemed extremely eager to test their mettle with the UCPL.

On the face of it, there was truly no reason why the Laotian Army should not have thought itself sufficiently strong to destroy the Pathet Lao in battle: The only Pathet Lao force in the field was about 500 men strong who had among them less than 400 weapons, and they had to face a "national army of 25,000, trained and staffed for modern warfare, and supported by air transport." The only thing that was wrong with that appraisal of the situation was that the kind of war about to be fought was not "modern warfare" but a far more insidious kind of war that, for want of a better term, is best described as "revolutionary war."

Much has been said lately, both by specialists and laymen alike, about various types of covert operations designed to bring about the collapse of an enemy without resorting to the horrors of nuclear war. The tactics used to achieve such an end have been variously dubbed: guerrilla warfare, special warfare, unconventional warfare, sublimited warfare, and, most recently, "internal war." As in the case of some mysterious diseases, its name became the fancier as the extent of our ignorance about the subject became better known. Yet that old specialist in that kind of warfare, Mao Tse-tung, had given it its proper name as early as 1936: That name was "revolutionary warfare." It was left to French Army officers, whose dire experience with the subject in Indo-China and Algeria is a matter of record, to give the problem more than passing attention. In particular, one Colonel Gabriel Bonnet made it the subject of a well-researched book—*Les Guerres insurrectionnelles et révolutionnaires* (1958)—which, although almost completely unknown in the United States, is the "bible" on that particular subject. Bonnet defines revolutionary warfare as "the application of guerrilla warfare principles to the furtherance of an ideology or the extension of effective political control." In other words, in the kind of war which the West had been fighting against the Soviet bloc since the first Berlin blockade of 1948, the major target is not square miles of Laotian jungle or the beach-front hotels of Havana but the minds and allegiance of billions of people who have yet to make up their minds as to whether the Communist system or our way of life is more likely to fulfill their aspirations. For that kind of war—the only kind of "modern war" that continues to pay handsome dividends even in the face of nuclear arsenals—the Royal Laotian Army was woefully unprepared and no lavish amounts of American surplus weaponry were likely to close the psychological armament gap.

In addition, the very technology of guerrilla warfare made the task of the Royal Laotian Army a hopeless one. In a study prepared by the United States Army Special Warfare Center at Fort Bragg, which included a survey of all guerrilla wars fought throughout the world over the past twenty years, it was found that a single guerrilla fighter can tie down ten or more conventional soldiers, can kill fifteen conventional soldiers for every guerrilla fatality, and will only spend twenty percent of the ammunition required to effect a casualty as compared to the conventional soldier's expenditure, thanks to the guerrilla's motivation, training, and courage.[4] Those hard statistical factors have proved correct in the case of the Soviet partisans behind German lines in Russia, of the French *maquis* and of the Yugoslav partisans, of Fidel Castro's followers and of the Viet-Minh, and finally of the Pathet Lao. Once the Pathet Lao rebellion hit its stride in the late summer of 1959, and its fighting swelled to over 2500 men, as a result of reinforcements by large parts of UCPL

Battalion No. 1, which, as will be seen, slipped out of Xieng-Ngeun on August 8, 1959, and by Black T'ai mountaineers from both sides of the North Vietnamese border, it would have taken (on the basis of the tie-down ratios established at Fort Bragg) the *whole* Laotian Army merely to break even in a fight with them.

Unfortunately, it was very obvious that the Laotian Army could not be entirely concentrated in the northern areas where most of the Pathet Lao were operating because—and this is a fact that was hidden from the American public at least until late 1961—much of southern Laos was as badly infiltrated as the better publicized north. Furthermore, the problem of feeding and supplying 25,000 men in the roadless jungles of northern Laos would have far exceeded the logistical capabilities of the Laotian Army. Another fact that had to be taken into consideration was that no one knew exactly what the size of the Laotian Army *really* was; in all likelihood, it was probably closer to a figure of 20,000 men than to the theoretical 25,000 who were supported by United States aid. (Later, as the crisis got worse, defections and desertions, along with the disaffection of some of the paratroops and other units under the command of Captain Kong-Lê, reduced the combat strength of the royal Laotian troops under the effective control of Premier Boun Oum to about 10,000—although at one time the United States paid salaries for almost 40,000 Lao troops and policemen).

While the equipment of the Laotian Army certainly was "modern," i.e., composed of standard-issue infantry weapons and field artillery, little effort had been made to adapt either the equipment or the troops to the missions they most likely would have to fulfill in case of an armed conflict. Here, the French, who, by virtue of the 1954 Geneva Agreements, were the only foreign instructors allowed to remain in Laos, cannot escape a certain measure of blame. Falling from one extreme into the other, the French, in order not to be accused of exercising command prerogatives in an army which no longer was theirs, allegedly also failed in providing the Laotians with sufficient training leadership. Moreover, in order to avoid any possible clashes of national pride, most of the officers with previous experience in Laos were transferred out of the country and replaced by training personnel largely devoid of fighting experience in Indo-China.

But there existed, aside from the training problem, a definite morale problem in the Laotian Army. The widespread corruption which prevailed in the civilian government circles in Laos also had contaminated the military; soon, most of the senior army officers owned newly built villas in the $50,000-plus class and even the simple lieutenants at least enjoyed the illicit use of an army vehicle for their private needs. With such little moral guidance to go on, the troops reacted in kind: In 1959 it was discovered that all the paratroops boots in stock had been sold on the black market, and the commanding general of the northern army area had to take money out of his headquarters funds to buy basketball sneakers from the Chinese merchants in Vientiane as substitute paratroop boots until new ones could be found. In another instance, verified by American observers, Laotian paratroopers refused to carry out a particular operation, announcing that "they would not march through the jungle like common infantry,"[5] because they could not be parachuted directly on the target. If one couples to those observations the fact that the bulk of the troops were raised from among the lowland Laotians whose experience with the jungle highlands was slight, one has here all the makings of a military defeat *regardless* of the amount of foreign aid and the quality of the foreign military advisers. Thus, it can be said fairly that the Sananikone government and its American advisers definitely overestimated the ability of the Laotian armed forces to solve by military means a politically unsound situation.

"Pathet Lao"—Round Two

Much already has been said about the Pathet Lao and its leader, Prince Souphanouvong, but with the battle now joined, a brief explanation of its organization is necessary, for thus far no Western source (outside of some intelligence agencies) has thought it useful to study the movement in any great detail. This is particularly regrettable in view of the fact that the Pathet Lao is precisely what its official name of *Neo Lao Hak Xat* indicates—a *front* for a hard-core Communist cadre party. The latter, known as the *Phak Khon Ngan Lao* (PKNL) or "Laotian Workers' Party,"* is an extremely small elite organization of which practically nothing is known and which has a total estimated membership of less than one hundred. This, of course, is not surprising in view of the lack of political sophistication of the Laotians in general. It is the PKNL which in fact seems to be the commanding body behind all the operations of the UCPL,

---

* *Editor's Note:* Subsequent to Fall's research, it has been learned that the cadre party is actually the *Phak Phasason Lao* (Lao People's Party), about which little is known. It is thought that Kaysone Phoumvihan is its Secretary-General.

and Sisouk is correct in estimating that Prince Souphanouvong may not be the central leader of the whole movement but may merely be its eye-catching front man, much after the fashion of Bulganin in the Soviet Union in the "B-and-K" combination of the 1950s. In Laos itself, persons who have seriously studied the Laotian Communist movement tend to believe that Nouhak Phoumsavan is the Secretary-General and real over-all leader of the PKNL-UCPL movement. The main job of the PKNL is "political preparation."* It carries out no guerrilla activities or overt sabotage of any kind, but it probably acts as a political coordinator with the North Vietnamese and Thai Communist organizations. Some of its members have at times been reported by the Thai police as having been seen in northeastern Thailand, particularly among the Vietnamese ref-ugees who have lived at Mukdahan for the past twenty years. Its main job inside Laos is to direct activities of the broad support organizations grouped inside the *Neo Lao Hak Xat* (NLHX).

With a solid political and military base, the Pathet Lao has rarely lost its momentum in Laos since 1955. On the eve of the Bandung Conference on April 13, 1955, the royal Laotian government, headed then as later by Prince Souvannaphouma, issued a long and detailed report describing violations of the 1954 agreements by the Pathet Lao and by the Viet-namese people's volunteers who apparently had not departed from Laos.[6] Contrary to expectation, the administration of the two northeast-ern provinces had remained totally in Pathet Lao hands. Military and civilian schools in Sam-Neua had begun to turn out trained cadres for further operations. In short, the Pathet Lao behaved, in the apt image of a Rand Corporation report, as if its position were, "though on a much reduced scale, similar to that of the Chinese Communists in 1945. . . ."[7]

With the penetration of the Viet-Minh into northern Laos in 1953 be-gan the establishment of a full-fledged "parallel hierarchy" of Pathet Lao administrators and cadres throughout the country, which reached down through most of the small villages. Like similar movements in other Com-munist countries, the Pathet Lao practices the rule-by-committee system, ranging from the central level down to the individual villages (*see* chart). The committee system shown repeats itself at all echelons, with the com-mittee members of the higher echelons being at the same time the leaders

* *Editor's Note:* Much of the following discussion has been adapted from Bernard B. Fall, "The Pathet Lao: A 'Liberation' Party," in Robert A. Scalapino, ed., *The Com-munist Revolution in Asia: Tactics, Goals, and Achievements* (Englewood Cliffs, New Jersey: Prentice-Hall, Inc., 1965), pp. 180–82, with the permission of the publisher.

Chart

PATHET LAO ADMINISTRATIVE STRUCTURE*

Central:	*Neo Soun Khang*	(Chairman, Central Committee)
		Nanhok Neo Khoueng (chairman)
Provincial:	*Neo Khoueng*	*Long Nanhok* (deputy)
		Kommakan (committee members, 1 secretary)
District:	*Neo Muong*	(Same organization)
Township:	*Neo Tambol,* or	*Houa Na Neo* (chairman)
	Tasseng	*Pho Kong Tin* (administrator)
		Tha Han Ban (self-defense chief)
Village:	*Neo Ban*	(Same organization)
Affiliated groups:	*Samakhom*	

Sao Hay	*Sati*	*Say Noum,* etc.
(Farmers)	(Women)	(Youth)
	Nouey	
	(Cells)	

* Adapted from Bernard B. Fall, "The Pathet Lao: A 'Liberation' Party," in Robert A. Scalapino, ed., *The Communist Revolution in Asia: Tactics, Goals, and Achievements* (Englewood Cliffs, New Jersey: Prentice-Hall, Inc., 1965), p. 182. Reprinted with the permission of the publisher.

of the lower echelons. For example, most of the *Kommakan* (i.e., committee members) of the provincial echelon will be in fact the *Nanhok Neo Muong* (presidents of subordinate district front committees), and so forth. The key echelon is that of the township (i.e., *tambol,* or *tasseng*); the best-trained Communist cadres are said to operate there. Very often, the NLHX village administrative official, the *Pho Kong Tin,* is at the same time the official village head for the royal Laotian government. In other words, the local administration in Laos is often completely entwined with the Communist underground organization. Thus had developed a system of "parallel hierarchy" which is harder to bring under control than the more usual situation where the legal administration is under open attack.

The Pathet Lao administrative organization is in turn under the surveillance of an entirely separate and secret (even to the Pathet Lao administrators) watchdog organization known as *Kene Sane* ("he who sees"). Each of the Kene-Sane—their number is unknown—in turn appoints several deputies who report only to him, while all the Kene-Sane report directly to the central committee of the NLHX. Since the Kene-Sane do not know each other, they unwittingly also report about each other's activities, which completes the full circle of mutual control on which every Communist organization thrives.

Contrary to the impression given by most sources in Vientiane and Washington, the country-wide organization of Pathet Lao administrative structure did not begin after the outbreak of hostilities in 1959 but in fact had never ceased to exist since 1953 and had almost never lost much ground even when on the surface the Laotian government seemed to be actively engaged in anti-Pathet Lao operations. This became patently clear when the "young Turks" of the CDIN attempted to set up their own counterpropaganda in the villages with the help of psychological warfare teams and rural action groups. While this made some convenient headlines at the time and temporarily assuaged some members of Congress who were rightly worried about the way things were going in Laos, it never had more than a skin-deep effect in Laos itself. As a Laotian report was to say at the time: "In their immense majority, the NLHX cadres stand up under the stress, lower their heads under the storm, but refuse to yield."

By late 1957 (that is, before the conclusion of the November integration accords), the Pathet Lao had at least one secure "base" in every one of Laos' provinces, each containing several villages with a Pathet Lao township or district (*Neo Tambol* or *Neo Muong*) organization, a school or two, a mimeograph machine which reproduced leaflets for a rudimentary newspaper, and in many cases a small group of armed regulars. Each base area was surrounded in turn by a string of infiltrated villages which could be counted upon to notify it of the approach of royal Laotian troops in time to enable them to remove anything that was even faintly suspicious.

Until late in 1959, there seemed to have been no orders for the base areas to prevent at all costs temporary occupation by Laotian troops; on the contrary there seemed to have been orders to give such Laotian troops or government administrators the "deep freeze" treatment. They were received with great reserve; any offers for material aid such as rice, school books, or medicine were either accepted with the barest thanks (if the Pathet Lao base was in need of them) or altogether rudely refused. The fact that the Laotian Army in many cases treated the village population very roughly[8] further added to the favorable picture of itself which the Pathet Lao succeeded in giving the population. This, too, was realized in some Laotian government circles but never with sufficient urgency to bring about the much-needed reforms. This attitude was well described in a Laotian government report of 1957, as a result of which the Laotian government felt compelled to set up with American help the so-called "Civic Action" groups throughout the country:

> The NLHX propagandist knows how to present himself like a friend who helps and advises and who works with his own hands. He is unselfish, honest, enthusiastic, and knows how to get along without creature comfort. The success of his work lies in those qualities and in the hard fact that he is always there. . . . He does not fear the ephemeral effect of the mobile propaganda groups of the royal government. . . .

The existence of those permanent base areas became well known to Laotian government officials in 1957. By 1959 the base areas had nearly doubled in size and had spread away from the inhospitable mountain regions along the Vietnamese border to new sites deep in the interior of Laos which often were within barely a day's march to the country's major population centers. Every Laotian provincial governor was fully aware that certain parts of his own province were beyond his control and was willing to point them out on the map merely for the asking. Yet again no American journalist ever bothered to ask that simple question, with the result that in official briefings as well as in the press the myth was maintained until late in the spring of 1961 that while perhaps things were not going too well in northern Laos, the southern "panhandle" of the country at least was quite secure and free from Communist infiltration. Pathet Lao infiltrators spread the tentacles of their control beyond the impregnable wilderness of the Bolovens Plateau and soon made large areas of the southern provinces of Saravane, Champassak, and particularly Attopeu almost impassable except to protected road convoys.

The armed forces of the Pathet Lao, the UCPL, had as their hard core the two battalions of regulars that were to be integrated into the Royal Laotian Army. Composed of a deliberately and carefully selected mixture of lowland Laotians and tribal mountaineers (which ensures at least partial acceptance of the unit wherever it may go in Laos—a fact that took the Royal Laotian Armed Forces and its advisers about five years to learn) those units could count on a ready and trained reserve of about 5000 men who had been with the UCPL prior to the November 1957 accords. In addition to those trained ready reserves from tribal areas within Laos, the UCPL could always rely upon some additional support from

White and Black T'ai mountaineers from neighboring North Viet-Nam, whose racial and linguistical similarity to their brothers across the border in Laos makes them completely indistinguishable to lowland Laotians and foreigners alike.

The training of those troops at the basic level took place in the local protection units of each permanent base. The more promising elements were then filtered north to the Pathet Lao-held provinces of Phong Saly and Sam-Neua for further advanced training. The Pathet Lao was also not loath to have its officers trained by French and American advisers wherever this was feasible, and there is some evidence to the effect that Pathet Lao elements joined the regular Laotian Army merely to benefit from Western training. In August 1959, for example, the French military adviser to the Laotian Battalion Commanders' School discovered that at least four out of the twelve battalion commanders he was training were openly sympathetic to the Pathet Lao. The Laotian Defense Ministry, however, requested his transfer when he made his discovery public.

In terms of armament, there was not the slightest doubt that the more than 4000 weapons surrendered after the integration agreements of 1957 were but a fraction of the weapons held by the Pathet Lao. With the resumption of hostilities in 1959, the Pathet Lao apparently experienced no difficulty in finding sufficient weapons for its again expanding forces. It was adept in using for its own purposes all the American-made ammunition and weapons which it captured in large amounts from its adversary.[9] Until the Pathet Lao acquired full control of Road No. 7 from the Vietnamese border to the Plaine des Jarres in the spring of 1961, it did not own a single vehicle; the lone Peugeot panel truck in the hands of UCPL Battalion No. 2 in May 1959 was left behind, minus its battery and with its tires slashed, when the battalion retreated into the hills. Until the onset of the regular Soviet airlift between North Viet-Nam and Xieng-Khouang in 1961, the Pathet Lao fought all of its battles with its normal infantry equipment, its "artillery" being composed of 81-mm. mortars.

This situation was to change rapidly when the United States provided the Royal Laotian Air Force with helicopters and planes armed to intervene in ground combat; a miniature "escalation" process began in the course of which the Communist bloc provided the UCPL with rapid-firing and antiaircraft artillery as well as with some self-propelled antiaircraft guns. But as the summer campaign of 1959 began, the Pathet Lao did not yet have access to this relatively sophisticated equipment, and small groups of jungle-trained guerrilla fighters were being pitted against large bodies of oversupplied and overpaid garrison troops. And in that kind of war, as a British colonel had said almost twenty years earlier after small groups of Japanese jungle fighters had literally made hash of his regiment north of Singapore, "quality always wins and wins incredibly."*

* *Editor's Note:* Bernard Fall wrote in 1965, "Estimates of the over-all numerical strength of the movement are widely divergent. The 1959 consensus, based on extensive surveys and interviews throughout Laos, was that there were at least 1500 full-time armed Pathet Lao guerrillas. By 1964, there were estimated to be about 20,000 Pathet Lao troops in the country, backed up by perhaps 5000 North Vietnamese regulars. At least 10,000 Laotians and mountaineers left Phong Saly and Houa Phan [Sam-Neua] provinces for North Vietnam when they were temporarily integrated with the rest of Laos in November, 1957. Table 1 shows the estimated strength of the permanent cadres of the NLHX administrative structure in 1960. The figures are very unlikely to have been revised downward by 1965."

NUMERICAL ARRANGEMENT OF PATHET LAO ADMINISTRATION

Lan-Xang (provinces of Luang Prabang, Nam-Tha, and Sayaboury)	500
Vientiane (city and province)	700
Tran-Ninh (Xieng-Khouang and eastern Vientiane)	400
Central Laos (Khommouane and Savannakhet)	1000
Southern Laos (Bassac and Attopeu)	400
	3000

"In addition, small groups of specialists are being trained abroad. Soviet and Communist Chinese sources mention Laotian students in Moscow and Peking, some of whom are Méo . . . mountaineers. Their total number seems never to exceed 100, and another 100 study in North Viet Nam. Recent reports speak of military specialists (a large proportion of them tribesmen from central and southern Laos) who are being trained in [Pathet Lao] schools in Sam-Neua and Khang Khay in Laos. While those figures may not seem impressive at first glance, they are sufficient—within the Laotian context of scarce and poorly trained leadership material—to tilt the balance of strength dangerously to the [Pathet Lao] side.

"By 1965, the *administrative* hold taken by the [Pathet Lao] power structure over large areas of Laos was, in fact, more dangerous to the survival of a non-Communist Laos than the military situation, although Western observers blithely disregard it. As of 1965, there existed at least eleven full-fledged [Pathet Lao] provincial administrations (out of a total of sixteen Laotian provinces), and these successfully overshadowed the legal but ineffective [royal Laotian government] administration. There even exists an openly known [Pathet Lao] governor of the province of Vientiane: Say Pethrasy. Significantly, all those [Pathet Lao]-held provinces abut directly on North Viet Nam, and actual [Pathet Lao] control limits itself to the mountainous areas for the time being. However, it is sufficiently flexible to expand or retract, according to the fortunes of the political and military situation, without losing its structural integrity.

"In those provinces which [Pathet Lao] forces do not entirely control, they nevertheless maintain base areas (i.e., *Phun Than*) composed of village groups that are solidly under the control of the NLHX or the [Pathet Lao] forces. This does *not* mean that they no longer are accessible to Royal Army forces or even to periodic inspections

The Diplomatic Byplay

In the meantime, Vientiane seemed totally oblivious to the seriousness of the situation. On May 23, 1959, Foreign Minister Khamphan Panya, while negotiating a treaty of friendship and commerce with the South Vietnamese government in Saigon, expressed hopes for the further tightening of the many bonds with South Viet-Nam and averred that the ICC was dissolved for good. He re-emphasized that the Sananikone government would not be bound by any restrictions placed on the country at Geneva—thus again contradicting not only the note of caution injected into the ICC debate by his own government in March of that year but also the declarations made to the press by his colleague at the Information Ministry, Sisouk na Champassak.

This was neither the first nor the last time when various Laotian government officers simultaneously were to issue declarations and communiqués whose tenor was diametrically opposed. Thus, while Khamphan Panya was making a strongly pro-Western bid in Saigon, the Information Ministry in Vientiane, in the face of the breakthrough of UCPL Battalion No. 2 to the Communist North Vietnamese border, issued a communiqué on May 24, 1959, which stated flatly that "there has been no serious development within the country. The former Pathet Lao forces had agreed to serve in the National Army," while a communiqué issued on May 27 admitted the events that had taken place on May 19 but reasserted that

by government civil servants. On the contrary: Such personnel is received politely, but with sufficient reserve to show that such visits from outsiders are unwelcome. Gifts are refused, and offers of help are turned down with the explanation, 'No aid is needed. We're helping each other and can get along very well without your aid.'

"In a base area, Communist indoctrination is continuous. The schools are Communist-run. There generally exists a dispensary and at least one good radio receiver capable of listening to the Lao-language programs of Radio Hanoi and Radio Peking. Some bases have their own short-wave transmitters. Propaganda periodicals and newspapers are edited, printed, and distributed. For a time, the *Lao Hak Xat*, with a print run varying between 25,000 to 40,000 copies, was by far the largest Lao-language publication in the country.

"A friendly Asian military observer who had an opportunity to tour parts of back-country Laos in the spring of 1960 reported, upon his return, that 'The Pathet Lao in hundreds of villages had almost reached the stage of political organization that enabled the Viet-Minh to defeat the French in Viet Nam.'

"That, unfortunately, turned out to be no exaggeration." [Bernard B. Fall, "The Pathet Lao: A 'Liberation' Party," in *The Communist Revolution in Asia: Tactics, Goals and Achievements,* Robert A. Scalapino, Editor, © 1965. Reprinted by permission of Prentice-Hall, Inc., Englewood Cliffs, New Jersey.]

any rumors to the effect that a civil war might break out in Laos were "completely untrue." Having said this, the Ministry of Information nevertheless hedged its bets by adding that all this was the handiwork of the Viet-Minh, bent upon launching a "new aggression soon by seizing the opportunity caused by the present disorders and chaos."[10]

Yet, for the time being, everything remained uncannily quiet. Communist North Viet-Nam, which as late as January 1959 had been involved in repeated border incidents with Laos in the Tchépone area in central Laos, maintained relative silence, and only on June 8 began to react publicly to the military operations carried out by the Vientiane government against the Pathet Lao. Even then—as in the case of an earlier statement of June 1—all broadcasts were purported to be mere amplifications of statements attributed to Pathet Lao sources. Particular emphasis was placed upon the fact that those statements did not issue from Hanoi but allegedly from within Laotian territory. As one of the highest-ranking NLHX leaders not under detention in Vientiane, Faydang, the vice-chairman of the central committee of the NLHX, in his statement of June 1, 1959, appealed again to the Sananikone government to restore the *status quo* of one year ago, when the Pathet Lao held two cabinet positions and nine seats in Parliament. It was substantially the program which Prince Souvannaphouma had implemented prior to his resignation, with the exception of one point: The Pathet Lao now wanted the return of the ICC whose departure from Laos Souvannaphouma had successfully induced.

The Sananikone government did not bother to reply directly to that offer, and limited military operations directed at mopping up the now dispersed units of UCPL Battalion No. 2 continued. As late as June 15, Pathet Lao broadcasts emanating from Hanoi still professed to be interested in a peaceful settlement of the dispute; but the Sananikone government, carried away by the very dynamics of a situation in which it seemed to have, for the first time, the initiative over its adversary, was not in a mood to negotiate, the less so as it felt that it had received explicit assurances of wholehearted support from both South Viet-Nam and Thailand along with the United States. The statement issued by the Department of State on May 29 rejected as a "fabrication" all allegations of American inspiration of the events in Laos but expressed strong support for the stand taken by the Sananikone government. This position was further reinforced by a joint declaration issued by Khamphan Panya and Thanat Khoman, the foreign minister of Thailand, during the latter's visit to Vientiane on May 29, which advocated "extending and enlarging the measures of co-operation already existing between the two countries." The negotiations between Laos on one hand and South Viet-Nam and Thailand on the other, resulted in a series of Lao-South Vietnamese agreements on transit payments, customs, immigration, etc., signed on June 11 in Vientiane, and in similar agreements with Thailand signed in Bangkok on July 22.

The reactions in Hanoi and Peking to those events, while not explosive, were certainly sharp.[11] In any case, it became clear that—like the United States in the Laos crisis of March 1961—the Soviet bloc had to do something about the Pathet Lao lest it lose complete control over the events in Laos. In view of what was to develop later, it is also possible that at least Hanoi and Peking, if not Moscow, now began to believe that the United States was seriously considering making Laos "an American base." By July 1, 1959, the Pathet Lao and its substitute leadership had worked out a new program which no longer pretended to seek a reconciliation with the Vientiane regime as it now existed; the program consisted of eight points which, with due allowance for local conditions, were to become an almost standard charter for the Communist view of what constitutes a "neutral" government:

1. Strict implementation of the Geneva Agreements; reactivation of the ICC; execution of the 1957 Vientiane agreements.

2. Policy of peace and neutrality; establishment of diplomatic relations with all countries—"especially with neighboring countries" (i.e., with Red China and Communist North Viet-Nam)—on the basis of the five principles of peaceful coexistence; renunciation of "U.S. imperialism."

3. Creation of a coalition government including NLHX members.

4. Guarantee of all democratic freedoms and respect for the powers of the National Assembly and the Constitution.

5. Immediate end of persecution and repression of NLHX party members and release of Pathet Lao members from detention.

6. Return of Pathet Lao administrators to Sam-Neua and Phong Saly provinces.

7. Establishment of a "policy of economic independence and acceptance of economic aid from 'any country.'"

8. Development of national culture; respect of Buddhism; preservation of "national customs"; and banning of various types of literature and recreation.

It is not without interest that the "National Front for the Liberation of South Viet-Nam" which was created on December 19, 1960, by North Viet-Nam to attempt a similar neutralization of South Viet-Nam prior to an eventual reunification on Communist terms, proclaimed a ten-point program which, save for its more detailed provisions and differences in sequencing of the points, bears a marked resemblance to the Pathet Lao program of July 1959.[12] From that day onward, the pattern on the Communist side was fully set: The Sananikone government had to be replaced and its American backers expelled from Laos. Throughout Asia and Eastern Europe, Communist propaganda took its cues, while on the eastern border of Laos, UCPL Battalion No. 2, now regrouped in North Viet-Nam opposite the Sam-Neua salient and reinforced by T'ai-Dam warriors, grimly settled down to fighting a jungle war.[13]

The Summer Campaign

The Pathet Lao counteroffensive began with a series of skirmishes on July 18, 1959, in the peripheral areas of Sam-Neua province, where the UCPL had had several of its bases for almost seven years. In this phase, which was to last from July 18 to July 31, the Pathet Lao forces attacked successfully the Laotian army posts at Muong Hiem, Muong Peun, Muong Sone, and Phong Satone, inflicting in each case a few casualties. In most cases, however, fighting was extremely brief, with the Royal Laotian troops withdrawing into the hills rather than being caught in their posts. At the same time, several minor incidents occurred in the "panhandle" area of Laos, including the kidnaping of village chiefs and local self-defense militiamen by Pathet Lao elements. And, as we have seen earlier, during the night of July 29–30, 1959, it was Lieutenant Déo Van Khoun's turn to die at Sop-Nao.

From over-confidence in the previous weeks the atmosphere in Vientiane nose-dived into complete panic. On August 1, the Laotian government cried, "invasion," and Vientiane began to consider an appeal to the United Nations. In Vientiane, the French-language newspaper of Vice-Premier Katay Sasorith, *La Voix du Peuple*, editorialized on the same day as follows:

> We are determined to do anything to preserve for our country its moral integrity so that our beautiful kingdom may live in freedom. . . .
> For this we shall face all situations and shall seize every opportunity to take the measures that are necessary and are ready to make any sacrifice

to remain ourselves and to repel the open supporter of a party which would lead us to subversion and to death: we are speaking of the ICC. . . .

No, we shall not be subjected to blackmail. Let this be known.

On the following day, August 2, Foreign Minister Khamphan Panya declared that "should the situation become graver in the next forty-eight hours, the Laotian government would call upon the United Nations." And reiterating a line that was to haunt him over the next two years, Khamphan Panya stated, as had Katay Sasorith the day before, that the real objective of the Pathet Lao was to force the government to accept arbitration by the ICC and the revision of the military assistance accords with the West. He added: "This objective shall never be reached because we are an independent government which shall never yield to blackmail by force."[14]

By August 4, the incidents had spread further inland to Luang Prabang province and also to the Thakhek area, but—and this must be emphatically underlined—none of the fights had cost more than perhaps a dozen casualties, with the average being around four, according to the Laotian government's own report later submitted to the United Nations. But on August 4 Khamphan Panya sent a lengthy telegram to United Nations Secretary Dag Hammarskjöld in which he judged the situation in Laos to be "very grave" and formally accused Communist North Viet-Nam of having supplied arms and provisions to the Pathet Lao. Having sent off the telegram, the Foreign Minister then told a press conference that "the telegram was not a request, nor even the first step in a protest to the United Nations."[15]

On the following day, London proposed the sending of United Nations observers to Laos in order to safeguard the territorial integrity of the country without necessitating recourse to the intervention of SEATO or to the reactivation of the ICC, and the headlines of the American press began to scream "Red Invasion in Laos." In the words of the previously cited research report prepared for the United States Air Force, "from the start the American public was given to expect some degree of Viet-Minh participation. For this reason, Vientiane's accusation before the United Nations in September that there was a large Viet-Minh participation in an otherwise undistinguished local affair was accepted in the United States. . . . This accusation, made in advance of evidence, made from the start of the campaign and reiterated in New York, was presented in the most casual ways."[16]

Laos
PATHET LAO ATTACKS
1959

|||||| Communist base areas
⋯⋯⋯ Guerilla areas
⟶ Escape route
⟹ Royal Lao forces
➤ Pathet Lao attacks

CHINA

BURMA

Phong Saly

Muong Khoua

Sop Nao

Nam Tha

M. Het

Sam-Neua

Sam Teu

Luang Prabang

PLAINE DES JARRES

Xieng Khouang

VIET-NAM

MEKONG

Kam Kheut

RIVER

R.N.13

VIENTIANE

Muong Nhonimarat

Thakhek

Muong Phalane

Séno

Tchépone

Savannakhet

Dong Hene

THAILAND

Saravane

BOLOVENS PLATEAU

Pakseng

Attopeu

CAMBODIA

This uncritical acceptance of the story was evident even in the American liberal press, which usually tends to shy away from saber-rattling. As early as August 9, 1959, the Washington *Post* editorialized that "the possibility cannot be ruled out that the dispatch of troop help in response to the Laotian request may become imperative even before the UN reaches a decision." (During that second week of August 1959 according to the Laotian government's official report to the United Nations, the Lao army's own losses amounted to twelve men as against the Pathet Lao's nineteen).

And while the chanceries of the world were being stimulated into action over the Laos crisis, Laos was getting ready to celebrate the marriage of Princess Dala Savang Vathana, daughter of then crown prince Savang Vathana, to the son of a high dignitary of the court of Luang Prabang. Beginning on August 1, four high officials of the royal court spread the tidings of the marriage throughout the kingdom in accordance with established rites. Then on August 8, at the precise hour and minute chosen by the astrologers, the engagement ceremony was celebrated. Finally on August 10, the official marriage ceremony took place, to which high dignitary and diplomatic representatives from Laos and from the surrounding countries were invited. Marriage rites began at precisely 4:40 in the afternoon, while a chartered aircraft, diverted from its usual supply runs to encircled outposts of the Laotian Army, spread multicolored confetti over the city of Luang Prabang.

The ceremony ended late in the evening with a theatrical presentation from the Ramayana. The senior army officers were also invited, and in most army posts the happy event was also celebrated by banquets. This was also the case at Xieng-Ngeun, where the former Pathet Lao troops of UCPL Battalion No. 1 were stationed. At Xieng-Ngeun, also, festivities had taken place and, since the camp was fairly close to Luang Prabang, many of the officers had gone there to watch them. That night, about one-third of the former members of Battalion No. 1 quietly left camp with their weapons and equipment and disappeared into the nearby jungle. News of guerrilla activities of that new group of rebels soon began to appear in Laotian reports, as the posts of Sop Sang, Paphay, Ban Napa, Nalane, and Pakseng were attacked in succession.

At the same time, what the French like to call *la guerre des communiqués*—"the war of the press releases"—continued in Vientiane and elsewhere. In an interview granted by Phoui Sananikone on August 14, 1959, the Laotian Prime Minister now used the Pathet Lao attack as an *ex post facto* rationale to justify his previous policy, confirming at the same time that he would send his brother Ngon Sananikone to New York to request

United Nations observers (probably without realizing the irony of this request since any such commission, as it turned out, would in all likelihood contain at least some representatives from non-committed nations, just as the old ICC did) and expressing his certitude that such observers would be "soon fully educated as to the effective aid given by the DRVN [Democratic Republic of Viet-Nam] to the rebellion." When asked about precise evidence of Viet-Minh interference, the Prime Minister declared that "the Viet-Minh are much too smart to let themselves get caught in a flagrant violation," adding that he did not think that regular Viet-Minh units had intervened but that there was "considerable indirect aid." Interestingly enough, Phoui Sananikone also confirmed that Prince Souphanouvong had several times offered to act as a mediator between the government and the UCPL units but that his offers had been *rejected by the government.*[17] Then, as suddenly as they had begun, Pathet Lao attacks upon Lao army positions almost ceased after August 14, and another wave of unjustified optimism—just as unrealistic as the intervening despair—swept through both Vientiane and Washington. The official Laotian view was that the rebels had wanted, and failed, to spark a popular uprising to support their attacks, while according to the New York *Times,* it was felt in Washington, "that the pullback came quickly on the heels of a statement by President Eisenhower at his Wednesday news conference that he intended to take up the attack on Laos with Premier Khrushchev."[18] And even as level-headed a study as the previously cited Rand Corporation report came forth with the surprising bit of intelligence that the "Pathet Lao columns broke under the mild resistance of the Royal Army." That lull—along with the optimism—was to last only three days before a new wave of bad news disturbed the midsummer doldrums.

The Second Wave

While the reassuring news of the slowing-down of the fighting was still on the news wires, new skirmishes were being reported in Vientiane, at the very same moment when Ngon Sananikone, brother of the Laotian Prime Minister, was on his way to the United Nations to present the Laotian charges of aggression to that august body. The Laotians were again trying the "one-two" punch method of diplomacy which had stood them in such good stead on earlier occasions—at Bandung and in India, for example, when visits of Laotian emissaries were accompanied by the presentation of reports of hostile activities. Here again, the news in itself was not alarming; in fact, a close reading showed that the alleged attacks had taken place on or before July 25, and had been delayed in transmission until August 16. Even so, the Sunday calm of August 16, 1959, was shattered by headlines to the effect that wounded from the border post of Muong Song had reported that they had been attacked by Black T'ai and Kha tribesmen who were being commanded by "Vietnamese officers."

That particular propaganda gambit had of course been used by every cold war belligerent in the last fifteen years—there had been allegations of MIG jet pilots in Korea speaking Russian to each other, and the Israelis in the 1956 Sinai campaign had alleged that Russian had been heard in the radio communications between the Egyptian tank crews—but no one asked the simple question how Vietnamese commands could have been distinguished in the din of an infantry night battle. In any case, not to be outdone, Peking charged on the following day that American pilots were "active in the Laos battle" and that the United States was "instigating other Asian nations to carry out a big conspiracy of military intervention against Laos."

On August 20, Ngon Sananikone arrived in New York and paid a twenty-minute call on UN Secretary General Hammarskjöld, in the course of which he transmitted to the United Nations *not,* as was expected, an official complaint of aggression against Laos' Communist neighbors but merely an invitation "to suggest procedures in such measures as might be considered suitable to achieve a peaceful settlement of differences at present experienced by Laos." And again as if to back up the new Laotian move in New York, the Laotian Ministry of Defense issued on the following day the first communiqué after a whole week of silence, which prophesied that the enemy "would unleash a large-scale offensive. In this second phase of his offensive, his activities will be general and extend to the whole territory of the kingdom." Such an advance notice of the enemy's future intentions, coming from a young army whose intelligence branch was of very recent creation, surely must be considered as remarkable.

The same communiqué also spoke of the presence of two Viet-Minh regular battalions of Regiment 174 of the 316th Division, allegedly operating deep in the province of Sam-Neua. Lastly, the communiqué referred to an encounter that had taken place on August 18 near Muong-Khoua, in which the enemy had lost three killed while the Laotian Army had taken sixteen prisoners of whom the majority were Viet-Minh, i.e., North Vietnamese Communists. Here again, the American press did its job well; news that "Reds Mass in North for Offensive" was carried in banner headlines in the United States. Yet, when the Royal Laotian Government presented its itemized day-by-day report on Communist attacks in Laos to the United Nations three weeks later, *no mention whatever was made of an attack on August 18 or of the Communist casualties inflicted or Communist prisoners taken!*

Nevertheless, Communist pressure was building up, particularly in Sam-Neua province where Laotian government units, often more frightened by cries of alarm from Vientiane and the world press than by Communist pressure in their own sector, pulled back from outlying positions until the government-held area was little more than an elongated pocket around the city of Sam-Neua, precariously supplied by a constant stream of C-47s of the Royal Laotian Air Force and of sturdy Canadian-built "Otters"—single-engine aircraft flown by French pilots of "Air Laos" and the "Veha Akhat," civilian-owned and -operated airlines.

As for "home-front morale"—to the extent that this term can be applied in Laos—things were also deteriorating, for King Sisavang Vong, the old courageous ruler of Luang Prabang who in 1953 had defied both the French and the Communists in his determination to hold out in his capital, lay near death in his small palace after a reign of more than fifty-five years. Much had at one time been made in the world press (and even in some congressional hearings on foreign aid) about the "fact" that the name of the King was known only to sixty percent of the population, as if the affection of the Laotians for their sovereign could be measured by statistics. Naturally, assuming for a moment that this figure was accurate, it was totally misleading since at least fifty percent of the population in Laos is made up of non-Laotian tribesmen. The fact remains that the old King was, within the modest confines of his country, a "King's King"—courteous, wise, kind, and to the last endowed with a glimmer of humor and worldliness in his eyes that earned him the esteem of Laotians and foreigners alike.

But now on August 22, 1959, having reigned a record time of more than fifty-five years, the old monarch decided to transfer the mantle of royalty to his son, Prince Savang Vathana. Savang, an able and honest man of conservative leanings, had for years been overshadowed by the more outgoing personality of his royal father. As he now stepped forward to assume the regency for King Sisavang Vong, many Laotians associated the decline in health of their sovereign with the gradual disintegration of the kingdom. Gone was the buoyant optimism of barely a week ago as a profound gloom settled down over Luang Prabang and Vientiane.

On the war fronts little that was significant was happening—which does not mean that it was not being abundantly reported. Thus, new and severe attacks were reported on the Laotian post of Muong Peun, lying deep in the center of Sam-Neua province on the trail leading to the rear. The fact that Muong Peun was situated on that trail was of some importance—assuming that one wanted to march on foot from the interior of Laos to Sam-Neua, which no one in his sane mind had ever attempted during the rainy season. Thus, the fall of Muong Peun would not have materially affected the defense of Sam-Neua itself, since the latter, like Muong Peun itself, depended entirely on airborne supplies. In other words, the Communist probe on Muong Peun was more likely to impress the armchair strategists outside of Laos, who still tended to look at jungle warfare in European terms of overland communication lines, and the reporters of several newspapers and wire services who had begun to congregate at the "Hotel Constellation" in Vientiane.

The Muong Peun army post, as I know from my own stay there in August 1959, was typical of the Laotian field position of the time: Two little bamboo and wood barracks constructed on a small hillock overlooking the surrounding plain, encircled by a six-foot-high breasts of sand bags and wooden planks which were surrounded in turn by a few harmless strands of barbed wire—"just enough to keep the buffaloes from coming into the encampment," as the wags used to say. When the surrounding posts had suffered Communist probing attacks, the lieutenant who commanded at Muong Peun added a few shallow communication trenches leading to the sandbagged machine gun or mortar positions. In other words, Muong Peun was what the British in Malaya called a "jungle fort" but not a military position designed to withstand a concerted attack of any size. Throughout the whole 1959 crisis, Muong Peun itself never came under direct enemy fire and whatever evidence there was of Communist penetration in the peaceful valley consisted of assertions by tribesmen in the surrounding hills that they had seen "some Communists."

On August 21, the Laotian government undertook to reinforce the company-strength garrison of Muong Peun. This being the rainy season, the airfield at Muong Peun was too soggy to take on twin-engine heavy aircraft and it was decided to parachute in the reinforcements. These reinforcements consisted of two "sticks" of paratroops, or about forty-eight men. They were dropped on August 21 without incident, with the ex-

ception of a few ankle fractures due to the fact that the men were jumping
with basketball sneakers instead of the regulation paratroop boots which,
as has been explained before, had unaccountably disappeared from Laotian Army stocks in Vientiane. When the news hit the Associated Press
tickers in the United States, it was presented as follows:

> The government is dropping hundreds of paratroopers on Sam-Neua's
> Muong Peun fortress, surrounded by steep palisades and depending en-
> tirely on air drops for its supplies.
>
> Observers say the fortress looks like the famed battlegrounds of Dien
> Bien Phu, where the French failed in the last major battle of the Indo-
> Chinese war.

The New York *Times,* which tended to be less impressionable, fleshed
out the AP dispatch with news from its own sources and reduced the number of paratroopers to 125. It also cited a Laotian Defense Ministry dispatch which stated that "Muong Peun was not surrounded by rebels," but
it did swallow and propagate the hoary fairytale that the two hilltop
wooden shacks of Muong Peun resembled the fiery hell of Dien Bien
Phu where 16,000 French elite troops had been literally smothered by
concentrated artillery fire of 340 Communist cannon backing 50,000 in-
fantrymen! Here again, the official Laotian government report presented
to the United Nations Mission in September is more eloquent and truthful
than the combined might of the American news media represented in
Laos: Throughout its whole day-by-day recital of Communist attacks or
engagements, *not once* is Muong Peun even mentioned.

But the news reporting (if not the war) was getting worse rather than
better. August 22 and 23 had been extremely rainy in the Mekong Valley.
Thus, my friend Bernard Lafont, the delegate of the Ecole Française
d'Extrême-Orient in Vientiane, and I were not unduly surprised when
the Laotian servants reported at breakfast that the combination of truck
and bus which brought in fresh vegetables every day from the downriver
town of Ban Pak Ca-Dinh had not arrived that morning. "I guess the rains
washed out the bridge again," remarked my friend who had traveled over
that flimsy bridge many times, and without further alarm, breakfast continued.

The bridge washout turned out to be a true estimate of the situation at
Ban Pak Ca-Dinh; the bridge was precariously propped up a few days
later and we were again fully supplied with fresh vegetables. That prosaic
incident, however, would scarcely have made headlines anywhere. One

can just imagine the New York *Times* topping off a page-one story with "Rains Cut Laos Vegetable Supply." It seemed much more sensible to attribute the washouts to a Communist breakthrough, and the title duly read "Laos Insurgents Take Army Post Close to Capital," with the lead paragraph containing the ominous lines: "Pro-Communist insurgents have attacked and infiltrated parts of Vientiane province, Western military sources said here today."[19] What gave the story an additional international flavor was that the New York *Times* was able to report that General Amkha Soukhavong, then the Laotian northern sector commander, had observed that the Ban Pak Ca-Dinh "attack" had had the support of Communist Vietnamese who had been residing in refugee camps in northern Thailand and who supposedly had crossed over into Laos to support the rebel thrust in that river town. I happen to know General Amkha personally; he is a level-headed man who had risen to the rank of major in the French Army—a unique feat in Laos, I believe—and who also was the only senior Laotian officer to be of the Christian faith. While those events were reportedly happening at Ban Pak Ca-Dinh, General Amkha himself was bottled up in Sam-Neua some hundred and fifty air miles to the north. Thus, any comment he might have had on the "attack" on Ban Pak Ca-Dinh was most likely to have been a speculation stimulated by questions put to him by a journalist. The story made him endorse as fact an event about which he could not possibly have had direct knowledge. Needless to say, the Laotian report to the United Nations was totally silent on the Ban Pak Ca-Dinh affair as well.

In New York, in the meantime, the conversations between Ngon Sananikone and Dag Hammarskjöld continued. It was quite apparent that the United Nations, a body certainly extremely sensitive to threats to the peace, real or fancied, was not yet ready to intervene openly in the Laotian problem. In any case, the United Nations Secretary-General made no preparations to send observers to Laos. And whatever arrangements had been made between the Laotian special envoy and the United Nations, they did not include an immediate appeal to the Security Council (whose specific job it is to maintain world peace)—or for that matter to the special session of the General Assembly. And as if to further downgrade the urgency of the Laotian crisis, Hammarskjöld made ready to pay a courtesy visit to several Latin American countries.

Once more, it seemed that the Laotian crisis was simmering down, in spite of a declaration by a spokesman of the Department of State at a Washington press conference on August 24 that the "situation in Laos was grave." Nevertheless, the spokesman took care to leave his audience with the impression the Communists were mainly carrying out "raids" rather than trying to occupy an army post permanently. In the course of his own press conference of August 25, President Eisenhower declared that the United States was considering the request for additional financial aid made by the Laotian government, at the same time denying that Laos was seeking American troop commitments. During direct conversations between the Laotian special envoy and J. Graham Parsons, the new Assistant Secretary of State for Far Eastern Affairs and former American ambassador to Laos, the details of that aid were hammered out, but direct American participation in Laos war effort was at that time limited to a few battered civilian aircraft flying supply runs to Laotian outposts.

On the Communist side as well, August 25 was a day for diplomatic activity. A North Vietnamese spokesman warned the Laotian government that if it continued to "toe the line of the United States in expanding the civil war," both Laos and the United States would have to bear the full responsibility for all the disastrous consequences. At the same time, the Hanoi spokesman branded as "crude slanders" the Laotian assertions that at least two regular Viet-Minh battalions had been operating in Sam-Neua province. Peking reported simultaneously that Ho Chi Minh was about to return to Hanoi after a month-long visit in the Soviet Union and several briefer talks with Chinese Communist leaders.

These diplomatic moves were matched inside Laos by new reports of attacks along the traditional invasion routes from North Viet-Nam to the royal capital at Luang Prabang, where the old King lay dying. Here again, it can be said that near-total ignorance of French verb forms led the American journalist up another garden path. On August 26, the official Laotian government report, couched in precise French, mentioned that an engagement "might have taken place near Pakseng, forty-five miles east of Luang-Prabang," which resulted in "what might have been a certain emotion" among the population of Luang Prabang. The key word in that French-language communiqué was the conditional auxilliary *serait* which can be translated as "would have been" or "might have been."

But the Associated Press, on August 25, saw the situation as follows: "Some fifty families yesterday were reported fleeing Luang Prabang as reports of approaching rebels touched off some panic in the city." I happened to have been in Luang Prabang on August 26 and 27, 1959. If ever there was an unpanicky town, this was it. Clouds were lying low over the narrow valley, partly interdicting air traffic. Nobody was feverishly digging trenches as in 1953 when the invasion had been real, and "Mister" Heintges, the civilian-garbed American general who headed the "Program Evaluation Office (PEO)," the local version of the American Military Advisory Group, could be seen reviewing the Laotian guard company near the airfield. The French-built fortifications of 1953–54 were quietly rotting in the jungle, unmanned; there was no airlift carrying in reinforcements— in brief, if there was fighting, particularly that which threatened the royal capital, its sounds were certainly muffled around here. The only panic observable was at the French Advisory Group's mess, where the spate of bad flying weather had produced a distinct shortage of red wine. And thus ended the second wave of the Laos crisis of 1959.

September High Tide

I have been told that one of the most important virtues of the good journalist is that peculiar sixth sense which places him at the right spot when the news is about to break. It is precisely what now happened in tiny Laos. With the uncanny ability of the birds of prey who can sense the death throes of a still-living creature, journalists began to converge upon Vientiane from all over the world. There were long-haired Asia-wise Anglo-Saxons from Australia and New Zealand; close-cropped, cynical Frenchmen who had "seen it all once before"; former German general staff officers now working as military commentators who sought similarities between the Communist use of mortars at Muong-Het and Russian artillery preparations for the battle of Dnepropetrovsk; American pundits who even before they arrived in Laos, knew that the fate of the free world was being decided in the jungle hills of Sam-Neua; a little German girl who represented several ladies' magazines in her home country but wanted to take a crack at outdoing Marguerite Higgins; tiny Filipinos who, trying to model themselves after their own conceptions of an American journalist, were burdened down with huge sombreros, four cameras each and ten-inch cigars; and here and there in that motley assemblage one or two of the old canard-wise "Asia hands" or real war correspondents who could tell the difference between a shallow hole caused by a hand grenade and the conical crater of a 105-mm. HE shell. The output of reporting on Laos (if not the quality) shot up impressively.

On August 29, the New York *Times* asserted that Laos was beginning to "feel the strain of the fight" and that a "high-ranking briefing officer" had described the situation as "one of unrest bordering on panic." In the follow-up story filed by a newly arrived man-on-the-spot, the Laotian armed forces were estimated at "24,500 troops plus 16,000 'minute-men or constabulary troops.'" Although the article admitted that there were only 10,000 troops in the Laotian Army who were properly trained and equipped with modern weapons, the total figure of 40,000 Laotians under arms was probably the most inaccurate statistics yet reported.

As for the "strain" of the war on Laos, it was most visible in the hotel facilities of Vientiane where the price of French mineral water—the only kind of water considered safe for drinking by the Anglo-Americans— soon exceeded the price of the poorer brands of French wine. That strain "bordering on panic" likewise did not prevent the city of Vientiane from breaking out in gay red and white bunting and thousands of red flags with white elephants in order to greet, on August 30, Crown Prince Savang Vathana who arrived from Luang Prabang to take his oath of office as Regent before a giant gilded statue of Buddha at the ancient That Ong-Tu. But while those rather peaceful pursuits were transpiring in Vientiane, some real attacks (in fact, the first real attacks of the war) were being launched on the fringes of Sam-Neua province during the night of August 29–30, 1959.

September Fog

Night settles early and lasts long in the tropics, even in August. In the highlands of Laos, it is almost always followed by hours of dense fog at dawn, giving the countryside the delicate air of unreality of a Chinese ink painting. The night of August 29–30 was no exception along the Laotian posts on the Nam Ma. Although the Nam Ma (see map) is not a border river but for most of its course flows from ten to eighteen miles inside Laos, to all practical purposes the strip of Laotian territory located between the North Vietnamese border and the Nam Ma constituted more or less a no man's land in which the Laotian government did not seek to exercise its administrative and, above all, its military presence. Only the villages directly located along the river contained Laotian troops of any importance.

Among the most important of those garrisons—none of which exceeded about two hundred men in strength—were the posts of Muong Het, Xieng Kho, Sop Sai, Sop Bau, and Sop Hao. The smallest of these posts, Sop Bau, was held by a single platoon of thirty men. When dawn broke on August 30, the northern post of Muong Het was suddenly blanketed by

81-mm. mortar fire that was as heavy as it was unexpected. To be smothered with mortar fire when you expect it least and when your own mortars can find no suitable counter target is an unnerving experience. For the garrison in Muong Het, it proved to be too much, and within an hour after the attack, having flashed an alarm signal to the area headquarters at Sam-Neua, the garrison at Muong Het simply fled.

According to the accounts of the survivors (after about two weeks, the bulk of the garrison straggled into Sam-Neua with much of its individual equipment) the mortar barrage had *not* been followed by an infantry attack; or, if it had been followed by an infantry attack, the garrison was no longer there to witness it because it had begun its retreat much earlier. Exactly the same thing happened at the neighboring large garrison of Xieng Kho, which also pulled out under mortar fire, followed in the course of the same day by the garrisons of the other Nam Ma River line posts. The small post of Sop Bau was ordered to fall back before it was attacked. It is worth emphasizing that in nearly all those attacks in Sam-Neua province, contact between Royal troops and their adversaries was at a minimum; in almost all cases, such confrontations as occurred were limited to mortar fire of varying intensity and to sightings by villagers of "Lao-Viet" troops or T'ai-Dam mountaineers, or in many cases "dark shadows coming out of the fog."

With that kind of evidence to go on, the headlines in the American press erupted into banners that made the situation look one bare shade less alarming than the outbreak of the Korean War or the beginning of a new Berlin blockade. But beyond doubt the crown in alarmist reporting of what followed must go to the noted columnist of the New York *Herald Tribune* and the Washington *Post,* Joseph Alsop. With the uncanny sixth sense of the journalist which I already have referred to, Alsop had arrived in Laos at precisely the right moment and, like all the other journalists in quest of the "grim reality," he had made his pilgrimage to General Amkha's headquarters at Sam-Neua. His article, written on the spot, reflects perfectly the extent of inaccurate information that was being disseminated in 1959–61 in Laos and abroad; and, because he is a reporter marvelously able at ferreting out the pertinent details, his stories were elaborated with more liberty than most. Thus, in his article "The Strange War on Laos' Border," Alsop describes in graphic terms how the Laotian Commander in Chief, General Ouane Rathikoun, found out about the Nam Ma River line attack forty-eight hours after it happened, thus conveying the impression that no one outside those posts had known about the attack earlier and making the nice point that Laotian army communications in 1959 were only a trifle slower than those of King Harold of England at the time of the Norman invasion of 1066.

While that little story makes nice reading, it is not quite accurate. As Alsop reported, a French bush pilot, a former Austrian from the French Foreign Legion, Leopold Marold, had flown his small supply aircraft to Muong Het on August 31 and had drawn Communist machine-gun fire as he was about to set his wheels on the short grass airstrip near the fort. While this was happening I myself was flying to a destination fifty miles to the northwest of Muong Het in another Laotian aircraft piloted by one Captain Catry. Our pilot (as a matter of normal precaution in a country where airplane ground control is in its infancy) was in radio contact with Marold at that particular time and heard both his exclamation of surprise and the ensuing unprintable oaths uttered by Marold upon seeing a few holes appear in one of his wings. We not only reported that incident at our intermediate stop at Luang Prabang but also related it to the Laotian Army Command in Vientiane upon arriving there that same evening.

A few hours later, Marold who had successfully pulled out from the trap—for had the Communist gunners not been overeager, they probably could have captured on the ground his airplane with its precious cargo of ammunition and other supplies—reported the incident himself to the Laotian authorities. And as was mentioned before, almost all the Laotian outposts had by then been provided with United States Army field radios. I personally was to observe radio communications between Sam-Neua and far smaller units than the rather substantial garrisons of Muong Het and Xieng Kho. So much, then, for that part of the story.

The rest does not exactly constitute an improvement over the beginning. It deals with the sudden arrival from Muong Het and Xieng Kho of four "scrawny, wiry little villagers," one of whom had a "severe leg wound." According to Alsop, they had hiked all the way from Muong Het and Xieng Kho, a distance of sixty-one and seventy kilometers, respectively, to bring the news of the battle to Sam-Neua. We can trust Joseph Alsop, an M.D. by training, as to the severity of the leg wound; but in that case the ability of the villagers to cover forty miles of dense jungle, in the middle of the monsoon season, inside forty-eight hours surely borders on the miraculous. In fact, anyone who ever has had to hack his way through tropical jungle will consider himself lucky to have covered ten miles in a full day's march.

The story finally ends on another touching note: As Alsop and Generals

Ouane and Amkha were sauntering over to the officers mess, they encountered another group of villagers, including ten-year-old boys, who apparently also had beaten a world marching record in their flight from Xieng Kho to Sam-Neua. One of the little ten-year-olds was carrying his father's gun (pictures of ten-year-olds carrying submachine guns in Laos recurred throughout the American press from then on until May 1961), and General Ouane allegedly stopped to hand the boy a coin. It surely must have been a French colonialist silver piaster, because *none* of the governments in the area have issued anything else but paper currency in the past twenty years.

Since Joseph Alsop's desire to report the truth cannot be doubted, one can only conclude that he, along with dozens of other reporters, had simply been trapped by his tendency to view events in a manner that best suited his own preconceived notions and not as they actually developed in the field. Once the image of a large-scale invasion had taken hold, all the other pieces of the puzzle conveniently fell into place. In Alsop's subsequent column on the subject the story was embroidered with more lurid detail; the refugees now reported that "Vietnamese regulars also manned the heavy weapons"—as if that heavy equipment had been placed close enough to their objective for anyone to identify their gunners, particularly in the fog at six o'clock in the morning!

The columnist—whose experience with infantry weaponry apparently is somewhat limited—speaks of "80-mm. mortars" (he probably means the 81-mm.) and of "another important innovation of this war"—the 57-mm. recoilless rifle. The fact that the Pathet Lao and the Viet-Minh had such recoilless rifles since 1951 was a piece of first-hand knowledge to most Laotian veterans of the Indo-China war. The crowning piece of information in the military category was that Muong Het had been bombarded not only by mortars but by "125-mm. cannon from the North Vietnamese artillery post at Ban Dan about six miles across the border." Here again even a cursory check with the local American military personnel would have shown that 125-mm. was an odd caliber not readily found in anyone's military arsenal; and a somewhat more attentive check on a large-scale Laotian map would have revealed that Muong Het is more than ten miles and one mountain range away from the North Vietnamese border and thus almost unreachable by normal field artillery. Having declared that Muong Het fell within an hour after the attack had begun (i.e., at seven A.M.), the article then goes on to state that the "fifty boys in the village school fought with the defenders." One wonders how in the chaos of a dawn attack the schoolboys could have been mustered for a defense of the village when the army troops which were supposed to protect it were apparently not putting up too spirited a resistance. Lastly, the article speaks of the "key border post" of Tha Thom which, in reality, far from being a border post at all, happens to be located in the center of the Laotian "panhandle" and thus at least thirty-five air miles and two mountain ranges removed from North Viet-Nam. But this story and many others like it began to make the rounds of press wires and of Western chanceries, and the myth, supported by such first-hand "evidence," proved hard to kill.

It is therefore not surprising that as sophisticated a newspaper as the Washington *Post* would publish an editorial on September 5, 1959, in which the above hoary tale was cited as a "splendid example of alert, on-the-spot reporting," which "told how the hit-and-run guerrilla attacks have now been augmented with a full-scale artillery-backed invasion from Communist North Viet-Nam." In order to squelch in advance any of us doubting Thomases, that liberal newspaper was quite ready to apply some of the tar-brush techniques it had so often deplored in the past: "To doubt the circumstantial evidence is merely to abet the Communist disguise." On the Laos question at least, American public opinion was reaching a high level of what, in psychological warfare parlance, is called "self-intoxication." In a democracy, this is an unsound situation, at best.

Once more, the Communists refused to play the game according to the rules; practically within forty-eight hours after the Nam Ma River line disaster, the situation began to quiet down—helped in no small way by the fact that the Laotian General Staff had shut down all its offices for forty-eight hours in order to celebrate the Buddhist Festival of the Dead with all the dignity befitting the holiday. In any case, a realistic appraisal of the situation (as well as a look at a good map) would have shown that the royal government had thus far not sustained any decisive losses, both in terms of terrain and of man power. To be sure, it controlled little more in Sam-Neua province than the provincial capital and a few outposts whose sole connection with the outside world were the little "Otter" aircraft— but it had not controlled even those between 1954 and 1957.

In terms of military armament, the Communist attacks, such as they were, had given the United States ample reason to step up its program of military deliveries and military training in Laos and had at the same time, as Captain Lederer points out in his book, stifled all further congressional criticism of American operations in Laos. Hence, in spite of all appearances to the contrary, the crisis had thus far not brought any tangible international benefits whatever to the Communists but had helped a great deal the "young Turk" regime in Vientiane. Once more, Laotians had won through diplomacy what they were losing on the battlefield and they now proceeded swiftly to consolidate their gains in the international arena of the United Nations.

On September 4, 1959, the Vientiane government asked the United Nations to send an emergency force to help stop aggression by its Communist neighbor, North Viet-Nam. The Laotian complaint was formally circulated among all the United Nations members while Secretary-General Hammarskjöld, who was still on his South American tour, decided to cut it short by one day and to return to New York on Sunday, September 6. The tenor of the new Laotian note to the United Nations showed how much the climate had changed in Vientiane in less than two months. Gone were the days when the "young Turks" would bristle at the very idea of "foreign interference" or of a threat to Laos' "sovereignty." The new note specifically requested "the sending in the shortest possible time of an emergency force in order to stop the aggression and prevent it from spreading."

That weekend, the American press was once more carried away, although statements by more sensible souls, notably Senator J. William Fulbright and even senior officials from Thailand, preferred to preface their statement about the crisis with a cautionary "if." But to "our men in Laos" representing the bulk of the American press, the situation presented no shadow of a doubt. In another portentous first-hand report entitled "Is There Aggression?" Alsop made short shrift of the skeptics. Referring to Japanese reports indicating that a United Nations investigation would be desirable prior to labeling the situation in Laos an invasion, he said that "it would be hard to imagine a more ironically superfluous venture." And then, he developed his invasion theory into a parable which, in the light of what happened in Cuba in April 1961, would be sufficient for several minutes of hearty laughter—if the story were not so sad and if anyone save a political scientist or a historian bothered to read old newspaper columns. In that memorable column, Alsop conjured the absurd image of the CIA selecting "reasonably . . . combative . . . refugees," and argued, "imagine, further, the CIA training and arming these people as guerrilla units" in a neighboring country. As if the possibility of the CIA training refugees as guerrilla fighters against their own former country were not sufficiently unthinkable, Alsop wrote, "the imagination has to be considerably stretched to picture the peaceful Allen Dulles carrying out any such scheme as this." Alsop then concludes this perfectly prophetic image of things to happen two years later by saying that even the most respectable anti-Communist elements in this country, along with the United States Senate, would be "in full cry" against such "flagrant aggression."

It is perhaps an indication of the change in the national mood and of times in general that when the Cuban invasion aborted, not only the most respectable anti-Communist elements, but a considerable number of middle-of-the-roaders and liberals, tended to regret more that the operation had been bungled than that it had been attempted at all. And only the most determined and idealistic liberals (as well, of course, as the habitual left-wing elements) would stand by Alsop's definition of "aggression." Although Alsop did not know it, what was happening in Laos already had become part of that new shadow—and of "revolutionary war" in which sovereign countries seemed to be perfectly authorized, free, and immune to carry out warlike operations in neighboring countries without undue reprisals—be this the case of Tunisia in Algeria, Cuba in Nicaragua, the United States in Cuba, or Red China in Korea.

In the meantime, however, the United States had now decided to take the matter seriously, and, if possible, to use it as a battering ram in the forthcoming United Nations discussion. On Sunday, September 6, the headline read: "U.S. Links War in Laos to Moscow and Peking." The State Department released an official declaration on the same day which fully accepted the thesis of outside Communist intervention as proved by the following facts:

(1) The assistance evidently being received by the Communist forces within Laos, including supplies and military weapons that could be provided only from Communist territory;

(2) The false—and ridiculous—Communist propaganda . . . to the effect that the Laos government has been instigated by the United States to "stir up a civil war" within its boundary;

(3) The continuing flow from Moscow, Peking, and Hanoi of propaganda and false information . . . stating that the U.S. is using Laos as a military base; and

(4) The fact that the military outbreak in Laos has followed conferences in Moscow and Peking [between the senior Communist leaders of Russia, China, and North Viet-Nam].

The meeting of the Security Council which began at three P.M. on Monday, September 7, 1959, ended on a double ambiguity: Just as the meeting was coming to order, the Vientiane government announced that all the "foreign invaders" had departed from the province of Sam-Neua and that whatever Communist forces remained there now were native to Laos; at the same time, Prime Minister Phoui Sananikone proclaimed martial law throughout Laos in view of the gravity of the situation. Laotian Defense Secretary Phoumi Nosavan, again using the traditional Laotian one-two punch of negotiating, simultaneously told the Associated Press representative in Vientiane that Laos would not hesitate to call upon SEATO, should its request for United Nations forces be turned down.

The United Nations debate ran true to form, that is, the Russians immediately announced that they would vote against the sending of an inquiry commission to Laos. On the allied side, the United States, France, and Britian submitted a motion to the Security Council, requesting that a subcommittee of the Council, composed of Argentina, Italy, Japan, and Tunisia, be sent on the spot to Laos in order to inquire into the Laotian charges of aggression. The proposal was so worded as to avoid, if at all possible, a Russian veto; in particular, it avoided branding Communist North Viet-Nam as an aggressor. But caution in the wording alone was not sufficient to stop Soviet Ambassador Arkady A. Sobolev from threatening to use the veto, should the West insist upon its position. The next move hinged upon whether the West would be successful in making the appointment of a Security Council subcommittee a procedural issue not subject to Big Power veto, or whether the Soviet Union would succeed in its countermove to have the motion recognized as substantive. In the first vote on the issue, the tally went ten to one in favor of the Western position; whatever the Soviet delegate did now was merely a face-saving rearguard action which no longer could really affect the basic issue of whether or not the United Nations would send a mission to Laos.

While matters were turning in favor of Laos at the United Nations, Laotian Foreign Minister Khamphan Panya was pushing Laos' case forward at SEATO as well. Banking on the excellent relations existing between the Laotian government and Bangkok, Khamphan now attempted to marshal a unified SEATO position on the Laotian issue while the State Department was attempting to hammer out a similar position in Washington in the course of a "private get-together" of the SEATO ambassadors with acting Secretary of State Douglas Dillon. On September 8, 1959, the United Nations voted the fact-finding subcommittee into existence over the protesting (but non-veto) "nay" of the Soviet Union. This vote, considering the flimsiness of the evidence presented, constituted not only a tactical victory for the Western viewpoint but must be judged, from the viewpoint of Laotian diplomacy, as a major achievement.

The fact that on that particular day most of the Laotian spokesmen got their wires crossed and reported completely contradictory stories about what was going on in their homeland was completely overlooked in the general feeling of relief that, finally, "something was being done." Thus, the reliable British news agency Reuters reported from Vientiane on September 8 that the fort of Sam Teu, according to military sources, had been evacuated under heavy Communist pressure; while at the same time the then acting Foreign Minister Sisouk na Champassak stated that "seven hundred soldiers of North Viet-Nam" were still assaulting Sam-Neua province and "were believed likely to attack Sam Teu fort within the next few days." Foreign Minister Khamphan Panya announced in Bangkok, while on his way to United Nations headquarters in New York, that four thousand Communist troops had penetrated into Laos from North Viet-Nam, while on the same day the Laotian government informed its acting delegate at the United Nations by cable that "all North Viet-Nam troops had been withdrawn."

In the world press outside the United States, some of those contradictions were detected early and doubts as to the real extent, or even the existence, of a large-scale Communist invasion of Laos had been voiced in many responsible newspapers. No major American newspaper saw significance in the fact that the United Nations, while voting to send an inquiry commission to Laos had failed to act on the Laotian request for a United Nations police force—a fact mentioned on page 1 of the *Wiener Zeitung* of Austria on September 9. On that very day, the pro-Western *L'Orient* of Beirut (Lebanon) carried in its headlines the question: "The Laotian Affair—Political Maneuver Designed by the Partisans of the Membership of the Country in SEATO?" and also mentioned that Khamphan Panya would find UN Secretary Hammarskjöld reluctant to send United Nations forces to Laos.

In the United States itself, Senator Mike Mansfield, then assistant Senate Democratic whip, not only cautioned the Eisenhower Administration to go slow before getting overly involved in Laos, but confronted the Administration with several much-overdue, searching questions: Which American agency was responsible for the policies embarked upon in Laos? What were the reasons for the royal government's failure after the hundreds of millions of dollars expended there? What was the extent of American influence used in bringing about the withdrawal of the ICC? None of these questions ever received a public answer. Within less than two weeks, such and similar questions were to receive rather shattering answers both by the United Nations subcommittee in Laos and by a belatedly awakening American press.

Mission on the Spot

The approval of the United Nations had barely been given to establish a subcommittee for Laos when the four nations concerned began their task. Here again, the solidly pro-American character of that mission must be underscored in view of what was to follow. Italy was a member of NATO; Argentina a member of the Organization of American States; Japan was tied to the United States by its security treaty; and Tunisia was, until the Bizerte affair of 1961, the most pro-American of all the African states with the possible exception of Liberia. In other words, if there were any evidence that a Communist invasion had taken place, that mission would certainly not have been loath to report on it at great length. Yet as the Commission made ready to leave for Laos with a promptness that was, to say the least, unusual for an international body, events again took on a quieter turn in Vientiane.

Phoumi Nosavan, the "young Turk" strong man of the Phoui regime, had gone to Bangkok to take the pulse of things there and had spoken to his uncle, the strong man of Thailand, Marshal Sarit Thanarat. He returned to Vientiane after four days, having been told in friendly but nevertheless unmistakable terms that Thailand, for all its public determination, was not about to embark upon a military campaign without the absolute certainty of immediate American participation. In Vientiane itself, the breaches suffered by the American-Franco-British front during the summer were now mended, and the Pathet Lao were asserting that it was ready to negotiate with the royal government on the basis of the 1954 and 1957 agreements. Even the Red Chinese, while clearly unhappy about the arrival in Laos of a United Nations observation mission and still insisting that the "U.S. must not be allowed to usurp the name of the United Nations to intervene in Laos,"[20] apparently seemed prepared to view the Laotian problem in terms other than a junior edition of the Korean War.

A problem of a minor nature which nevertheless was to haunt the

anti-Communist government of Laos for the next two years was that of
trying to live up to its flamboyant communiqués of an earlier period. On
several occasions, the Laotian government had boasted that it had captured up to fifty Communist prisoners in a single engagement and claimed
that the North Vietnamese origin of those prisoners could be fully substantiated. With the arrival of the U.N. mission imminent, the problem
of producing credible evidence of foreign intervention became truly acute;
for already on earlier occasions some of the French and British reporters—
particularly those who had been veterans of the Malayan or Indochinese
wars—had driven Laotian government spokesmen into tight corners by
their refusal to accept mortar-shell fragments as artillery-shell fragments
and suspect Laotian villagers herded together by the Laotian Army as
bona fide North Vietnamese from across the border.

That problem of actual proof of invasion was, as will be seen, never
quite resolved. The Laotian government on the eve of the arrival of the
mission, declared that "it has not yet been possible to find a North
Vietnamese prisoner but no effort shall be spared to find one." One correspondent of the New York *Times,* who was later to mock himself for
swallowing another canard cabled to his newspaper that

> Briefings have noticeably played down the activities of North Viet-Nam in
> the conflict. This led some observers to believe that Laotian political tac-
> ticians were creating a background that would soften the blow if the ob-
> servers' report on intervention by North Viet-Nam was negative.

When the United Nations mission debarked at Vattay airport in
Vientiane on September 15, it was truly given a hero's welcome as only
the Laotians know to prepare it: Willowy, sloe-eyed Laotian girls with
their tilted hair buns, clad in white blouses and beautiful embroidered
skirts offered the visitors from afar flower bouquets in wrought silver
vases, while the few miles from the airport to the capital were lined with
school children waving Laotian and some United Nations flags. Without
further ado, the members of the mission settled down to work, while in
far away London, the British government received from Moscow a request for a reconvening of the 1954 Geneva conference powers to discuss
the Laos problem—reflecting, no doubt, Moscow's second thoughts about
its unsuccessful stance at the United Nations in New York. The fact that
Soviet Premier Nikita Khrushchev was arriving in the United States at
that exact moment and needed all the good will he could muster probably
also played an important role.

The United Nations subcommittee had barely assumed duties when it was faced with a new Laotian accusation, according to which the little post of Sam Teu had been overwhelmed on September 12 by eight hundred attacking Viet-Minh backed by Pathet Lao forces and three hundred mortar shells. That charge, formally submitted to the United Nations, was described as "completely inaccurate" by the New York *Times* four days later.

The same problem of ambiguity, of contradictions in information provided by equally "official" sources, and of unbridled hearsay which had dogged the journalists and diplomats, now became the scourge of the United Nations subcommittee. The fact that the Laotians had not been able to marshal their evidence for the mission in time for their arrival also did not help matters; the Laotians requested a delay of several days in order to complete the documentation they wished to submit to the members of the subcommittee. Considering the haste with which the subcommittee had been assembled and the character of extreme urgency that had been given to its mission, the typical Laotian calm and laxity with which the whole war was viewed from Vientiane surely must have been anticlimactic to the Japanese, Italians, Argentines, and Tunisians sweltering in the monsoon heat and scant facilities of Vientiane.

Unfortunately for the Laotian government, it was not aware of the haste with which the mission had been dispatched to Laos; instead of concentrating in a businesslike manner on the essentials, the Laotians resorted to a diplomatic stratagem which to them may have been original but which that noted diplomatist and diplomat George F. Kennan has found to be an age-old gambit. Speaking of the Czarist Russians as they were faced with an allied mission in 1917, Kennan wrote in his recent masterpiece *Russia and the West:*

> They defended themselves against Allied curiosity and Allied demands in the traditional manner: by a combination of extravagant promises . . . and a formidable barrage of banquets and other social ordeals. . . . This was a combination guaranteed, by the experience of centuries, to get even the most sanguine Western visitor out of town—exhausted, bilious, empty-handed, but grateful for his escape—within a matter of weeks, if not days. . . . This technique superimposed on the general pallidness of Western curiosity worked very well.[21]

Exactly this was happening to the United Nations subcommittee, who were now being obliged to keep pace with a social calendar of two engagements a day. As Kennan pointed out in his book, the Allied missions soon had a vague feeling that they "were being had," but could do very little about it. The same kind of feeling was said to have prevailed very soon among the members of the United Nations subcommittee. Finally, on September 20, the Laotian government presented the fact-finding commission with twenty pages of documents which the New York *Times* described, without having seen them, as "damning" but which, upon publication by the United Nations later in the year, proved to be nothing but a day-to-day chronology of events in Laos since July 1959.

Oudone Sananikone, another spokesman of the Laotian government, also promised on the same day to present to the United Nations subcommittee seven former North Vietnamese soldiers from the "330th Division"—a unit that cannot be found on any of the available records of the North Vietnamese Army. At the same time, Sisouk na Champassak, in his capacity of acting Foreign Minister, repeated once more that his government "would never agree to the International Conference to consider Laotian problems along the line of that proposed by the Soviet Union." Less than eighteen months later, that very same Laotian government would be pleading for such a conference to be opened as soon as possible in order to save it from total destruction.

Second Thoughts

As if the Laotian tangle were not complicated enough with its various battle lines in Laos as well as at the UN, another problem was to reach an acute stage at this time. This concerned cooperation between the Laotians and the Americans on one hand, and the French on the other. Until then, relations between Laos and France had been more than cordial; as long as the health of the old King permitted it, he was a yearly guest at the French spa of Vittel. Laos, alone of all the member countries of the ill-fated French Union, had ratified all of the treaties and had participated fully in all the deliberations of its organs, and when nationalism in South Viet-Nam became tainted with Francophobia, many Frenchmen from Saigon transferred their businesses to Laos where they were received with open arms.

At the United Nations, Laos had defended France many times when most of the other Afro-Asian nations found it expedient to engage in the usual anticolonial rhetorics and platitudes. On the French side, there was little in Laos—once rich and populous Viet-Nam was lost—that made it profitable for the Paris government to maintain a presence there. Pre-occupied with events in North Africa, France had not even brought its bases and training mission in Laos up to the strength permitted by the 1954 Geneva Agreement, all statements to the contrary notwithstanding.[22] The French base as Xieng-Khouang had never been occupied and the French Air Force Base at Séno (mockingly called by the French themselves "our calling card at SEATO") had barely enough troops for the maintenance of the immediate security of the base, let alone the surrounding Laotian territory.

French commercial interests in Laos can best be described as "limited"; security had never been sufficiently re-established after World War II to permit the regular exploitation of two tin mines in the northern part of the Laotian "panhandle" and the few French importers and Corsican black marketeers were not the kind of citizens for whose economic rights the French Foreign Office would make a fighting stand. In fact, the French Ambassador to Laos at the time of the 1959 events, Olivier Gassouin, was ostracized by the French colony in Vientiane in part because he had allegedly said he would be a great deal happier if at least one-half of the French in Laos were repatriated.

The French view of the Laotian situation in 1959 was that Laos was by and large militarily indefensible—as they themselves had learned painfully in 1953 and 1954 during the horribly futile battle of Dien Bien Phu —and, that the neighboring Communist states would not tolerate a resolutely anti-Communist government, and that under the circumstances, a pro-Western Laotian government under a leader acceptable to both sides would be the best solution all around. It was the French view, largely shared by the United Kingdom, which was to prevail in 1961. In the meantime, however, the French opinion was dismissed as either "sour grapes" or simply as another case of French paranoic anti-Americanism. Joseph Alsop, never at a loss for a well-turned phrase, had defined this French mental state as "the dog-in-the-manger attitude of the French." Once this view of the French had taken hold, it was easy to dismiss all they were doing or saying as either inaccurate, biased, or even mischievous. And that was exactly what some Americans and the great majority of the Laotian "young Turks" now proceeded to do. Sisouk explained the process quite clearly in his book:

> French officials always thought that since they had been pushed out of South Viet-Nam by the pro-American Vietnamese in 1955, they would

suffer the same fate in Laos. This naïve but persistent idea made French diplomats suspicious of American efforts [and] led to different interpretations of the events of the summer of 1959, when the Viet-Minh crossed the Laotian border. . . .

The French press hardly helped to enlighten public opinion about the justification of the Laotian complaint against Viet-Minh aggression. French newspapers were skeptical and asked for proof. Did they have proof of Chinese intervention at Dien Bien Phu? Yet that intervention was never questioned by them.[23]

That statement, while it reflects views then popular in government circles in Vientiane, suffers from several inaccuracies. First of all, while some French officials in Laos no doubt found their American allies, in Sisouk's own words, "slightly cumbersome and perhaps somewhat boisterous," the French Ambassador himself proudly told everyone who wanted to hear it that U. S. Ambassador Horace Smith was his personal friend and not merely a diplomatic colleague. As far as the Chinese intervention at Dien Bien Phu was concerned, no serious-minded French writer or military expert had claimed such in the same sense as the Laotians were now speaking of a Viet-Minh invasion of Laos. The presence of technicians was known from first-hand visual evidence; a mutual assistance agreement between the Chinese People's Republic and the Viet-Minh existed openly and in writing since 1951.

As to the skepticism of French newspapermen about the stories with which they were presented by the Laotian information services, it was not born out of any sinister plot on the part of those journalists, but merely out of years of experience with similar bungled attempts of the French Information Services during the Indo-China war to utilize the press as an additional instrument of psychological warfare (failing at it just as much as the Laotians did). Those French journalists who covered the 1959 Laos crisis—Lucien Bodard, Max Clos, and Robert Favart, as well as André Lebon, the newsreel cameraman who lost a leg at the battle of Dien Bien Phu—had been too long at this game not to be able to detect the flaws and contradictions in the stories which they were told every day.

They were not trying to downgrade the *real* threat which the Laotians were facing—internal chaos, aided and abetted by a pro-Communist movement supported from the outside, whose combined effect really made the country come apart at the seams—but the story the Laotian government expected them to tell abroad would have hurt that government much more in the long run (as it did when the American newspaper writers found out that they had been led down the garden path) than the healthy grain of salt which the French reporters injected into their writing right from the beginning. In the meantime, however, and for the next eighteen months to come, to be a member of the French press in Laos was not exactly considered a choice assignment.

It is interesting to follow the letdown (or should one say: the comeuppance?) of the more superficial of the American reporters as it was revealed in their dispatches from Laos. As late as September 21, the reporter from the New York *Times,* citing the arrival of some wounded, asserted that "their arrival discounted private French Embassy assertions that no real fighting had taken place and that press reports of the conflict were gross exaggerations, based on Laotian and United States propaganda." That, of course, was perfect nonsense, since no one had denied that people were being attacked and killed; civil wars—and the Civil War in the United States is a perfect example of this—can be just as bloody as foreign wars; the fact that there were Laotian wounded clearly established the fact that there was fighting. It did *not* establish the fact that there was an organized North Vietnamese invasion.

On the following day, the Laotian Army barred all correspondents whether French or American, from all combat areas and forbade them to interview or photograph wounded soldiers. The step was declared to have been taken because of "distorted and untrue" dispatches sent out by those correspondents about the military situation. Here again, according to the New York *Times* of September 23, "the principal complaint had been against French correspondents who had written reports challenging the Army's account of various actions. . . . These were described as demoralizing for both civilians and military personnel."

What really had happened was that *American,* and not French, journalists had been able to go to Sam Teu which allegedly had been the scene of fierce seesaw fighting in the course of which 800 alleged Viet-Minh had "smothered" the post with more than 300 mortar shells. Among those American reporters was Richard Dudman from the St. Louis *Post-Dispatch,* a veteran of several war reporting jobs and a former captain in the United States Marines. Dick Dudman's report of what he saw at Sam Teu was a typical example of the "demoralizing" news that the French reporters had been sending out for several months. Instead of the 250-man garrison at Sam Teu, there had only been 140, of whom 30 men were in the post itself and the other 110 scattered in patrols over a 30 mile radius. After an interview with the Laotian lieutenant who commanded the garrison, Dudman summed up the situation as follows:

> As for the reported five hundred to six hundred attackers, the lieutenant's estimate was two hundred. He personally had seen only enemy patrols.
>
> The lieutenant said he and his men withdrew into the hills without waiting for an enemy attack. They returned the next morning and, seeing no one but assuming the enemy had been there in the night, re-entered the fort without firing a shot. . . .
>
> As evidence of foreign intervention for the UN Fact Finders, the lieutenant had already sent to Vientiane a gunny sack of mortar shell fragments some bearing the marking of "USA," as well as two homemade "potato masher" hand grenades made of tin cans attached to foot-long bamboo sticks, which he said had been found twenty miles away. This is part of the evidence, presumably, that led Admiral Arleigh Burke, Chief of Naval Operations, to conclude that this Communist "gnawing at the vitals of the free world" was "another extension of the Soviet Union's continuing peripheral efforts since World War II."[24]

As for the North Vietnamese troops allegedly involved in the attack, the only evidence which the commander at Sam Teu could think of was that "strange" soldiers had passed a village ten miles away and had not thanked the young Laotian girls who had offered them flowers, as was the custom. (And what Dudman did not know was that the likelihood of *Laotian* girls—rather than Méo or T'ai mountaineer girls—living ten miles from Sam Teu was remote.) Dudman's observations came to the attention of the undaunted New York *Times* which, on September 23, quoted other correspondents as saying that Sam Teu was "practically unscathed" and that it had never been occupied by enemy forces.

On the same day also the New York *Times* quoted an Associated Press dispatch (but not its own reporter there) from Vientiane which stated that the Laotian government *"had avoided accusing Communist North Viet-Nam of aggression in documents put before the special United Nations Fact Finding Committee."* On the following day the Laotian government withdrew another step from its previous position by simply failing to submit further documentation to the United Nations subcommittee and by not setting a date for the interrogation by the United Nations group of the seven alleged North Vietnamese prisoners held by the government.

It was obvious that as a propaganda gambit for the position of the Phoui Sananikone Administration and the "young Turks" of the CDIN, the U.N. subcommittee in Laos was unlikely to prove to be an overwhelming success.

The Laos debacle was not only straining American relations with France, it was also straining the relations of the Asian allies with the non-Asians within the Southeast Asia Treaty Organization (SEATO). SEATO, contrary to Communist charges, had certainly not acted as an "aggressor" or even as a "warmonger" in the Laotian crisis. On the contrary, the body of experts on Communist subversion and jungle warfare from the United States, Europe, Asia, and the countries of the South Pacific assembled in Bangkok proved to be a group of hard-headed men less likely to be swayed by "breathless" reports of idle press correspondents in search of a war than any other group of specialists working for any single government.

The annual conference of SEATO military advisers which began on September 20th and ended on September 24, 1959, dealt for obvious reasons almost entirely with the problem of possible SEATO intervention in Laos. As was to be expected, the Asian member countries of SEATO, with Thailand in the lead, carried the ball for immediate intervention in Laos. The stand of the members from Europe and the Pacific (Britain, France, Australia, and New Zealand) was that the situation beyond a doubt bore watching but did not warrant immediate intervention. France in particular stuck to the rather unpopular position that a return to the *status quo ante* of May 1958 was probably the most desirable of the solutions available under the circumstances.

The United States basically backed the position of the smaller Asian powers, with the important difference, however, that it was willing to consider SEATO intervention only if United Nations mediations had failed altogether. A conference of the SEATO foreign ministers or their representatives on September 28 produced little more than a confirmation of the wait-and-see policy adopted by SEATO at the insistence of the European and Pacific members. In the final paragraph of the official communiqué, the SEATO Council simply stated that it supported prompt action of the United Nations Security Council in response to the appeal of the royal Laotian government.

"Why They Called Off the Dogs"

The Laotian government in Vientiane certainly had read the SEATO communiqué and most certainly must have been aware of the impression the presentation of its case had made upon the United Nations subcommittee. But while it knew those facts, it may not have realized their implications, in a case of naïveté worthy of simpler times. Or perhaps, and this is probably more likely than any other explanation, the "young Turks," like the proverbial sorcerer's apprentice, had unleashed something they could no longer control.

They simply continued to go on on their old track of "full-scale Viet-Minh invasion" even though it became increasingly unlikely that either the UN or even Laos' closest allies were going to follow her along that path. On September 30, Foreign Minister Khamphan Panya gave the United Nations General Assembly a detailed report of North Viet-Nam's depredations in Laos, but it was obvious that Laos had now lost a good part of its audience. Even the hitherto gullible New York *Times* now printed the term "North Viet-Nam aggression" with cautionary quotation marks around the word "aggression," and in a type of journalistic sleight-of-hand worthy of a much smaller paper, the editorial of the New York *Times* of October 4 simply wrote off in advance the United Nations subcommittee's prospective report in the following terms:

> One may as well be honest about it. There never was much likelihood that this hastily improvised mission could come up with a definitive analysis of the situation and a strongly documented group of findings. . . . The odds were against such an achievement from the start.

In Laos itself, its local correspondent also did his best to retrieve himself from the limb onto which he had so blithely climbed a few weeks ago. He reported on the same day that all the prisoners who had been questioned by the Security Council subcommittee in Laos had turned out to be, as was expected, Laotians. And two days later again, it developed that whatever North Vietnamese prisoners were in the hands of Laotian authorities were no more than *deserters* from the North Vietnamese forces who, sick and tired of Communism, had voluntarily come over to the Laotians. What the report did not say (and, as far as I know, this has never been said publicly) was that those deserters had fled from North Viet-Nam as early as June 1959; in other words, they had *not* deserted from Communist Vietnamese units operating inside Laos. That was the real reason that the Laotian government finally decided against interrogations by the United Nations subcommittee.

For the Laotians, it was most fortunate that the chairman of the sub-committee was Shinichi Shibuzawa, a Japanese fully aware of the problem of face-saving. Beyond question was the fact that the interrogation of even those deserters would provide significant information because it could have established whether plans were afoot in the North Vietnamese Army to give aid and support to the Pathet Lao. On the other hand, the inquisition of those prisoners could have produced the startling intelligence that at least as late as the beginning of June 1959, the Communist High Command had given its troops in the Sam-Neua salient strict orders to avoid clashes along the border with Laos. The problem of how to avoid confronting the prisoners at all was nicely solved by both sides: The chairman of the Laotian liaison office dealing with the United Nations team, Mr. Inpeng Suryadhay, declared that he would authorize interviews of the prisoners if the committee requested it; whereupon the Japanese chairman of the United Nations team replied that his group would interrogate the prisoners only if the Laotian government requested it to do so. Since no one made a move that would have upset the applecart, the whole issue was allowed to die quietly.

But a long-range rationale had to be found to explain the "numbers game" that had been going on in Laotian government circles all summer long. After all, too many high Laotian officials had given precise and detailed figures as to numbers, units, and locations of North Vietnamese prisoners taken. The explanation that was finally given can be found in Sisouk's book. Since he wrote this book while he was an official of his own government and its delegate to the United Nations, it must be considered as rather startling: Sisouk candidly affirms that the Laotian soldiers "usually 'liquidated' the Viet-Minh prisoners they captured."

While no one apparently is too squeamish these days in the application of the rules of land warfare, it is rather rare to find a nation in the "Free World" camp that candidly admits to the massacre of prisoners. If that explanation were even remotely true, and I believe it is not, it would do away with the well-worn saw of the "fun-loving Laotians" whose Buddhism prevents them from shedding blood. I cannot help but feel that the cause of both Laos and the Free World would have been better served had the royal Laotian government simply admitted that it had erred in its reports on captured prisoners; but in the curious process of face-saving, it apparently seems to be preferable to stand in front of history as a murderer of prisoners than as a liar.

With the same poor timing as Foreign Minister Khamphan Panya's speech before the United Nations, Laotian Prime Minister Phoui Sananikone attempted in October to influence both American policies and the

United Nations report by undertaking a personal trip to the United States, accompanied by his Defense Minister Colonel Phoumi Nosavan, and a vast retinue of other officials; while at the same time, again in the one-two punch method of Lao foreign policy, deputy Prime Minister Katay D. Sasorith in his newspaper *La Voix du Peuple* launched a bitter attack against what he called the "inquisitorial and vexatious" controls of American-aid funds by United States officials in Laos.

Katay, whose own personal liberality with foreign-aid funds was proverbial in Laos, charged that credit was "always granted with parsimony. . . . We must implore like a poor beggar."

"At the time of the French administration the treasury was never capable of meeting its payments. Today with the generous aid of its friendly powers this has become frequent."[25]

United States officials could do very little else but simply express "puzzlement" at the unexpectedly strong Laotian reaction to American accounting methods.

All this, in addition to the arrival in the United States of almost the entire royal Lao government, gave the Laos crisis a renewed news impetus at the precise moment when it needed it least since both sides were apparently working at a behind-the-scenes settlement. Sisouk himself did not hesitate to qualify that particular venture of his own government as the "worst conceivable diplomatic blunder" that could be made under the circumstances. And so it was: At the very moment when it already had become clear to most of the better-informed persons that the UN report would probably backfire badly on the Laotian contention of a Communist "invasion," the Laotians themselves again began to harp away at the old theme.

New reports of large-scale subversion in the southern panhandle of Laos began to appear in the press, culminating finally in the assertion that no one else but Red Chinese Field Marshal Peng Te-huai was masterminding Communist operations in Laos and that Red Chinese troops had captured a Lao army post in Phong Saly province. Needless to say, those reports were denied twenty-four hours later.

But all this could not stave off the bitter truth of the report which the United Nations Security Council Subcommittee made public on November 5, 1959. In order to soften the blow on the Laotians and the United States, advance excerpts of the report had been circulated for two weeks prior to publication, thus allowing the newspapers—particularly those who had gone all-out in their acceptance of every unconfirmed rumor—to prepare for more or less graceful exits along the line of "What-did-you-expect-from-the-UN-anyway?"

The New York *Times,* as we have seen, already had dismissed that "hastily improvised mission" as of October 4. The Washington *Post* and some other papers waited until October 25 (i.e., when advance copies of the UN report began to leak out) to brand it editorially as a "soft pedal" whose "muted" findings came as "no surprise" and were due to the fact that "there is a disposition in the UN not to rock the boat in relations with the Communists."

The fact is that the UN fact finders had worked a great deal harder to get at the truth of the Laos situation than the vast majority of the American press, who had not even bothered to ask the right questions —let alone really tried to get the right answers. The Security Council Subcommittee indeed had put into its report every shred of evidence that had been submitted to it; the previous pages have shown how precious little that was. Thus, the conclusion of the subcommittee's report to the effect that "certain of these hostile operations must have had centralized coordination," was a fair and accurate statement of the situation on the basis of the available evidence. It is likewise noteworthy that the UN report does not make any mention of the possibility that such "centralized coordination" might have come from non-Laotian elements outside the Pathet Lao.

There is not the slightest doubt that as in the development of events in Laos during much of 1959, the United States had suffered a severe setback both in protecting Laos from civil war and Communist subversion, and in bringing its case to the public. It would have been desirable and—considering the events of 1960–61 in Laos—helpful all around if the Laos fiasco had been given a thorough airing so as to prepare for the next round that was inevitably to follow.

Instead, the attitude that seemed to prevail after the UN report was that, "after all, things could have been worse." From there, to whitewash the whole thing as a Western success and to attribute it to "American firmness" was but a logical next step. It was again Joseph Alsop who was to argue that case with his usual eloquence in a column modestly titled "Why They Called Off the Dogs." With dramatic crispness, he describes "The Moment of Truth" of September 4, 1959, when, according to Alsop, President Eisenhower gave the U. S. Commander in Chief, Pacific, Admiral Harry D. Felt, orders to place all his forces in a state of immediate readiness. In particular, the U. S. 7th Fleet was given orders to "assist in the defense of Laos," and two days later its ships "began steaming grimly and majestically southward."

The question may arise in the mind of the more unsophisticated reader how a high-seas fleet armed for nuclear war can come to the help of a landlocked country whose only means of naval access is a river which can accommodate a 15-ton launch (during the rainy season). The usual answer seems to be that such support could come from helicopter-borne Marine forces aboard the 7th Fleet, as well as from carrier-borne fighter-bombers. A brief look on a map would, of course, show that the shortest route from the sea to Laos would involve a flight over either South or North Vietnamese territory. In the case of South Viet-Nam, this would constitute a breach of the 1954 Geneva cease-fire provisions; in the case of North Viet-Nam, a rather uncomfortable *casus belli*. There always remains the round-about way via Thailand, but that is available in any case and was used, in fact, in 1961—but it is entirely overland and has nothing to do with the usefulness of the 7th Fleet in a revolutionary jungle war far away inland.

Yet, according to Alsop, the deterrent apparently worked for once. Coupled with "careful, methodical, quiet political action" to get the SEATO nations into line, the American Government had gotten ready for the worst. The Communist "probe in Laos was met with unexpected firmness, on the spot and in Washington" and thus checkmated.

The Italians have a saying for that kind of history-writing: *"Si non é vero, é bene trovato"*—"Even if it isn't true, at least it sounds good."

In Laos itself, the carefree happiness of the old days was dying with the old leaders. On October 14, Viceroy Phetsarath, oldest of Laos' three princely stormy petrels, died in Luang Prabang, followed by King Sisavang Vong on October 29, after a reign of fifty-five years. Katay Don Sasorith, the energetic and resourceful pro-Western politician who had swung many an internal Laotian political battle in American's favor, died on December 29, 1959, at the early age of fifty-five. The year 1959 had not been kind to the small country.

VIII

The American Stake

———————◀◆▶———————

As you have no doubt surmised, I see the most serious fault of our past policy formulation to lie in something that I might call the legalistic-moralistic approach to international relations. . . .

George F. Kennan
American Foreign Policy
1900–1950
University of Chicago Press
1951

There is, let me assure you, nothing in nature more egocentrical than an embattled democracy. It soon becomes the victim of its own war propaganda. It then tends to attach to its own cause an absolute value which distorts its own vision on everything else.

George F. Kennan
Russia and the West
under Lenin and Stalin
Atlantic, Little, Brown
1961

Much has been said in recent years about American foreign policy in the Far East that was often inaccurate and many times downright malicious—and often the most uncomplimentary or harshest criticisms came from America's allies or from Americans themselves. For years, American foreign policy in the Far East was purely and simply paralyzed by what can best be described as a "self-inflicted injury"—the loss of mainland China to the Communists, which conservative Americans tend to ascribe not to any grievous errors committed by the Chinese Nationalists under Chiang Kai-shek but merely to the nefarious activities of a group of State Department officers devoted to the Communist cause. Before the dust had fully settled, as the unfortunate phrase went, over the loss of the Chinese mainland, the invasion of South Korea by the North Korean Communists was ascribed again to foreign policy errors (the question of how Communist preparations for an invasion could have taken place without being detected by military intelligence was never asked in public).

The changeover from a Democratic to a Republican administration in 1953 changed the style of the press releases but not the realities of the Far Eastern situation. The Korean war ended where it had begun three years and 29,000 American dead earlier—on or near the 38th parallel. The much-proclaimed "unleashing" of Chiang Kai-shek (i.e., the permission given Nationalist troops on Taiwan to invade the mainland on their own) remained very much a dead letter, made even more so by the subsequent evacuation of the Tachen outpost islands. And the loss of the Indo-China war by the French in July 1954, after a halfhearted last-minute American attempt to give some substance to the "massive retaliation" concept,[1] further rounded out the dismal picture of Western fortunes in the Far East.

With each successive blow, the American determination to make a stand somewhere became stronger. A success in the Far East, far from remaining essentially a political, military, or diplomatic objective, became an internal American issue. "Firmness" became a policy *per se* rather than a style of policy, since all flexibility was immediately associated with previous periods of "weakness." The result was to be that while changes still had to be made when a particular policy proved unworkable, they were now made *in extremis* and preferably in a way which left the American public largely unaware that they had taken place. A keen observer of that process described its results in the following words:

It is indeed remarkable how often and how significantly American diplomatic postures have been forced by circumstances to shift and how therefore we are caught with petards we were the first to hoist.[2]

In the case of Laos, that particular type of policy implementation occurred in almost schoolbook fashion: America stepped into a situation that was essentially precarious, proclaimed a policy of firmness, was forced by a variety of factors to back down from it, and then had to go through a dizzying series of diplomatic acrobatics to emerge from the tangle without too much damage to American prestige. All this was accomplished —but at the price of a retreat from even the modest initial position, not to speak of a monetary outlay which, by the end of 1961, was nearing the $500 million mark.

The question, then, naturally arises: If this is so, who must be held responsible for the failure? The American diplomats in the field? The desk officers at the Department of State? The policy-shaping Assistant Secretaries and Under Secretaries? The military in the field or in the Pentagon? The various intelligence agencies and particularly the CIA? Congressional pressure? A "Laos lobby"? Weak-willed or, on the contrary, overeager allies?

In all likelihood, the answer lies somewhere in between those various poles of influence—although it is certain that the existence of a Laos lobby or of a congressional pressure group in favor of that little country can be dismissed, having been cited for reference only. In any case, it is of prime importance to define once and for all *what* exactly those American policies in Laos were before they become forever shrouded by subsequent events or self-serving "official versions" of the facts.

From Bastion to Buffer

There exist at least three distinct definitions of American policy objectives in Laos. Two of them emanate from the Department of State; the third directly from the President. All three differ radically from each other and all three cover different time spans. Thus, it cannot be said that they contradict each other but rather that they reflect important changes of policy.

The first policy period lasted roughly from the inception of direct American operations in Laos in 1955 until the collapse of the Laotian counteroffensive against the Pathet Lao at the end of 1960. The second can be considered as merely a transitional phase until the new Kennedy Administration had had time to find its bearings in the maze; and the third represented the position of the Kennedy Administration in the light of the further military reverses suffered by Prince Boun Oum and General Phoumi in the early spring of 1961.

The first policy can be summed up simply as the "bulwark-against-Communism" approach to the Laotian problem. A Department of State comment to a congressional report defined that policy as follows:

> . . . to assist the Lao (1) in keeping the Communists from taking over Laos, (2) in strengthening their association with the free world, and (3) in developing and maintaining a stable and independent government, willing and able to resist Communist aggression or subversion.[3]

While it must be kept in mind that the comment was written for congressional consumption, its overwhelming emphasis on politico-military anti-Communism is noteworthy. No mention is made of such pressing matters as helping the Laotians to gain a measure of economic stability, or of giving the country the kind of educational and administrative underpinning that would permit it to withstand (more than with policemen and guns) the depredations of Pathet Lao subversion.

The fact that the policy statement is preceded by an underlined passage affirming that *"its major objectives have been and are being achieved with signal success,"* clearly shows to what extent the style of policy formulation had replaced its substance.

In the second policy statement, contained in the State Department White Paper on Laos issued on January 7, 1961, American objectives had clearly shifted from participation to explanation. Now Communism was not only the villain (which it had always been) but had put the United States sufficiently on the defensive to be in a position to extract promises:

> The United States believes that it can best contribute to a solution of the Laos problem:
>
> First, by attempting to further international recognition and understanding of the true nature of Communist intentions and actions in Laos;
>
> Second, by the United States itself continuing clearly to show that it has no desire to establish a Western military position in Laos;
>
> Third, by joining with other free nations to support and maintain the independence of Laos through whatever measures seem most promising.

The first point, for all its verbiage, is little more than a watering down of point (1) of the earlier statement; the second point completely annuls the "bulwark" concept contained in the passage of point (2) of the 1959 statement; only the third point, in still threatening joint action of the SEATO powers, contained the seeds of some sort of positive action in behalf of Laos. But here, previous experience had probably taught the Communists to judge such threats at their real value.

President Kennedy faced that particularly unpromising heritage in a press conference on March 23, 1961, with only few, if any, hopeful new leads in the West's favor. While, as will be seen, the public was still not told how bad the situation in Laos had really become, the policy espoused by the President at least had the merit of coming closer to reflecting actual American intentions and capabilities than any of the previous statements.

Specifically, the new American position, like its predecessors, contained three points:

First, we strongly and unreservedly support the goal of a neutral and independent Laos tied to no outside power or group of powers, threatening no one, and free from any domination.

This simple phrase alone showed how much American policy had shifted in less than three months. Part of the next paragraph was designed to re-establish *credence*—as against the much-overused and misunderstood term "credibility"—in American promises of non-interference in Laos:

. . . And if in the past there has been any possible ground for misunderstanding of our desire for a truly neutral Laos, there should be none now.

It is noteworthy that *not one* American news source picked up the full import of that apparently innocuous sentence. It was evidently addressed more to America's own allies, the Asian neutrals and, last but not least, the Soviet bloc, than to the tens of millions of Americans who watched the proceedings on their television sets. The hard fact was that the "misunderstanding" not only existed abroad where American performance in Laos was watched closely, but apparently also in Washington itself where the "desire for a truly neutral Laos" had come, if at all, as a much-belated piece of wisdom.

The second and third points of President Kennedy's statement further elaborated on the new policy. The second point embodied the elements of the SEATO counterthreat contained in the previous White Paper of the Eisenhower Administration; while the third swallowed the bitter pill of an international conference on the Laos problem as a prerequisite to guiding Laos "back to the pathway of independence and genuine neutrality."

In less than four months, American policies on the Laos problem had run the gamut from "bastion" to "buffer." All other factors of the problem were merely a more or less thinly drapped veil of minor tactical changes or policies-within-a-policy laid over that essential set of facts.

Why America in Laos?

As one considers the development of the American commitment in Laos, the question often arises as to why and how America became so deeply involved in such a peripheral and basically indefensible area. There are, of course, several complicated answers to that question, involving the "over-all American strategic posture" in the Far East. A somewhat simpler and not inaccurate answer is that the French asked the United States to step in.

In view of later Franco-American disagreements over Laos—particularly over the extent of American involvement in the training of the Royal Laotian Army—this point needs to be nailed down with sufficient emphasis so as not to be forgotten again. While the French military (who had witnessed the same process in South Viet-Nam) were cautioning Paris against requesting American military personnel for Laos, the diplomats of the Quai d'Orsay considered it one of their better achievements to have succeeded in persuading the United States, as one wag put it, "to pick up the tab while leaving us the glory."

Had the Algerian war, which consumed French military manpower and financial resources like an ever-spreading cancer, not taken place, perhaps this arrangement might have worked with a certain amount of success (it did work successfully in neighboring Cambodia, but for somewhat different reasons). But the Algerian war demanded exactly the kind of junior infantry commanders which a sound training program in Laos required—and Algeria had top priority. The French Military Mission in Laos never even reached one-third of its statutory strength set by the 1954 cease-fire provisions (1500 men), and French cash outlays in Laos could have never met even the barest civilian needs of the small kingdom, let alone those of its military defense.

Two choices thus were open to the United States after the cease-fire of July 1954: Let Laos take care of itself and hope that the Communists would find it as uninviting a piece of real estate as we do; or literally "underwrite" the country in full. Any halfway solution on that score would have been comparable to giving a very sick patient a half dose of antibiotics. In the light of the over-all policy stand of "firmness" that had been decided upon by the Eisenhower administration after the Asian setbacks of 1953–54 (Korea, Indo-China and the Tachen evacuation), Laos—being the one country "on the swing" in that area of the world—became the pilot project in which an American success was the goal hard on the rim of the Communist bloc. That policy decision was made late in 1954 and implemented as of January 1, 1955. From then onward, American intervention in Laos took on the preordained air of a Greek tragedy. Its only logical outcome could be an "escalation" of the American effort commensurate with the increase of the Communist threat and the gradual disintegration of native government processes (just as was to happen somewhat later in South Viet-Nam), culminating in the commitment of American troops or, conversely, a total backdown. Until late in 1960, all the American bets were on "escalation" —political, economic, and military.

Once the decision had been made to hold Laos, the important next step was to determine which of the Lao government's agencies was most likely to be able to bring salvation to the country at large. In the case of Laos, the decision was made that the Royal Laotian Army (and not any of the civilian agencies) was the best means of reaching the bulk of the Laotians and of reforming the country's deficient administrative and economic structure.[4] As J. Graham Parsons, who was American Ambassador in Laos during the critical 1956–58 period, testified in the course of the Senate hearings on his appointment as Assistant Secretary of State: "In the case of Laos . . . the Army is virtually the only branch of the Laos government service . . . which reached the countryside . . . in remote places."[5]

The decision to make the Laotian Army the center of all American efforts in Laos was therefore *political,* and not military. In fact, it should be underlined—and might come as a shock to those who tend to think of the higher echelons of the Pentagon as a group of wild-eyed saber-rattlers—that year after year until 1959, the U. S. Joint Chiefs of Staff, who statutorily determine the force levels of foreign armies to be supported by U.S. funds, *refused* to recommend a force level for Laos! As late as fiscal year 1958, Laotian forces were still considered by the Department of Defense as not being "within force objectives," and when the House Committee on Government Operations investigated U.S. operations in Laos in June 1959, it emphatically made the point that

> . . . *U.S. support of a 25,000-man army [and] of the entire military budget . . . is, in fact, based on a political determination, made by the Department of State contrary to the recommendations of the Joint Chiefs of Staff.* In Laos, the only country in the world where the United States supports the military budget 100 percent, military judgments have been disregarded.[6]

In its rejoinder to the Committee's report, the Department of State argued that "subsequent events have justified from a military as well as a political standpoint the determination of the force level." While it is always unfair to argue with the benefit of hindsight, it can nevertheless be stated objectively on the basis of Laotian events subsequent to both the report and its rejoinder, that the U. S. Joint Chiefs' view, had it prevailed, would have saved the United States both from a political fiasco and a needless expenditure of almost a half billion dollars; for close to nine-tenths of all American expenditures in Laos went into the financing and maintaining of the Royal Laotian Army.

To finance that Army without completely wreaking havoc with Laos' precarious economy required the creation of an artificial economic current similar in substance to that which exists in other underdeveloped countries supporting oversized military establishments: Goods are imported with U.S. aid dollars via normal commercial channels and sold on the local markets for local currency; that local currency, minus taxes and profits, is deposited in a counterpart fund from which the local government pays the expenditures of its armed forces; and those armed forces, in turn, spend their pay on the local market which, in order not to be completely swamped by the huge purchasing power of the military, must import even more consumer goods.

In an advanced country, to be sure, a very sizable part of the counterpart funds would be derived from the import by local merchants not of consumer goods, but of tractors or industrial machines which, in turn, would increase the national output and thus absorb in a healthy manner the excess purchasing power generated by American aid. In Laos and other countries of a similarly primitive economy, that type of aid created a literal flood of the local market by luxury goods of every kind. In strictly economic terms, it was immaterial whether the funds necessary for the payment of the Laotian Army came from the sales to the population of much needed agriculural implements or of somewhat less useful Mercedes-Benz luxury automobiles (at one time in 1958–60, all taxis of Vientiane were of the $6500 Mercedes-Benz 220 S variety). From the socio-political viewpoint—and in an underdeveloped country, competition with Communism is socio-political before it becomes military—it proved disastrous.

Graft and Corruption

In Laos, the problem was complicated further by the fact that Laotian regular troops are among the highest paid in the world. That problem, too, was in part inherited from the French, but less than it had been made to appear. In fact, the Laotian government had granted the Army three pay raises between 1954 and 1961, and at least in one case over the objections of the United States. In such cases where pay raises were effectively blocked on a general basis, they were in effect put through by mass promotions to higher ranks. The Laotians also had successfully resisted both French and American attempts at actual head counts of existing units, with the result that various Laotian disbursing officers and unit commanders could pocket the difference between their real troop strength and the officially reported strength.

Estimates of total troop strength under government control have varied from between 40,000 to as little as 10,000. If it is realized that the per-capita cost to the United States of a Laotian soldier was above $1000 per year (as against a worldwide average of $848, and such per capita costs as $485 per year for a Pakistani or $424 a year for a Greek soldier) it is obvious that both the opportunities for and the size of graft were enormous.

Much has been said already about corruption in Laos and to repeat it here would be tedious, since this is probably the only aspect of the Laotian problem that has been given some public attention.[7] Every person who had been in Laos between 1956 and 1960 had his own particular tale of corruption in Laos: TV receivers ordered in a country without a transmitter; the contents of CARE packages sold on the black market, its empty boxes being shipped by air to the provinces, so that inspectors from that organization would find "proof" of the aid's proper use; previously penniless officers suddenly owning $100,000 villas (not to speak of comfortable retreats in France)—yes, all this, and more, had indeed taken place. And perhaps most dishearteningly of all, even Americans had succumbed to the madness, pocketing bribes for contracts, dealing in illicit currency transactions, delivering faulty equipment, defaulting on signed contracts, etc. Here again, Sisouk—as pro-American a Laotian officer as there was—states the case bluntly in his own book: "Black market deals in American aid dollars reached such proportions that the Pathet Lao needed no propaganda to turn the rural people against the townspeople."[8]

Americans and Frenchmen who denounced these abuses of aid were railroaded, intimidated, or called names, when their sanity was not altogether questioned. A Frenchman could, of course, always be accused of "colonialism." In the case of an American, things were slightly more complicated but usually worked out well in the end according to the time-tested formula of "Woe unto him who causes the scandal to become public." An American foreign-aid end-use auditor, Haynes Miller, who had first made public the abuses in the program was removed because his "general attitude and conduct had demonstrated his failure to adjust to the requirements for successful execution of his responsibilities in Laos."[9] A French Army major who had openly protested to his own French superiors and to the Laotian Defense Ministry that out of the twelve Laotian battalion commanders he was training, four were Communists and likely to join the other side as soon as their training was completed, was removed at the request of the Laotian anti-Communist government and replaced by a man whose general attitude and conduct made him more likely to adjust to the somewhat nightmarish conditions under which he was to operate: i.e., see no evil, hear no evil, speak no evil.

Yet, when J. Graham Parsons was appointed Assistant Secretary of State by President Eisenhower after spending two years as American Ambassador in Laos (in other words, as head of all American operations in that country), he testified that he had no knowledge of corruption there, particularly among ICA personnel, until one former mission employee had testified that he had received bribes totaling $25,000![10]

In fact, as one reads the rather voluminous record of congressional hearings on Laos, he can sense throughout it all the frustration of legislators who realized that they were being denied the whole truth about a situation so grave that only the most radical change could head off disaster. Unfortunately the situation already had deteriorated beyond the point of no return when the Pathet Lao put the whole Laotian house of cards to the military test.

Rationale for a Policy

Still, corruption or the maintenace of an unpopular government in power should not *ipso facto* condemn a foreign-aid program. If this were so, precious little would be left of foreign aid in general. Thus, the test of ultimate success becomes paramount in justifying an aid program, particularly when it is meant to be of indefinite duration.

Experience has shown that there are three ways of successfully defending an aid program: (1) if it is truly successful, simply pointing to the facts will suffice; (2) if the situation has remained bad in spite of massive American aid, the appraisal usually proceeds along the lines of "this is not bad at all, considering where it was when we came in"; and (3) if the situation is going from bad to worse, the program can probably be defended on the "denial value" of the country—"we don't need the place, but we can't afford to let the Communists have it." The latter argument also permits the injection of altruistic motives of the "legalistic-moralistic" kind of which George F. Kennan spoke and which are usually very hard to refute.

In the case of Laos, the argument most often invoked until President Kennedy announced the United States' support of Laotian neutrality was that of "denial"—the Communists had been prevented from taking over Laos, if nothing else. Again, it is the Department of State's rejoinder to congressional criticism of the Laos program which makes the case for "denial" most persuasively:

> . . . The admission of past shortcomings in administration cannot dis-qualify us from asserting an uncontrovertible fact, namely, that the Mutual Security program has succeeded and is succeeding in its basic and vital objective of assisting Laos to remain a member of the free world com-munity of nations.

That thesis became the mainstay of the rationale for American opera-tions in Laos. Under the ambassadorship of J. Graham Parsons and his subsequent tenure as Assistant Secretary of State for Far Eastern Affairs both under the latter Eisenhower and the early Kennedy administrations, vigorous attempts were made to put it into effect. The Laotian govern-ment strived to concentrate power in as strong an anti-Communist group as could be formed. The United States in its turn committed itself in late 1958 to the support of that group by overt and covert means and it did so with great energy.

Some American writers, notably those of *Time* magazine and Keyes Beech of the Chicago *Daily News,* have tried to describe to American readers some of the difficulties Parsons' successor, Ambassador Horace H. Smith, experienced in keeping a rein on CIA operatives in Laos, who, according to Beech, did not make Smith's job "any easier" by overriding Smith's own decisions. At the same time, the American military advisory group which, until the Spring of 1961, operated under the thin disguise of the "Program Evaluation Office" (PEO) of the economic aid mission in order to skirt the provisions of the 1954 cease-fire, injected a new dimen-sion into American operations in Laos. Everyone knew that the mission was here—ill-fitting civilian slacks with loud Hawaiian shirts whose tails were left to flap in the wind were as much of a "uniform" as the khakis, patches, and rank insignia which they replaced—and its introduction into Laos gave the Communists an excellent pretext to avail themselves of similar stratagems.[11]

One last factor which influenced American policies in Laos was the open antagonism which reigned between the Frenchmen and Americans on the spot and, at a higher level, between the foreign offices of those two countries—at least as far as Laos was concerned.

By virtue of their own bitter experiences, the French were persuaded—and the British often to a greater degree than the French—that the only workable Western policy for Laos should be all-out support of a truly neutral country. That particular kind of concerted Western backing of neutrality had done wonders in once-divided Austria, and there was an outside chance that it could work in Laos. But American-French friction at all levels in their missions in Laos interfered with the free communication of ideas.

Haynes Miller reported as early as November 1958 that "many of the Americans have adopted an openly scornful attitude toward the French," and this writer, a Frenchman, was able to verify this out of personal experience. While in Laos in 1957, I paid an informal call at the house of a senior American official. In the absence of her husband, the lady of the house invited me in, but, apparently confused by the combination of my American crew cut and my French tropical shorts and knee socks, blurted out: "I hope you're not one of those goddamned French?" Upon my assurance that I was one of those goddamned French, we both chose to make light of the phrase and the incident was closed.

Another such incident in 1957 occurred during the drive of the Lao Junior Chamber of Commerce in support of the "Operation Brotherhood" hospital then being built near Vientiane and staffed by a group of devoted young Filipinos. The Lao "Jaycee" was composed of a truly international group ranging from Americans to Chinese, Thai, Frenchmen, and even a sprinkling of Laotians (the latter mostly younger government officials). Its drive was a great success and to crown its ending, the American Ambassador gave a party from which—on an erroneous evaluation of Lao "anti-colonialist" feeling—all French "Jaycees" were pointedly excluded. On the following day, all the French Jaycees handed in their resignations, and it took a great deal of apologizing all around to patch up ruffled feelings.

Even when such thoughtless incidents did not mar the picture, there never existed anything that could truly be called comradeship (in arms, or otherwise) in spite of the fact that both France and the United States were deeply interested in seeing Laos resist Communism. As one realistic French official told me during the 1959 crisis: "Let us have no illusions. If the right-wing Lao government gets licked in this fight, we stand to lose a great deal more than the Americans. They just pack up and go home—we've got almost eight thousand civilians here, many of the ex-soldiers eking out a living as mechanics or truck drivers. We'd be really stuck." But there were many Frenchmen in Laos to whom the American presence in Laos was only a shade more agreeable than that of the Pathet Lao. In short, a situation of total non-communication existed between the two communities at a particularly crucial time.

How serious the absence of constructive interchanges was is best revealed in the testimony of executive officials before congressional committees. When asked by legislators as to the extent of French involvement in training and aid operations in Laos, none of those officials was capable of giving even a remotely accurate reply—much less a coherent picture of whether such operations overlapped or dovetailed with American operations in the same field.

To a question raised by Congressman Walter H. Judd as to whether the French Military Mission and the PEO were on good terms or "more or less *persona non grata* to each other," the reply was that there was "not what you might call a close intimacy." And to Mr. Judd's additional question concerning French help in supervising Lao Army expenditures and requests, the answer was that "we do not know, but we have a feeling they do not."[12]

As the crisis mounted, mutual recriminations became more vehement, and some American correspondents began to carry lists of American and French officials whom both sides allegedly desired to remove from the scene on an "exchange" basis for the sake of better allied cooperation. And one of the better-known pundits let it be known both in Vientiane and Washington that he considered removal of all the French (save a small embassy staff) to be an essential step toward curing all the ills of the Indo-China peninsula.

At working level, however, both in Laos and in the two nations' capitals, American and French positions were not always as far apart as they seemed. In fact, relations improved considerably during the tenures of U.S. ambassadors Smith and Winthrop G. Brown. At the "country desk" level throughout this period, the United States had an extremely able and conscientious officer who had served in Laos and Viet-Nam and thus knew what the score was*—and it already had been shown that the Pentagon labored under few, if any, illusions as to the fighting capabilities

* *Editor's note:* This officer was Christian G. Chapman.

of the Laotian Army, particularly when pitted against the jungle-hardened Pathet Lao and their Viet-Minh mentors.

Through a sheer process of elimination—leaving aside the usual snide remarks addressed to the "activists" of the CIA whose covert operations sometimes backfired in Laos as well as elsewhere—it becomes readily apparent that the two Assistant Secretaries of State for Far Eastern Affairs, Walter S. Robertson and J. Graham Parsons, who held office between 1953 and 1961, were the main inspirers of American policies in Laos. Robertson had the well-earned reputation of a tough and steadfast man who could be counted upon to carry out Far Eastern policies in the Dulles manner. He was to the last an advocate of the "hard line" on every Far Eastern issue.

Parsons succeeded him in May, 1959, after a continuous career of more than twenty-three years in the Foreign Service. He, too, was thoroughly prepared for his job, having previously served as Counselor of Embassy in Tokyo and later as U. S. Ambassador to Laos. Most Western (including French) diplomats who had met him at various times agreed that he was a friendly man, easy to get along with, and devoted to his job. He was also anxious to succeed where others had failed.

Laos, for that purpose, was an ideal place. From 1954 until Parsons' arrival in 1956, Laos had been a true diplomatic backwater, about on a par with Nepal, Yemen, or Paraguay. American fortunes there were neither rising nor falling, and American prestige certainly was not riding on making Laos a "success." All this now changed rapidly.

Within a few months after his arrival, Parsons deduced accurately that Laos was being led toward neutralism by Souvannaphouma. Where Parsons diverged from other expert opinion, however, was that he thought that *any other* policy would have a better-than-even chance of success in Laos—and he immediately proceeded to implement the "bulwark" policy that was to remain in operation until 1961 and whose results are now part of the record. In the process, it was obvious that Parsons and Souvannaphouma would inevitably clash head on, and they did. I do not know whether Parsons hated Souvannaphouma as a person or simply disliked the policies he stood for; but I do know that the latter despised Parsons and his policies, considering him to be the man who single-handedly had ruined six years of delicate negotiations designed to bring the Pathet Lao back into the fold without at the same time turning Laos into a Communist country.

Upon his return to the United States in 1958 and his subsequent appointment as Deputy Assistant Secretary of State (his appointment as Assistant Secretary coming one year later), Parsons was placed in the relatively uncomfortable position of having to defend his own handiwork as ambassador and to justify continuance of his previous policies, even though new events suggested some radical adjustments. This probably explains at least in part why official statements on Laos took on an air of unreality which, though swallowed whole by the bulk of the American press, did not escape notice by congressional committees, one of which had this comment:

> This subcommittee cannot understand how two experienced senior officials of the Department of State, Robertson and Parsons, working together closely day after day, having available to them identical information and field reports, could have reached and expressed . . . diametrically opposed views of the same situation.[13]

Indeed, Parsons now began to attach to his own cause, in the previously cited words of George F. Kennan, an "absolute value which distorts its own vision on everything else." Yet, this was precisely the negotiator whom President Eisenhower sent to Laos in October 1960 in order to attempt to persuade Souvannaphouma to abandon his policy of neutrality in favor of a pro-Western posture.

According to all available accounts, Parsons stooped to coercion, which culminated in an airtight aid blockade literally starving Vientiane of its most essential supplies. The Souvannaphouma regime was forced to accept the only alternative that was left and readily available: Soviet aid. American pressure exerted through the withholding of aid had been used twice before on Laos: The first time it was intended to stimulate Laotian efforts to dismiss the International Control Commission, and the second time to effect a more realistic exchange rate of the *kip,* the Laotian currency. Parsons himself, in his appointment hearings, had stated to the Foreign Relations Committee of the U. S. Senate that

> . . . The way in which we use the aid program as a device to bring pressure is a very delicate matter, and I think each particular case . . . of this kind has to be judged on the basis of the particular situation. . . .

In the case of Laos, the particular situation in October 1960 had included an alternative to the U.S. aid when that was not forthcoming. This should have been clearly realized before that kind of pressure was applied for a third time. Apparently it was not, and the whole scheme backfired; the USSR was recognized by Laos for the first time and even the subsequent right-wing regime of Prince Boun Oum could not muster sufficient will power to annul the measure.

The retention of Assistant Secretary Parsons by President Kennedy until March 31, 1961, more than anything else convinced the outside world that the new administration did not really intend to change its Laotian policy, all statements to the contrary notwithstanding. In light of the crucial events that transpired in Laos during that period, the disinclination to appoint a new figure to this important position became a policy decision in itself, one which affected events to no small extent.

On May 2, 1961, J. Graham Parsons was appointed U. S. Ambassador to Sweden by President Kennedy. With his departure from the Far Eastern scene began the laborious process of rebuilding American policies in Laos on a new basis.

IX

New Turmoils

The Year of the Sword

As far as Buddhist Laos was concerned, 1960 was the Year of the Buffalo, a peaceful and useful animal. But it might as well have been the Year of the Sword (fortunately non-existent in Buddhist mythology) for all the pre-eminence the military were to enjoy in Laotian politics, both externally and internally.

The American reaction to the military reverses of 1959 was to increase the size of the American training mission and to undertake its justification in the press. As early as October 6, the Washington *Post* reported that at certain training bases the "Americans outnumbered the French by five to one." The rather inane explanation for this was that "the French are not familiar with the American 50-caliber machine guns and 57-caliber [sic] recoilless rifles." The fact that the 50-caliber U.S. machine gun had been standard issue in French units since 1942 and the 57-mm. rifle since almost its inception in the late forties was conveniently overlooked.

A few weeks later, it was the turn of the New York *Times* to quote Washington sources as being "dissatisfied with the French contribution in Laos"[1] while still later the Associated Press was able to report that U.S.-trained Laotian troops not only fought U.S.-style but now greeted French generals in U.S. fashion and with U.S. close-order drill, which resulted in arousing the generals' ire.[2]

But those little spats of military primadonnas were of a rather minor nature in comparison to the series of military *coups d'état* the Laotians were preparing for themselves. Lest the reader be completely bewildered by the details of what is to follow, the situation can best be summed up in the following brief sketches:

Coup No. 1: The right-wing military, headed by all the Laotian generals, against Phoui Sananikone; from December 25, 1959 to January 5, 1960;

Coup No. 2: Paratroop Captain Kong-Lê, against the Tiao Somsanith government on August 9, 1960, bringing about the return to power of Prince Souvannaphouma;

Coup No. 3: General Phoumi Nosavan with part of the Royal Laotian forces stationed in southern Laos and based around Savannakhet, beginning on August 31, 1960, and ending with the capture of Vientiane on December 16, 1960;

Coup No. 4: Colonel Kouprasith Abhay and a group of officers and men from the armored squadron stationed at Camp Chinaimo near Vientiane, on December 8, 1960, against Captain Kong-Lê but in support of Souvannaphouma, followed by a counterattack of the paratroopers who drove Kouprasith's troops right back to Chinaimo;

Coup No. 5: Menaced on all sides and afraid of losing all freedom of maneuver, Prince Souvannaphouma fled to Phnom-Penh on December 10, handing over all powers to General Sounthone Patthammavong, who was unable to persuade Kong-Lê to evacuate Vientiane peacefully and thus failed to prevent the shelling of the city by both sides; and, finally,

Coup No. 6: In a lightning move Captain Kong-Lê threw his paratroopers from the outskirts of Vientiane into the vital Plaine des Jarres 150 miles to the northeast, thus securing for himself, the Pathet Lao, and their Soviet airlift an excellent airfield complex after a few perfunctory skirmishes on New Year's Day 1961.

Those military coups against whatever represented orderly civilian government in Laos were not a cause of the chaos that prevailed but rather a product of it; even while their country was literally slipping away under their feet, Laotian politicians kept fighting over each position as if the most important thing in the world was whether a member of the RPL or of the CDIN would get the juicy plum of the dollar-controlling Directorate of Foreign Commerce or the graft-ridden Directorate of Customs, where a reformist "young Turk" of the CDIN was accused by his detractors of having put more into his own pockets in six months than his "corrupt" old-line predecessor in three years. Perhaps, had there been no vast sums of dollars or huge stocks of consumer goods to parcel out, those same Laotians would have been more concerned with the fate of their country. But this is a moot question.

In the meantime, matters had come to a head once more between the old-line politicians and the "young Turks." The latter accused the former of having failed to mend their ways and in particular were incensed over Premier Phoui's impulsive trip to the United Nations and to Washington, which had ended in failure. The old-line politicians, in turn, accused the reformists in the CDIN of (a) having failed in their undertakings and (b) of having, by their virulent but essentially vocal anti-Communism, brought the whole country to the brink of military ruin.

The fact that the Laotian National Assembly's mandate was to expire on Christmas Day 1959 brought the whole problem to a head. Under the emergency powers voted Phoui earlier in the year under CDIN pressure, the Laotian cabinet decided on December 7 to extend the mandate of the present assembly until new elections could be held in April 1960.

When the "young Turks" protested against what they felt was a violation of the Laotian constitution, Phoui, in a burst of energy that he had not shown in a long time, fired the whole American-backed CDIN crew on December 16 while at the same time intimating that Laos would henceforth return to a policy of effective neutrality.[3] Two days later, the National Assembly held a special session in which it extended its own mandate until the new elections, now definitely set for April 3, 1960. The old-guard politicians seemed once more to have triumphed over idealisms, youth, and the CIA. Even the indestructible Phoumi ("Our Boy") Nosavan, recently promoted to Brigadier General, was eliminated from his cabinet post. If it had not been the case that the Pathet Lao leaders were still under detention and Souvannaphouma in comfortable exile as ambassador to France, one might have thought that things had returned to the halcyon days of 1957, when Laotians worked out their cabinet crises en famille and did not rock the global boat by announcing a new Communist invasion every second week.

But things had changed: The Laotian Army had entered politics for good. On December 25, the day the Lao National Assembly's original mandate was to expire, gendarmerie surrounded Premier Phoui's residence, at General Phoumi's orders, followed later in the day by three

M-8 armored cars, and the next day by tanks. At the same time Lao troops in mottled battle dress and arms at the ready began to appear in the streets. In a flurry of letters designed to save face all around, Phoui offered his resignation to the King on December 30, while the King himself sent one to Phoui—sources seem to conflict as to which letter reached whom first—declaring his stewardship at an end.[4]

When the diplomatic corps presented its traditional wishes to the King on New Year's Day, it found him surrounded by his usual court dignitaries, the caretaking Phoui government—and Laos' five generals. On the following day it became apparent that the small country was heading straight for a military dictatorship under strong man General Phoumi. This was more than the Western powers were willing to stomach under the circumstances. Phoumi, for all his genuine intelligence (he had graduated with top marks from the French General Staff College), was too closely identified with a "hard" policy incompatible with Laos' utter dependency upon United Nations support to be acceptable as a prime minister under the circumstances. That point was made in clear language to the King by the ambassadors of the United States, France, Great Britain, and the Australian chargé d'affaires during a personal call on January 4. The King (as well as Phoumi) fully understood,[5] and the premiership was entrusted on January 7 to Khou Abhay, a sixty-seven-year-old court official of moderate views, who agreed to head a caretaker government until the elections. Khou appointed a six-man cabinet which included three RPL and three CDIN members, including General Phoumi as Minister for Defense and Veterans Affairs, thus ensuring effective control of the government by the "young Turks."

The New York *Times,* ever willing to look at the brighter side of things, editorialized that "after a brief military rule Laos [had] returned to democratic ways under a civilian government."[6] In actual fact, nothing had been resolved, and at the most, divisive issues within the non-Communist camp were "frozen" until the April elections. Militarily, the Pathet Lao, while abstaining from spectacular campaigns, nevertheless succeeded in infusing its influence deep into the government-occupied southern panhandle of Laos,[7] thus making a complete mockery of earlier or later "ivory-tower" plans to partition Laos at a given parallel, in a manner which would leave the "infiltrated" north of the country to the Pathet Lao while giving a non-Communist Lao regime the "solid" southern part of the country.

In all this, the United Nations, which had saved the non-Communist

Laotians from the jaws of death barely a few weeks earlier, remained conveniently forgotten. But like Banquo's ghost in *Macbeth,* it was very much in evidence.

That "UN Presence"

The role of the United Nations in Laos had indeed not ended with the report of the special subcommittee; in fact, it had only begun. The late Secretary-General Dag Hammarskjöld, making use of what he himself called in September 1959 "a common-law development" of United Nations activities,[8] decided to leave in Laos a permanent observation mission which, as a sort of "personal emanation" of the Secretary-General, was not subject to the Russian veto[9]—although the Russians, of course, as in the case of United Nations operations in the Congo, objected violently to it.

The practice of sending an almost-unofficial (in terms of the UN charter) mission to a world hot spot is not new. It was to be United Nations Under-Secretary Ralph J. Bunche, who, in a conference in March 1960 in Tokyo, was to attempt for the first time to sum up the concept of the UN "presence" in a coherent statement:

> . . . Thus far, at any rate, the United Nations "presence" is a process or device, or concept, which has been employed by the United Nations exclusively in the field of peacemaking. It may be defined loosely as a common term used to designate all the various forms of functional representation which have been employed in pursuance of Chapter VI of the UN Charter, relating to the Pacific Settlement of Disputes. . . .[10]

Agreement on the term "presence" followed its use for the first time in the report on the 1958 crises in Lebanon and Jordan, made to the UN General Assembly by Secretary Hammarskjöld, who felt that such terms as "UN Ambassador," "UN Representative," and others were far too precise and likely to arouse the ire of one interested party or another. In Bunche's view, among such presences must be counted the UN Truce Supervisory Organization in Palestine (UNTSO), the UN observers in Kashmir, the UN observer group in Lebanon (UNOGIL) and even the 5400-men UN Emergency Force (UNEF) in the Sinai and, naturally, that huge 17,000-man operation in the Congo. In Bunche's words,

> . . . Those who constitute and lead the "presence" operation . . . are expected to play their role pretty much by ear. . . . As there is no set

form for the United Nations "presence," neither is there any established pattern for its functioning.[11]

In the case of Laos, Bunche felt that it was "probably the best example of the effectiveness of a presence in the vaguest sort of guise."

. . . After the short visit of the Subcommittee, and a visit by the Secretary-General himself [in November 1959], *all with the purpose of maintaining a continuity of United Nations "presence" in the area,* the process was further pursued by a quite informal and perhaps quite deliberately imprecise designation of first one senior United Nations official, and later another, to come to the country to study and consult about its economic needs and, most important, to *be* there. Finally . . . a more permanent designation was made, and now Dr. Edouard Zellweger is out there as Special Consultant to the Secretary-General for Co-ordination of UN Activities in Laos, and is in the process of forming a staff.

As shadowy as all this may have been, it did—one might say almost miraculously—succeed in restoring quiet to the area.[12]

Dr. Bunche's optimism (for he spoke in March 1960) alone shows how badly the UN presence in Laos had failed in the end, and needlessly at that.

Indeed, the presence of the UN fact-finding subcommittee in Laos had contributed a great deal to slowing down overt Communist operations in Laos. In fact, it is not impossible that the Soviet bloc quietly acquiesced to the maintenance of a permanent UN representative in Laos because it considered this to be a lesser evil than an overt and effective U.S. presence —but most certainly it was not going to accept both. And there hinges the tragedy of the UN's failure in Laos.

Dag Hammarskjöld had been blunt with the Laotians during his visit in Vientiane in mid-November 1959. He had told them in effect that the UN would not stand for any more "wolf-crying"; nor would it brook being used as an instrument for anything but an effective policy "of independent neutrality and democratic progress."[13] The Laotians, badly shaken by the absence of Western or SEATO troops when the chips were down, were happy to agree to any and all conditions, and Dag Hammarskjöld stayed in Laos long enough to introduce personally his incoming representative, Sakari Severi Tuomioja, a former premier of Finland bearing a striking physical resemblance to Hammarskjöld, to the Laotians.

Tuomioja immediately set to work to hammer out an effective UN economic and political program for Laos. Calls went out for economic and administrative experts, often to be recruited on a crash basis within the first month after the call, and the mission head himself, known as "persistently, rather than restlessly, ambitious," began to observe the Lao political scene. He did not like what he saw, for the Laotians, like improvident children, seemed to return immediately to their usual political games now that the worst of the danger seemed to have passed: Playing with foreign aid and military coups.

This brought about a sharp message, sent from Brazzaville by Hammarskjöld, en route to the Congo, in which he reminded the King of the promises the Laotians had made that "no changes" would take place "which would raise doubt with regard to the basic foundations of the policies of the country and the confidence they have created."[14] In plain English, this meant: "If you want us to stay between you and the Communists, stay neutral or else."

The Hammarskjöld reprimand brought the Laotians to heel in January, but its effects began to wear thin as comparative peace prevailed and as the intelligence "activists" once more began to work on the Laotian "young Turks"—again falsely raising their hopes that in the case of yet another crisis with the Communists, they could bank on immediate and effective succor from the outside. The fact that General Phoumi was the nephew of Thailand's strong man, Field Marshal Sarit Thanarat, may also have encouraged them to adopt that totally erroneous view of the world situation.

Upon the completion of Mr. Tuomioja's mission in January 1960, he was replaced by a Greek official, Philip Messinesi, who suffered from the Laotian climate, difficulties of staff recruitment, and the fact that he was holding the post only *ad interim,* until the new chief of mission, a Swiss national by the name of Edouard Zellweger, arrived in the country. The arrival of Zellweger at the end of March 1960 did not change the situation much: The Laotian government saw to it, by delaying or withdrawing approval of UN staff specialists, that almost no one was appointed to Laos who had had previous experience in the country; and the real difficulties of monsoon season travel were repeatedly invoked to keep UN staff members from poking their noses into anything Laotian outside Vientiane or Luang Prabang. Far from being able to make its peacemaking influence felt, the UN presence in Laos was considered to be merely a new avenue to foreign aid. Zellweger himself, as able and conscientious a UN official as could be wished for, was able to report to his superiors only what he saw and heard, but could do nothing to influence

the situation as it once more began to snowball into a civil war com-
pounded by foreign intervention.

Zellweger experienced firsthand the latter situation when right-wing
rebels machine-gunned Vientiane from the Thailand side of the Mekong in
the fall of 1960. From his house on the Laotian side of the Mekong,
Zellweger saw the tracer bullets (the American Ambassador's residence,
incidentally, also found itself a hapless target of those machine guns)
clearly originate on the other side—but by then it was obvious that the
charm of the UN presence had fully worn off. Messages of warning from
Hammarskjöld were airily brushed aside; and in New York, the Secretary-
General's office clad itself in embarrassed silence whenever the subject of
the UN presence was brought up.[15] In fact, since January 1960, the only
known time when the UN presence made its weight felt in the Laotian
crisis was in the winter of 1960, when Zellweger made a final attempt to
mediate between King Savang Vathana, Souvannaphouma, and the right-
wing group. His arguments were listened to but not heeded. The United
Nations had failed miserably in Laos.

What was so remarkable about the UN presence in Laos was the near-
perfect hush-up job done on it by the American press. Once the UN had
indeed pulled the Western chestnuts out of the Pathet Lao fire of 1959,
not one word of appreciation or support for the UN's job in Laos was
spoken. Inquiries among well-informed correspondents in 1961 as to
whether they were aware that there still was a UN mission in Laos were
met with surprise, if not with outright incredulity: "You mean they're
still there? I thought they'd gone back long ago," was the standard reply.

No, indeed. The UN presence is still in Laos, still observing and still
reporting, in spite of the complete breakdown of peace and the death of
the man who sent it there, doing a modest job in the field of village
improvement in Central Laos (where its vehicles are courteously checked
by Pathet Lao sentries and let through without harm).

In New York the reports of the UN mission in Laos are still coming
in and are, presumably, still being read; although, as a high United Nations official told me in August 1961, it is not discreet to talk about them.
In fact, it may not even be discreet to remind the world that there is
a UN presence still tucked away somewhere in the jungles of Southeast
Asia.*

* *Editor's note:* The mission of Edouard Zellweger as "Special Consultant to the
Secretary-General for coordination of United Nations activities in Laos" was terminated in May 1961. The UN Development Program, however, continues to maintain
a resident representative in Vientiane.

In Laos, there was a better than even chance for the UN to do a good job in maintaining the peace. It was *we,* and not the Communists, who failed to make it work.

The 1960 Elections

With the Khou Abhay government firmly in the saddle, the Laotians now directed their attention to the nationwide legislative elections whose date had finally been set for Sunday, April 24. Elections in Laos, as in a great many other areas of the world, had always been the object of more or less overt manipulations, but this one was to set new records even by Laotian standards. With disarming frankness, Sisouk describes the process in full: Gerrymandering of electoral districts, thus breaking up those where the Pathet Lao could be counted upon to make a good showing; changing of eligibility requirements by adding property or educational qualifications which not many Pathet Lao could hope to fulfill; and, above all, the detention in jail (now for almost a full year) of the major Pathet Lao leaders.[16]

In addition, and this at least was understandable under the circumstances, the Army suppressed Communist propaganda in the provinces and made anti-Communist propaganda instead. The Army's psychological warfare program was personally directed by General Phoumi.

Contrary to what was expected, the electoral campaign proceeded without undue violence. One UN official of French nationality was assassinated by the Pathet Lao who had intended to murder an American (and said so, apologetically, to the wife of the victim),[17] and a total of 141 candidates stormed the countryside, doing everything but kissing babies. At the same time, nine Laotian battalions swept southern Laos, where the Pathet Lao had quietly taken over the whole countryside leaving the major towns alone untouched; the Army proceeded with sufficient ruthlessness to further antagonize the tribal minorities inhabiting the backlands.[18]

Once more, the non-Communists quarreled over the number of seats to be allocated to each faction. The CDIN felt that the old-guard politicians were exerting more effort to squelch the "young Turks" attempt to control the next parliament than to avert a possible good showing by the Pathet Lao. The latter, by the way, deprived of its major leaders, nevertheless entered nine candidates in the election, while Bong Souvannavong's *Santiphab* ["Neutrality and Peace"] party ran on the National Union list.

The election results left no doubt to anyone but the blindest optimist that large-scale fraud and rigging had taken place. Of the fifty-nine seats at stake, the CDIN won thirty-two and the old-line RPL the remainder. The neutralists and the NLHX won none at all and were defeated by margins that bordered on the ridiculous. In the Communist stronghold of Sam-Neua, the Pathet Lao candidate got exactly four votes, while in another Pathet Lao stronghold, its candidate also garnered four votes—against his CDIN opponent's 18,189.[19] Margins in other districts were of a like nature, while in one district the government candidate got 2000 votes more than there were registered voters.[20] The defeated neutralist candidate, Bong Souvannavong, reported charges of rigging to the UN presence. It is not known what the latter did with the information.

In any case, none of the Western chanceries fought the election results too hard, either, although none of them labored under any illusions as to their representativeness. This was best shown by the fact that the three major Western ambassadors in Vientiane again went to see the King and put a stop to any ambitions of General Phoumi to become more than the "gray eminence" behind whomever the King chose to be prime minister—although the election results themselves would have largely justified the appointment of Phoumi to that post.[21] Instead, the mantle fell upon the shoulders of Tiao Somsanith, a forty-seven-year-old prince. Souvannaphouma, who had been mentioned for the post, and who in addition having won an easy unopposed victory as legislator for Luang Prabang had been appointed to the important position of President (i.e., speaker) of the National Assembly.

The CDIN, now holding the absolute majority in the legislature, was in the embarrassing position of still not being a "political party." It now remedied this slight defect by transforming itself into the Social Democratic Party, or *Paxasangkhom* (PSK), of which the CDIN remained the hard-core political directorate.

Things seemed to return to some sort of normalcy in Laos; there was even talk, once more, of building up a few modest industries. Some of the U.S.-aided road projects got going again, and if there still was talk of the Pathet Lao, it was in more abstract terms. After all, its top leaders were securely in jail; their trial for treason and rebellion had been postponed several times because no Laotian judge could be found who had the death-defying courage to preside over the proceedings. And perhaps this indefinite situation was more in keeping with Lao mores than a drumhead trial. Things were back to being settled the Laotian way—*en famille*.

All that was to change during the night of May 23–24, 1960.

Souphanouvong's Escape

For ten months, Souphanouvong, Singkapo, and their thirteen associates had been almost model prisoners at the Phone Kheng police camp on the outskirts of Vientiane, tending their little garden and doing physical exercises, avidly reading newspapers and mail and, above all, discussing politics. That is, not as much among themselves as with their guardians.

The net result was that Souphanouvong and his aides escaped from prison exactly when they wanted and under the best conditions of safety, since the bulk of their guardians followed them right out of town and into the jungle hideouts. The choice of the date also was not fortuitous: As long as there had been any hopes that someone other than an extreme right-wing group was going to control Laos, the Pathet Lao leaders had no reasons to leave Vientiane since they were the logical interlocutors for a cease-fire between the Pathet Lao and the royal government.

But at the end of May, it was obvious that it was the CDIN which was going to hold the reins of government, and among them there were several people who might not have been loath to dispose of the Pathet Lao leaders once and for all and without the benefit of a public trial. And May 23 was exactly one year and one day after the first arrest of the Pathet Lao leaders, and to escape on the anniversary of their imprisonment would further emphasize the willfulness of the gesture and the powerlessness of the government even over its own elite police force.

With the escape of the Pathet Lao leaders, the royal authorities lost their very last trump card, or almost. From now on, the struggle for control in Laos was to become a test of military strength, and in that, the government still had an edge—and the fine hone of that edge was the 2d Lao Paratroop Battalion (BPL) commanded by an energetic and popular young officer, Captain Kong-Lê.

X

Coup and Countercoup

The Kong-Lê Phenomenon

What happened next in Laos was completely beyond the imagination of
the diplomats, intelligence experts and anthropologists: A young army
captain took over the reins of power in Vientiane for no other reason
than that he was "sick and tired of it all"—the graft and corruption,
the fratricidal war, the loss of Laotian values, and foreign control of Laotian affairs.

Kong-Lê was the almost perfect antithesis of what would make for
a successful member of the Lao elite: By ethnic origin he was a member of one of the proto-Malay minorities to whom the lowland Lao like to
refer contemptuously as *"Kha"* ["slaves"]; he was not a member of the
dozen or so princely families who usually play the political game of
musical chairs in Laos;[1] he had not been educated in France (in fact
Kong-Lê himself admits to not even speaking the "literary" Lao of the
educated man but the low-class Lao of the small merchants and arti-
sans[2]); and he was extremely young (being born in 1935) in a country
where age as such, regardless of wisdom, is an important asset.

On the positive side of the ledger were some factors which played in
his favor; some of them were traditional, while others were part of the

patterns of social innovation introduced by the influx of American and French ideas. One of the traditional factors in Kong-Lê's favor (and one that his Pathet Lao allies do not particularly stress) is that he is married to the niece of General Phoumi Nosavan, the standard-bearer of right-wing pro-Americanism in Laos. They have six children, and his family remained in Vientiane, unharmed, while Kong-Lê fought the Vientiane regime.

A non-traditional factor in his favor was that he belonged to the para-troops which—considering other military mutinies in Algeria and South Viet-Nam during the same period—are the military aristocracy of many armies. He enjoyed popularity not only among the Laotians but also among the American and French military instructors in his homeland. Kong-Lê had risen through the ranks of the French-controlled Laotian Army prior to 1954, had distinguished himself as a combat soldier and had followed French advanced paratroop and commando courses in Hanoi and Quang-Yen. In 1957, he was among the first Laotian officers to be selected by the United States to follow Special Forces training in the Philippines. He spoke very good French and acquired a passable command of the English language.

Fine-boned, with an infectious white-toothed grin, and barely five feet two inches tall, he was small even by Laotian standards; but Kong-Lê was certainly considered an "up-and-coming" man by everyone who had met him. The American advisers attached to the paratroop battalion considered him not only as very intelligent but also as very much pro-American. Conversely, the French had lost some of their enthusiasm for him as his reputation for pro-Americanism grew. Both the Americans and the French agreed, however, that Kong-Lê was, above all, "a soldier's soldier," interested in doing a good job but much too unsophisticated for playing the favorite Laotian game of political musical chairs. In fact, Kong-Lê was one of the few officers of his rank in the Laotian Army who did not own a private automobile (Mercedes-Benz or Chevrolet, prefer-ably), although he would, now and then, use a jeep from his battalion to drive his wife and children for an afternoon's outing to nearby Thadeua.

Yet, one day something happened that made this young man sufficiently angry to become a mutineer and a revolutionary. And whatever that was has been puzzling Western intelligence experts ever since. Was it the open or covert humiliations Kong-Lê no doubt had suffered because of his humble origins? (According to a Communist source, Kong-Lê had complained about having been treated as a "colored man" by Americans in the Philippines.[3]) Or was it because he had repeatedly complained that his battalion had to occupy quarters whose roof leaked while at the same time millions were spent for useless expenditures or simply disappeared in graft? Or, after almost ten years of continuous fighting in which his paratroopers had borne the brunt of the sweat and toil and casualties, was he simply sick and tired of the whole endless mess? Or did he, as one American psychologist gravely opined, suffer from a "runt complex" such as Napoleon was said to have had? Any one or all of those reasons may have had something to do with his act. The hard fact is that it profoundly affected the history of Laos.

The early days of August 1960 had been quiescent in Laos. The Pathet Lao held its own but was not exactly in a fighting mood, and the royal government was likewise ready to sit out the rest of the rainy season in comparative peace. In Luang Prabang, the body of King Sisavang Vong still awaited final cremation until a particular sandalwood tree could be found whose century-old trunk would be completely free of rot and also large enough to be hollowed out so that it could contain the King's body in a sitting position. At the beginning of August, such a tree had finally been located and brought to Luang Prabang with great difficulty, and now the King convoked the whole cabinet to the royal residence to discuss the extremely elaborate burial ceremonies that were soon to follow. On August 8, the most important cabinet members and some of the Army generals flew to the royal capital.

In Vientiane, the officers and men of the 2d Lao Paratroop Battalion went through their routine chores, except that Captain Kong-Lê and some of his staff officers went through a special tactical problem with their American and French advisers: How to hold and defend a major city. This problem, even in the case of a modern and well-trained force, is not as easy as it seems (as the Germans found out at Stalingrad) and the Laotians watched with great care and took many notes as their advisers went through the exercise step by step; and in order to make it useful as well as realistic in Laotian terms, the city of Vientiane was chosen as an example.

As the Laotians soon found out, it was not simple at all for a small force to hold a large city: The airfield had to be secured, as well as the radio station; the waterworks and power plants had to be protected from sabotage, and the post office with its telegraph transmitter and central telephone switchboard was essential to such an operation. And, of course, the various government buildings with their files had to be secured from looters and potential enemies. In a large city, a unit can soon fractionate into small defenseless groups if no strong central coordination exists, and the occupying commander must see to it that he retains full control over his troops while the city is being secured. All this the Laotians duly noted down.

At 0300 of August 9, Kong-Lê and his paratroopers struck: In quick succession and after only a very brief firefight in which six soldiers were killed, they occupied Vattay airfield, the radio station, the waterworks and power plants, the post office and, by dawn, all the most important government buildings. They were soon joined by the armored squadron stationed at nearby Camp Chinaimo. By 0700, the paratroopers were in full control, and Radio Vientiane was blaring out orders and communiqués of the newly baked *Chef du Coup d'Etat,* as Kong-Lê now styled himself.

In fact, Kong-Lê and his paratroopers added a new twist to army communications which will bear imitating: Each of the soldiers carried medal-fashion around his neck a small transistor radio set (imported thanks to American aid) which was constantly tuned in to Radio Vientiane. With the radio station under control of the rebels, the latter simply directed their soldiers by individual platoons or squads to their assigned targets.[4] This was combat control of the kind that many a modern army commander might well have envied.

What came out over the radio waves from Vientiane was far from reassuring. In fact, it was downright anti-American. The little captain with the high-pitched voice was exhorting Laotians "to quit killing other Laotians"; he advocated Laos' return to a "policy of genuine neutrality"; and worst of all, he directly attacked "a great power" which was infiltrating "every organization in the country."

"Even my own battalion," said Kong-Lê, "has ten Americans attached to it, whom the Government has allowed to infiltrate us."[5]

A few days later, the young captain was to be even blunter, as the outside world watched the unfolding spectacle with horrified fascination:

> What leads us to carry out this revolution is our desire to stop the bloody civil war; eliminate grasping public servants [and] military commanders . . . whose property amounts to much more than their monthly salaries can afford; and chase away foreign armed forces as soon as possible. . . .
>
> It is the Americans who have bought government officials and army commanders, and caused war and dissension in our country. . . . All Laotians must remain wide awake and not allow themselves to be led like ignoramuses. We must help each other drive these sellers of the Fatherland

out of the country as soon as possible. Only then can our country live in peace.[6]

Kong-Lê formed a forty-man "Provisional Executive Committee" which included left-wingers such as Quinim Pholsena as well as General Amkha Soukhavong and Prince Souvannaphouma (who one day later announced that his name had been used without his authorization), which he said was to govern the country until a new regularly formed administration could be installed.

In Luang Prabang, Tiao Somsanith and his cabinet made the usual declarations about "drastic action," and three cabinet ministers made a hasty visit to neighboring Thailand, while General Phoumi, bypassing Vientiane, flew to his southern stronghold of Savannakhet. In Vientiane in the meantime, the Laotian National Assembly had been called into session by its president, Souvannaphouma, to decide the fate of the Somsanith regime.

Theoretically, there was little the latter had to fear: After all, the CDIN held an absolute majority of seats and most of the legislators had been hand-picked for their anti-Communist and pro-Western leanings. But two factors were operating which, unfortunately, had not been taken into account when the elections were so shamefully rigged in April: One of them was that the majority of the legislators represented little more than themselves and thus had no compunctions about selling their party label down the river; the other was that close to one thousand troops, many of them in the paratroopers' mottled battle dress, were ringing the Assembly buildings, along with a few armored cars and tanks. In less than three hours it was all over, and on August 13, Tiao Somsanith's government was "voted" out of office by a heavy majority. The second attempt to impose a right-wing pro-Western regime upon Laos had met with failure.

Neutrality's Narrow Path

What followed next was the kind of total chaos and confusion which in Laos takes the place of political stocktaking. For a brief period, Laos was the seat of at least four or five centers of power, each jockeying for a stronger position and each totally incapable of defeating not only a coalition of the others but even a single one of its rivals: There were the Pathet Lao, holding much of the backlands but too short of supplies to do more; the remnants of the Somsanith regime around the King in Luang Prabang, with little more than legality to its name; Kong-Lê with his paratroops and Souvannaphouma; and, once more, Phoumi Nosavan in Savannakhet, still thirsting not only for the reality but also the appurtenances of power; and, finally, there were the xenophobic Méo mountaineers who, for a brief moment in October 1960, seemed ready to exploit the chaos among the lowland Laotians in order to create a "Méo state" or at least an autonomous area such as those which exist in Communist North Viet-Nam.

What kept the situation from really getting out of hand and becoming a bloody free-for-all were the monsoon rains which isolated physically each of the factions and left it dependent on its rivals' good will to keep a minimum of communications open. Had American aid *really* been proficient in its road-building program, then Kong-Lê would have had no trouble in trucking his paratroopers to Luang Prabang; or General Phoumi in getting his artillery to Vientiane.

This presumably left Souvannaphouma, like the Penelope of antiquity, free to begin reweaving the unraveled threads of attempted negotiations with all concerned—starting exactly where he had left off two years earlier, except for the fact that in the meantime the Pathet Lao had gained considerably in military strength and Vientiane could no longer be sure of benevolence on the part of Peking or Hanoi. But before beginning negotiations with the adversary, Souvannaphouma had to be certain of a clear mandate at home; that could only be obtained if the King administered the constitutional oath to the new cabinet and if the contending leaders on the non-Communist side were willing to support Souvannaphouma during the next round. This was not to be, for new forces had entered the picture on the non-Communist side as well; forces which sought a solution to the Laos problem in bringing the crisis to a head. In the words of a cover story of the well-informed *Time:*

> . . . Though the U.S. had recognized the Kong-Lê–Prince Souvanna government, it soon shifted the bulk of its aid to General Phoumi. The aim, explained the CIA, who called Phoumi "our boy," was to "polarize" the Communist and anti-Communist factions in Laos.[7]

If that was truly one of America's main objectives in Laos in the autumn of 1960, then it can only be said that it succeeded rather too well, for the "polarization" process occurred at an alarming rate. By the time it was completed on December 16 with the artillery bombardment of Vientiane, it had repelled into the waiting arms of the Pathet Lao, the Soviet Union, Red China, and North Viet-Nam not only Captain Kong-Lê and his tough paratroops (who all had won their spurs, or rather, wings, fighting the Communists) but also Souvannaphouma who in the past had done more to extricate his homeland from Communist domination than all the leaders put together of the so-called "right-wing"—for in fact they had no political views.

Small wonder that Western sources quote Aleksandr Abramov, the USSR's first ambassador to Laos, as having said ironically: "Had the Americans been our best friends, they could not have acted otherwise."[8] In the meantime, "polarization" was the new catchword and one could hear its effects tick away throughout the Laotian body politic with the inexorable regularity of a time bomb. On August 29, King Savang finally gave Souvannaphouma the official go-ahead for the formation of a "government of national union" to include five pro-American leaders, among them General Phoumi as Vice-Premier and Minister of the Interior (i.e., police and security), Culture, and Social Welfare. A Méo leader, Touby Lyfoung, was made Minister of Justice, while the Defense post was given to conservative General Ouane. To be sure, the neutralist Quinim was appointed as Information Minister, but all in all the new combination showed the usual "spread" around the political center that had been the hallmark of most cabinets of Souvannaphouma.

The latter, with the formalities completed—the new cabinet was sworn in by the King on September 2, with General Phoumi conspicuously absent from among the ministers—immediately addressed an appeal to his Pathet Lao half brother to come out of hiding and proceed with peace negotiations. Simultaneously, the provincial governors received instructions to put into effect local cease-fires in the areas under their control. That gesture was reported in the liberal Washington *Post* under the headline "Way Paved for Reds."[9]

The Pathet Lao's reply to that offer demonstrated as little willingness to compromise as ever. Souphanouvong asked for nothing less than the dismissal of General Phoumi and his friends from all government posts; the establishment of diplomatic relations with all nations "regardless of their form of government"; and the acceptance of foreign aid from any country.[10] Souvannaphouma turned those conditions down in almost the same terms as he had done in 1957; if any proof was needed that he was not "soft on Communism" at that time, the proof was now on the record. But apparently it was not proof enough for General Phoumi in his southern stronghold of Savannakhet.

On September 10, 1960, General Phoumi and Prince Boun Oum of

Champassak—as we have seen previously, the traditional ruler of southern Laos—broadcast an appeal which proclaimed the formation of a "Revolutionary Committee Against the Coup d'Etat" and declared a state of "martial law" in the country. In Vientiane, Souvannaphouma answered the challenge by declaring a state of emergency, but the means at his disposal to put it into effect were pitifully few, since for reasons of security the largest Laotian Army matériel stocks (particularly the artillery) had been channeled into the southern part of the country. In the meantime, the Pathet Lao were taking military advantage of the situation by completely asphyxiating the few remaining royal Laotian army posts in the northern border provinces, mainly those of Sam-Neua and Phong Saly.

The fact that the Vientiane government was in control of most Laotian aircraft while Savannakhet had the necessary supplies only added to the tragi-comedy of the situation. Once more, the Savannakhet group announced a "Communist invasion."[11] But it is significant that this time the news was received abroad in stony silence. Two invasion scares had apparently sufficed.[12] In actual fact, the military situation was serious at the end of the monsoon season and the Pathet Lao was making alarming progress, but that no longer seemed to be of importance to the "polarizers." They were merely intent upon eliminating the middle-of-the-roaders.

On September 18, Vientiane was subjected to a mortar and machine-gun barrage from the Thai side of the Mekong, while at the same time Marshal Sarit in Bangkok launched an airtight blockade of all supply lines into northern Laos. The effectiveness of the latter soon became evident in the severe shortages of food and fuel in Vientiane and the accumulation in Bangkok warehouses of 10,000 tons of U.S. aid goods destined for Laos.[13] Similar supply difficulties were not suffered by the right-wing rebels in Savannakhet, who now began a leisurely "campaign" upriver in the direction of Vientiane. Their singular lack of military luster should have tipped off General Phoumi's American supporters as to the fighting qualities of his troops. In a sharp skirmish between a few hundred of Kong-Lê's paratroops and a tank-supported 1200-man force of General Phoumi at Paksane on September 22, the latter simply abandoned the battlefield, leaving behind for the paratroops an important booty of new American weapons.

By the end of September, the Laos crisis had degenerated into a bitter three-cornered fight, in which practically everyone concerned lost sight of his initial objectives. The pro-Savannakhet commander of cut-off Sam-

Neua, for example, refused to accept supplies delivered to him by Souvan-naphouma's aircraft, stating that he preferred to accept death at Communist hands rather than to be supplied by "pro-Communists," while at the same time Savannakhet accused Vientiane of starving out the northern garrisons and thus playing the Pathet Lao's game. Vientiane, in turn, accused anti-Communist Thailand, the United States, and the Phoumi-Boun Oum group of undermining its bargaining position, and thus also playing into Communist hands! If ever there was chaos complete and insoluble, Laos could lay solid claims to having seen the worst of it.

And what, in the meantime, were the Big Powers doing? The available documentation does not seem to show that any of them was making its viewpoint known with sufficient determination to make it count. The U.S. certainly could have ordered Thailand to cease forthwith its blockade of U.S. supplies intended for Laos; France and Britain, whose views in favor of a neutral Laos along Souvannaphouma's proposal were well known, could have impressed the United States with their opinion in a more explicit manner (as they were to do later, when it was almost impossible for the U.S. to pull back from its position gracefully); the American press could have informed its public and Congress in clear terms about what was being done (or not done) in Laos; and, last but not least, Mr. Edouard Zellweger's UN mission in Laos could have, by merely threatening to make public what it must have observed, exerted a moderating influence on the activities on both sides. But no one raised his voice.

Instead, the terrain was left wide open to the paratroopers of Kong-Lê, the guerrillas of Souphanouvong, and the lackadaisical regulars of "Our Boy." The results of that total absence of policy were not long in developing.

The Parsons Mission

The deteriorating situation throughout Laos at the end of September— on the last day of the month, the Sam-Neua troops who had vowed "to fight to the death" against Communism, were fraternizing with a pro-Vientiane force that was largely composed of Pathet Lao—finally compelled the Eisenhower administration to take some sort of concerted action with regard to Laos.

Not that such moves had not been attempted, but thus far they had been left in the hand of lower-level operators or simply the military, because of the size of their commitment in Laos, and actions taken therefore suffered from a lack of central command. This was particularly visible during the "on-again-off-again" flurry of statements on United States aid to Laos.

On September 25, 1960, General Williston B. Palmer, director of the Defense Department's military assistance programs, declared in Bangkok in a statement that was completely ignored at the time that United States aid to Laos would be "slowed down" pending a clarification of the situation.[14] When he amplified his statement in Manila on October 1, adding that all military aid to Laos was "suspended," it was officially denied over the "Voice of America," which broadcast to the Far East that press reports had "misrepresented General Palmer's intentions and misinterpreted United States policy." The U.S. embassy in Vientiane further explained that American aid not only had *not* been suspended but was in fact being used to pay both the Laotian troops under control of the Laotian government recognized by Washington and those which, under the command of General Phoumi, were in active rebellion against that government—surely one of the most unusual instances of United States aid distribution.[15]

On October 7, however, Prime Minister Souvannaphouma denied that his government was receiving U.S. military aid or funds, and on the same day the Department of State reversed its own declarations of the previous days and admitted that aid to Laos (at least to its legal government) had indeed been suspended, thus again giving the outside world the impression that the United States was speaking with at least two voices, if not two minds.[16]

Phoumi, beaten militarily by Kong-Lê's paratroops at Paksane, again began to negotiate with Souvannaphouma. The latter, residing in a capital that was running out of food, fuel, and funds to pay civil servants and troops, only perfunctorily, if at all, supported by the monarch in far-off Luang Prabang, now had to face the Pathet Lao guerrillas as well at the negotiating table. For weeks, he had been pleading his case for a neutral but pro-Western Laos with anyone who wanted to hear it, had made several statements indicating clearly that he did not want to sell out Laos to his pro-Communist half brother and had, then and later, clamped down on impulsive and unsophisticated Kong-Lê when the latter uttered statements that went beyond what Souvannaphouma was willing to endorse.

But in reply, all that Souvannaphouma was ever offered was embarrassed encouragement on the part of the British and French and stony incomprehension on the part of Washington. Not that the latter was of one mind on the issue of Souvannaphouma and his proposed neutralization for Laos. In fact, diplomats in the American Embassy pleaded eloquently the case for Laos' neutrality and so did those in the middle echelon of the State Department in Washington. Higher up, however, the old "bastion" concept still held some appeal and the defeats it had suffered in 1959 only seemed to make its attainment more desirable.[17]

Secretary of State Christian A. Herter then made what probably was one of his most fateful decisions: He sent J. Graham Parsons to negotiate with Souvannaphouma. As we have seen earlier, Parsons had been the most ardent and vocal advocate of the "hard line" on Laos and he had been personally instrumental in bringing about the downfall of Souvannaphouma and his earlier attempt at neutrality in Laos. There was no love lost between the two men, and it cannot even be said that Parsons—under whose stewardship as U. S. Ambassador to Laos the most severe cases of aid mismanagement had occurred—enjoyed a great deal of popularity among the other Western diplomats accredited to Vientiane. Yet it was he and John N. Irwin II, Assistant Secretary of Defense for International Security Affairs, accompanied by Vice Admiral Herbert Riley, Chief of Staff at CINCPAC, who were entrusted with a last-ditch attempt to throw the rudder around in Laos.

What Parsons had to say to Souvannaphouma was never made part of the public record but in essence it boiled down to the following: Immediate cessation of all negotiations with the Pathet Lao, creation of a national union government in which Phoumi's CDIN would predominate, abandonment of attempts to put into effect a policy of neutrality, muzzling of Kong-Lê and his paratroops. In exchange for what amounted to a total capitulation, Parsons offered little more than the promise of resumed American aid with perhaps a somewhat greater emphasis on economic development. In order to make his case stronger, Parsons not only submitted it to Souvannaphouma but also made a special flight to Luang Prabang on October 13 to bring the King around to his views.

As Parsons had said to the Senate Foreign Relations Committee during his appointment hearings one year earlier, "the way in which we use the aid program as a device to bring pressure is a very delicate matter." In the case of Laos, as in the case of neighboring Cambodia, the device simply backfired: While Parsons was still in Vientiane, Soviet Ambassador Aleksandr N. Abramov arrived at Vattay airport and was given a rousing welcome that included not only the usual flower girls and garlands, but also Buddhist priests, school children, and a parachute jump by men of Kong-Lê's 2d Paratroop Battalion.

The weekend of October 14–16, 1960, brought the final break. As Assistant Secretary of State Parsons was grim-facedly dodging all questions on how the talks went—thus revealing their failure—Souvannaphouma held a press conference in which he restated that "we don't want to have Communism come to power here," adding: "If the Americans understand our position, that's all right. But if not—too bad."[18]

On the following day, *Pravda* opened up with a propaganda broadside against U.S. actions in Laos, comparing them with events in the Congo and calling for full support of the Souvannaphouma regime. In Vientiane, Soviet Ambassador Abramov had a long talk with the Prince from which he emerged smiling. He even had a kind word for the departed Assistant Secretary of State.

"I would have liked to meet Mr. Parsons," said Abramov, "but he left in such a hurry."

"Polarization"

The complete failure of the Parsons mission finally aroused America's allies from their torpor. Britain, France, and Australia began to exert pressure on Washington to reconsider its case against Souvannaphouma before making a final decision on the matter; but all that Washington was willing to do—acting once more under the prodding of Soviet moves—was to resume paying the salaries of the Laotian Army (both legal and rebel) as of October 22, while General Phoumi's forces and a new rebel group of Laotian officers in Luang Prabang resumed their military operations against the Vientiane regime. Thailand, in the meantime, continued to blockade the latter city, which completely ran out of fuel as of October 25; and on the following day Soviet Ambassador Abramov presented his credentials to the King, thus giving Russia for the first time an official foothold in the small kingdom. On October 27, Souvannaphouma announced that Laos would be "very happy" to accept Soviet offers of economic aid. Western fortunes in Laos were ebbing rapidly.

But still the various Laotian factions kept on fighting each other as if the greatest prize in the worldwide Cold War was to be prime minister of Laos. On November 12, Phoumi sympathizers, sidestepping Vientiane, made a putsch in Luang Prabang, thus securing for their side the person of the King and putting the hard-pressed Vientiane regime into a right-wing pincer. Kong-Lê's overworked paratroops, facing Phoumi's forces in the Mekong valley, now also had to face a new threat to the north. Wearily, Souvannaphouma ordered a column of loyal troops to attempt the hopeless task of recapturing Luang Prabang; at the same time he offered to meet with Phoumi at the royal capital in order to settle their differences. Phoumi did not even bother to reply to the letter.

Once more, the United States intervened directly in the internal struggle. It warned Souvannaphouma "in a strongly worded statement" against attempting to reconquer Luang Prabang as such a move "might facilitate additional Communist gains." The State Department's declaration remained silent on the question of how a three-cornered civil war might, on the other hand, hamper a Communist take-over.

In any case, the activists (both Laotian and American) in Laos also opened a second diplomatic front by initiating a whispering campaign which saddled France with the responsibility for almost everything that was going wrong in Laos. That tactic had worked once in Viet-Nam and seemed to have almost worked a second time in Saigon when Vietnamese paratroops rebelled against President Ngo Dinh Diem on November 11, 1960 (except that the Vietnamese press also accused the U. S. Military Advisory Group of having "aided" the rebels!). Thus, as the thirteenth meeting of SEATO military advisers opened in Bangkok on November 15, Thailand openly accused "a powerful country" of having backed both the Kong-Lê coup and the Saigon mutiny.[19]

In Vientiane itself, polarization rapidly reached its limit. On November 18, 1960, Souvannaphouma agreed to form a new coalition cabinet which would include not only neutralists but also members of the pro-Communist *Neo Lao Hak Xat* (NLHX)—and more than the two he had accepted in November 1957! If the whole situation began to have the same sinister overtones of helpless sliding to the Left as the Spanish Civil War, it was certainly not the fault of the Laotians who were uninformed about the fate of the Madrid regime in 1938 when, abandoned by the world's weak-kneed democracies, it had to face Fascism with the sole help of the Communists. But J. Graham Parsons, who had been personal secretary to U. S. Ambassador Grew in the early thirties and who already was a Foreign Service officer during that period, should perhaps have remembered. . . .

But Washington, embroiled in the throes of a bitter presidential campaign, had other things to watch than its own hotheads in faraway Laos; and the fact that the British and French (who perhaps had a somewhat clearer recollection of their failures between 1933 and 1939) were harping away at the theme that "support for General Phoumi Nosavan from the

United States [had] thrust Premier Souvanna Phouma into the waiting arms of the Communists,"[20] was simply dismissed as the typical "dog-in-the-manger attitude" of the French or the also typical "peace-at-any-price" stance of the British. In fact, it had become an axiom among certain Far Eastern experts that their policy moves were correct when "the French were bitching again." Allied warnings were glibly dismissed, while last-ditch concessions by the NLHX, which—under Souvannaphouma's prodding—had accepted the participation of right-wing elements in the government, were simply rejected as "political maneuvering" (which it no doubt was).

This was a time for action of the kind that was going to look good next spring at the budget hearings. General Phoumi's faltering military offensive against Kong-Lê's paratroops was again cranked up on November 30 and, now supported by American military advisers and additional equipment shipments, began to gather steam.

The attack began with a 105-mm. artillery barrage on Ban Sot, a village on the Nam [River] Ca-dinh, 100 miles to the south of Vientiane which, hitherto, had been the informal boundary between the troops from Savannakhet and the paratroopers of Kong-Lê who, faced with a material and manpower superiority against which they were helpless, calmly retreated northward. Meanwhile at Vattay airport the first Soviet airplanes began landing fuel and food supplies soon to be supplemented by heavy 120-mm. (4.2 in.) mortars and a few field howitzers.

This was no longer a time for neutrals. Having lost all leeway for maneuvering and unwilling to sell out a policy for which he had worked more than six years, Souvannaphouma chose a way out which many a politician before and after him had chosen: He went into exile. On December 9, in a move whose constitutionality was questionable, Souvannaphouma turned over the reins of government to a "Military High Committee" under General Sounthone Patthammavong, the Laotian Army Chief of Staff, who, in turn, transmitted them on Sunday, December 11, 1960, at noon to the remaining four cabinet members in Vientiane. Quinim Pholsena, the bookstore owner turned neutralist leader and now the senior cabinet official in the surrounded city, took over as "acting prime minister."

Grimly, the paratroops began digging trenches outside Vientiane, while the new Soviet artillery and mortars were rolled into position near the airfield. Colonel Singkapo, the Pathet Lao guerrilla leader, was seen in Vientiane in full American battle dress.

In Savannakhet, forty out of the fifty-nine legislators who had unanimously voted for Souvannaphouma's neutrality policies in August went into special session on December 12 to set up a new regime under General Phoumi and Prince Boun Oum, and in Moscow the Soviet news agency Tass published the text of a Russian note addressed to the United States, accusing the latter of "flouting the sovereign rights of the Laotian Government headed by Prince Souvanna Phouma" and hinting darkly that the "U.S.S.R. cannot ignore the threat to the peace and security of Southeast Asia" created by the new situation.

What happened next was absolutely unforgivable, the more so as it was totally avoidable: Both sides fought an artillery duel in and around the city of Vientiane, with the right-wing artillery being in position near Camp Chinaimo and Kong-Lê's men firing from near Vattay. Launched late on December 13, the "Battle for Vientiane" ended at dusk on December 16. The city was a total shambles; the native parts of the town, consisting of wooden houses covered with bamboo or rice straw thatch, went up in flames like tinder as incendiary shells ripped into them. The American Embassy's office buildings, which were located in the center of town right next to the Laotian Defense Ministry, also suffered badly and the military attaché's building caught fire.

Here also, the reporting in the American press differed widely from that of its British and French counterparts. While the former reported mainly the military aspects of the fighting, the latter emphasized the needless human suffering that had been caused by it: The fact that *five hundred* civilian casualties had been inflicted while the contending armed forces lost but a handful of dead;[21] the fact that the armored vehicles of Phoumi (Kong-Lê had no armor) literally used defenseless civilians in the streets for target practice;[22] that the French military hospital (one of whose two doctors went back on duty three days after having been operated on for appendicitis because of the overflow of Laotian wounded) had been the object of particularly vicious machine-gun fire in spite of the fact that its location was perfectly well known and that it flew a large Red Cross flag[23] —all that went unreported in the United States.

In one sense, the United States was lucky: It was certainly not the Communist press that was going to point to the similarity between what was happening in Vientiane and what had happened four years earlier in Budapest to a "neutralist" government under Imré Nàgy (whose program, incidentally, bore a remarkable resemblance to that of Souvannaphouma).

The fact, however, that perhaps some Europeans and many Asians were making a mental comparison along such lines remained largely ignored.

All that the editorialists of the New York *Times* could rouse themselves into saying about the whole affair was that

. . . the issue has been simplified by the fact that the forces of Captain Kong [-Lê] . . . have made common cause with the pro-Communist Pathet Lao forces, making the formerly three-cornered civil war a clear struggle between Communists and anti-Communists.[24]

What those genial oversimplifiers and "polarizers" overlooked in this sorry mess was that it had thrown into Communism's arms a great many people who essentially were *not* Communists (just as in 1946 many Vietnamese who at first merely wanted the French to get out as colonial masters in Viet-Nam, were finally pushed into Ho Chi Minh's Viet-Minh) but who, by deliberate action on our side, were left with no alternative.

No—"polarization" had not "simplified" the Laotian conflict any more than "polarization" of the fifty-odd uncommitted nations in the UN would "simplify" the Cold War. It had merely internationalized it.

Part Three:

THE SOLUTION

XI

Internationalizing the Crisis

—◄◆►—

It will be well to remember that diplomacy has rarely been able to
gain at the conference table what cannot be gained or held on the
battlefield.

General Walter Bedell Smith
(after the 1954 Geneva Conference)

Civil War

The Boun Oum-Phoumi regime received swift approval at home and
equally prompt Western recognition abroad, while the Americans, British,
and French began to airlift essential foods and medicine to the city which,
long before the shelling, already had been on short rations. For the first
time, the proverbially smiling Laotians looked downhearted; even during
the worst of the Viet-Minh attacks of 1953–54, no major Laotian city had
ever been shelled or burned down, and the damage done by both sides to
Vientiane had been severe.

Furthermore, the battle had not decided anything. Kong-Lê's paratroops emerged largely unscathed, battle-hardened, disciplined troops as
they were, and had withdrawn northward into the hills, taking with them
their heavy mortars and other weapons. They were supported in their
retreat by a constant stream of Soviet supply drops. The Pathet Lao, on
their part, had thus far not suffered at all, and the arrival of the paratroops, with their many well-trained non-commissioned officers, would add
to their tactical maneuverability. If anything, then, "polarization" had
added a great deal more military power to the pro-Communists than to the

anti-Communists, and it had made national heroes of the middle-of-the-roaders who hitherto had been rather lackluster.

Soviet aid—composed, incidentally, of a majority of American weapons delivered earlier to the French and captured by the Viet-Minh at Dien Bien Phu[1]—merely enabled the Pathet Lao and Kong-Lê forces to gain a slight edge in low-level firepower and keep pace with the Royal Army's mobility; their fighting qualities would do the rest.

In the ensuing military campaign (for it was that, for the first time in Laos' recent history) the anti-government forces were almost never to relinquish the initiative, all bombastic communiqués to the contrary notwithstanding.

Having drawn back from Vientiane, Kong-Lê took time to regroup his troops in a defense perimeter at Vang Vieng, about sixty-five miles north of Vientiane on the main road to Luang Prabang. It is there that the Pathet Lao "suggested" that he capture the vital airport complex at the Plaine des Jarres, lightly held by government troops. On New Year's Eve, 1960, a small airlift of Soviet Ilyushin-14's landed discreetly at Vang Vieng airstrip and picked up Kong-Lê and his men who then took the Plaine des Jarres garrison and its French advisers without a fight.[2]

A counterdrop of 300 paratroops of the 1st Lao Parachute Battalion, designed to retake the Plaine des Jarres from Kong-Lê, ended in a complete fiasco: Thirty of the paratroopers were killed or captured by Kong-Lê's men on January 3, 1961; the rest made their way back on foot to the government strongpoint at Tha-Tom a week later. The anti-government forces now had in their hands not only one of the best airfields in Laos, but also a direct overland line of communications with Communist North Viet-Nam, over which now a stream of Viet-Minh trucks carrying ammunition, artillery, mortars, and specialists began to flow into Laos, followed later by armored carriers with light automatic cannon.

In Vientiane, in the meantime, Prince Boun Oum was to declare on January 7 that a "general offensive on the rebels was imminent." The Pathet Lao, however, struck first against the strategic Vang Vieng strongpoint, which it was able to hold in spite of repeated strafing and rocket fire by the newly arrived T-6 U.S. aircraft with which the Lao Air Force had been provided. Under the guidance of American staff officers and training personnel, the Laotian Army now began to elaborate plans for a twin-pronged drive both northward from Vientiane toward Luang Prabang (still cut off and almost completely surrounded by an advance guard of Pathet Lao guerrillas), and in a northeasterly direction toward the Plaine des Jarres via Tha-Tom, just as the 6th BCL had in April, 1953, when the French-held Plaine des Jarres was surrounded by the Viet-Minh. Tha-Tom became the staging area for the latter drive, complete with helicopter landing field, message centers, and press briefings. The only thing that failed to work according to the rules of the book was the promised government offensive. A strong 1500-man government probe toward Ta-Vieng was routed by Kong-Lê on January 13, and another attempt, on the northern front, to push beyond the Nam Lik was stalled by determined resistance at Ban Hin Heup, later to become famous as the "Laotian Panmunjom" where royal and Pathet Lao delegations met endlessly to work out details of the cease-fire. On January 18, the Pathet Lao evacuated Vang Vieng after it had fully secured a new position around Sala Phou Khoun, the key crossroads where the Vientiane highway meets the road to the Plaine des Jarres; but at the same time the royal forces lost Tha-Tom.

Thus far, the royal forces had advanced exactly sixty-five miles in twenty-nine days, and *Time,* as willing as anyone to give the royal side a fair break, concluded glumly that "the spectacle of one pro-Communist captain with a nucleus of 300 paratroopers standing off a 29,000-man army nurtured and trained by the United States was bad enough."[3]

The Vientiane regime, feeling that it needed a respite, then resorted to their customary gambit: It announced a series of Communist invasions, which included thrusts by Red Chinese, North Vietnamese, and Russian troops, until the foreign journalists simply laughed in the face of Bouavan Norasing, the Information Minister who read the news to them and who, in his own defense, simply said: "Well, that's what it says here, anyway." When it was obvious that no one was quite willing to accept that information at face value, Vientiane resorted to the even more elementary tactic of inventing military victories. On February 1, Vientiane announced that Sala Phou Khoun had been captured, only to deny it four days later; then on February 27, General Phoumi announced that "the rebels were pulling out" of their key stronghold of Xieng-Khouang[4] because of fear of a major government attack.

In actual fact, Kong-Lê (who, in the meantime, had been appointed "President of the Supreme Military Council," i.e., commander in chief of the combined Pathet Lao and paratroop forces) was readying himself for the counteroffensive.

It came in what probably was a model of sound jungle tactics: Infiltration first, outflanking the enemy without a fight wherever possible, an intensive artillery and mortar barrage from all directions to confuse the defenders and, finally a brutally swift infantry assault with maximum use of automatic weapons and hand grenades. On March 7, the Kong-Lê forces emerged from the "bulge" around Sala Phou Khoun road junction and drove deeply into the royal lines around Vang Vieng, where the regulars of the Vientiane regime began to pull out in complete panic. Inside forty-eight hours, the Vientiane regime lost the military gains of two months.

This time, the reputation of the American military trainers of the Laotian forces was at stake. The counterattack of April 5 was a model of "three-dimensional planning," with Lao regulars being ferried via American troop carrier helicopters to a drop zone near Muong-Kassy which already had been secured by paratroops of the loyalist 1st BPL. Dubbed "Operation Noel," it was designed to cut off the Kong-Lê spearhead forces driving southward toward Vang Vieng. But again the royal forces, this time accompanied by American advisers, failed to make progress. Worse, on April 14, the whole force had to be withdrawn under heavy fire, with the New York *Times* noting that "many Westerners believe that the Laotian government is losing confidence in the United States," and adding a few days later that "it has now become clear to all observers here that the Laotian Army . . . has no will to fight."[5]

Still, the Laotians and their American advisers believed in the eventual success of a military decision. On April 20, 1961, the PEO finally stepped forth from behind its cloak as a civilian aid agency and became the U. S. Military Assistance Advisory Group, Laos (MAAG/Laos) under the command of Brigadier General Andrew Jackson Boyle. Four days later, Kong-Lê captured his first four Americans in uniform—a captain and three sergeants who, attached to the government's Vang Vieng force, had been left behind when their Laotian charges fled head over heels when the Pathet Lao suddenly overran Vang Vieng. Within twenty-four hours, the attackers were deep behind government lines which were finally stabilized along the last natural obstacle between the jungle and Vientiane, the Nam Lik and the village of Ban Hin Heup.

In the meantime, both sides were opening more or less secret "second fronts," supplied on one side by infiltrating guerrillas and on the other by Special Forces helicopters. An American Liaison Training Advisory Group (LTAG) began to train some of the long-neglected Méo mountaineers of northern Laos who long ago should have been a major object of American attention instead of being abandoned to the untender mercies of their lowland compatriots; and one of the Méo leaders, Vang Pao (who was later to be given the rank of lieutenant-general in the Laotian Army) organized several *maquis* in Xieng-Khouang and even faraway Sam-Neua province.

The Pathet Lao, in the meantime, systematically took over the whole hill hinterland of the Laotian panhandle until little else was left in royal hands except the Mekong valley bottom itself. Kam Kheut fell on March 30; on April 17 an attack on Muong Nhommarat nearly cut Laos in two, while during the same week Pathet Lao commandos carried out sabotages within three miles from the center of Vientiane. On April 29, Ban Keun, twenty-five miles north of Vientiane, was captured; and Muong Phalane, an important military post on Road No. 9 (which connects Laos with South Viet-Nam) collapsed on May 1.

In less than three months of fighting, the Pathet Lao and Kong-Lê, aided by the Soviet bloc just as the Vientiane regime was being aided by the United States, had made a total shambles out of any pretense that a victory over the pro-Communist elements could be won without a massive commitment of American ground forces in Laos.

To be sure, Vang Pao and his Méo still fought on against the Pathet Lao even after the cease-fire that went into effect on May 3, 1961, at 0800 local time; but their bases, overcrowded with noncombatant tribesmen and families, were dependent upon a constant stream of American supply aircraft. They were easy targets that could be surrounded and starved out or shelled and assaulted. As one survivor of British "Force 136" operations in Laos observed: "This is not the kind of behind-the-lines operations which we were taught to carry out. It's much too big and too brassy. I'm sure the Commies won't stand for the Americans flying regular supply runs behind their lines."

This prediction was upheld by subsequent events. One American H-34 helicopter carrying two American civilians and two U.S. soldiers was shot down, followed by the downing of a transport plane; and on June 7, the main guerrilla base of Ban Padong fell after the usual shelling followed by a massive infantry attack. The smaller bases of Pak Lat and Ban Hat Bo fell a week later.

To be sure, some American Special Forces operators will be able to hold out for some time; a few more perhaps indefinitely. After all, it took the far better organized Viet-Minh almost three years to kill off the last remnants of the French-organized mountaineer guerrillas in North Viet-Nam.[6]

Under such circumstances, any cease-fire accepted by the Boun Oum regime would be tantamount to a capitulation. What was left in non-Communist hands in Laos was indefensible anyway, and this time both the United States and the Communists knew it.

The West would once again reluctantly walk to a conference table at Geneva with yet another military defeat hanging like a dead albatross around its neck.

Neutrality Plans

What gives the Laotian problem a particularly heartbreaking quality is that at practically every turn of events since 1957 a perfectly sensible solution to the crisis was close at hand but was rejected simply because one or another of the contending Lao cliques found its own special interests threatened and was usually able to find one or another outside power who was willing to lend its support.

Assuming that Laos' membership in either the Soviet bloc or SEATO would be too repugnant to one or more of the contending groups to be considered a reasonable solution, Laos' *real* political problem seems to lie in the implementation of a neutral policy. There are several ways for a country to remain uninvolved in the power struggle: One is to be, like Sweden or Switzerland, willing and able to defend one's neutrality under most circumstances;[7] another is to be, like Monaco, San Marino, or Andorra, so miniscule and politically unimportant as not to warrant a power contest; a third way is to succeed, like Thailand between 1880 and 1939, in playing off contending forces against each other; and a fourth way consists in having one's neutrality guaranteed by international agreement among the contending powers. This was the rather unfortunate case of Belgium prior to World War I; it has, on the other hand, succeeded rather well thus far in the case of Austria, whose neutrality is guaranteed by a treaty signed by the United States, the Soviet Union, France, and Great Britain in 1955.

Today many small countries have succeeded in surviving along the rim of the two contending power blocs precisely by adopting one of the four courses outlined in the preceding paragraph. Sweden is dependably neutral thanks to its strong industry and armed forces—and thanks to the implicit certitude that neither of the two power blocs would let her iron mines and industrial plant go over "to the other side." Finland, as a defeated Axis partner, is in a far weaker position. Indefensible militarily and economically dependent in part upon Soviet purchases, she is nevertheless remarkably free in the field of politics and was even allowed to join the European Free Trade Area ("The Outer Seven"), as was Austria, without encountering Soviet objections.

In the Balkans, non-aligned Yugoslavia has, as a result of American largess, survived "unaligned." (Those for whom this is not sufficient justification for neutralists and who are mindful of Marshal Tito's pro-Khrushchev noises might do well to look at a map and ponder on what the situation in the Mediterranean would be if Soviet tactical missile bases were to line the 900-mile-long Yugoslavian shoreline.)

In the Orient, Afghanistan and Nepal teeter precariously between conflicting pulls, but neighboring India and Burma can easily bask in the righteousness of their neutrality, since the latter is enhanced by the mutual interest of both blocs in maintaining the *status quo*.

The lot of the neutral becomes harder when he is isolated within the confines of a single power bloc or when, having become a bone of contention between the two blocs, he is not certain whether both blocs will go to similar extremes in order to maintain or violate his neutrality (which comes out to about the same thing).[8] Thus, it was not easy to be a neutral Switzerland and shoot down German Luftwaffe planes violating Swiss airspace while the Axis controlled Europe from the Pyrenees to the Volga.

Neither is it easy to be a neutral Cambodia when right-wing regimes in neighboring countries feel strongly that many of their internal security problems would be made a great deal easier if Cambodia either ceased to exist or at least were also in the hands of a regime committed to an actively anti-Communist policy.

The case of Laos is, along with that of Hungary (whose attempt at neutrality lived exactly four days before it was crushed by Soviet tanks in the blood of its defenders), thus far the most tragic: Here is a country which, by virtue of its simple economy, largely unsophisticated leadership, and total absence of national cohesion, is most appropriately considered as a political backwater. Yet, by sheer accident of geography it is so situated that its neighbors (as well as the faraway contending bloc powers) believe that, though the country has no intrinsic value in terms of national resources or communications, it would make a handy springboard to further adventures. In other words, Laos has come to be viewed as possessing "denial value." Whether such an estimate has a basis in fact appears at this point to be irrelevant.

Thus, the only sensible way out of that dilemma is a neutrality based on international guarantees along the lines of the Austrian State Treaty. One Asian leader sensed this while Souvannaphouma, during his tenure as prime minister in the autumn of 1960, was still struggling with "unilateral neutrality." That leader was Prince Norodom Sihanouk, chief of state of Cambodia. Having successfully weathered some crises similar in character to those which shook Laos[9] and being in the position of an isolated neutral, he had watched with deep concern the ever-spreading turmoil which the situation in Laos was creating.

Sihanouk's plan, as presented on September 29, 1960, at the United Nations General Assembly, suggested the establishment of a neutral zone in Southeast Asia consisting of both Cambodia and Laos, whose inviolability would be guaranteed by all interested powers in both blocs. And he added:

> This would mean that the two blocs, by their common accord, would accept to remove Cambodia and Laos from the list of their zones of rivalry, and to consider these two states as buffer states intended to avoid direct contact, which is a constant source of conflict.

On October 13, Khamking Souvanlasy, Foreign Minister of Souvannaphouma's government, endorsed the Sihanouk proposal in an address at the UN, stating that "we see, in this proposal, the best guarantee of our independence [and] ask the United Nations to give it serious study."[10]

Both the proposal and its acceptance by the other country concerned were met with resounding silence by all interested parties: The General Assembly was much too busy watching the antics of Khrushchev and Castro, and the two contending power blocs were far too confident that the Laotian problem was going to be solved *their* way in the near future.

Yet, acceptance of the Sihanouk proposal then, even on a unilateral basis by the West, would have saved Laos from the horrors of civil war and perhaps the occupation of four-fifths of its territory by Communist forces; or it would at least have given the West a strong moral advantage without in any way prejudicing later military steps.

It is, therefore, not entirely without significance that two of America's largest and most respected newspapers almost simultaneously if belatedly came forth with editorials advocating the neutralization of Laos.

> If it were possible [said the Washington *Post*] to insulate Laos and establish the sort of neutrality that prevails, say, in neighboring Burma and Cambodia, that certainly would be preferable to the threat of continued or broadened embroilment.[11]

The New York *Times,* which was to express some less conciliatory opinions later on, wistfully reminisced on January 2, 1961, that

. . . the ideal arrangement for Laos was the neutralist, coalition government brought about by the International and Joint [*sic*] Commissions. . . . Before the end of 1957, Laos was a neutral, buffer state under Prince Souvanna Phouma. Internal coups upset this balance and led to the present dangerous international conflict.

Undeterred by his previous lack of success, Sihanouk, on January 1, 1961, came up with a new proposal. He suggested an enlarged conference on the Laos crisis which would include the following nations: Britain and the U.S.S.R. as the co-chairmen of the 1954 Geneva conference; India, Canada, and Poland as the members of the International Control Commission; Burma, Thailand, North and South Viet-Nam, and Cambodia as interested neighboring countries; France as a signatory of the 1954 cease-fire with special interests (bases and troops permitted under the treaty) in the country; and the United States and China as countries whose interests in Laos and Southeast Asia were in competition.[12]

Several non-Communist countries greeted the proposal with great interest; Red China, surprisingly enough, accepted it with alacrity on January 14. The Eisenhower administration gave a dilatory answer on January 18 which, in view of its caretaker character, was perhaps understandable but not to the liking of some of the Asians. The Cambodians, who in fact had considered the plan a neat way of saving America's face, were especially disappointed in Washington's reaction.

"I don't know what the State Department had against the plan," said a high Cambodian official to me later. "The West couldn't wish for a better-balanced membership—seven pro-Western nations; four Communist nations and three 'real' neutrals: India, Burma, and us. At the worst the West could always deadlock the conference."

Since the United States later agreed to accept the Cambodian plan, but only after the situation inside Laos had deteriorated beyond hope, the Cambodians were left to ponder the inscrutable ways of the mysterious West.

Other workable peace proposals were similarly regarded by the activists in Washington who seemed grimly determined to hand down to the incoming Kennedy administration as many insoluble crises as possible, or who, more probably, intended to close the books with at least one clear-cut "victory" (after Korea, Indo-China, Suez, Budapest, Sputnik, and Lebanon) on the record.

On December 23, 1960, India's Ambassador to Washington, M. A. C. Chagla requested a meeting with Secretary of State Christian Herter to express to him India's deep concern over the gravity of the Laos crisis. He attempted to gauge the United States' reaction should India propose a revival of the International Commission, if only in a fact-finding capacity (as it was eventually to function six months later).

Herter granted Chagla a sympathetic hearing, but when the latter called upon the Department a week later, he was informed by Acting Secretary of State Livingston T. Merchant that the United States was opposed to the ICC's revival. Other Washington officials (unnamed) stated that the U.S. "considered India's attitude unrealistic."[13] Since India shared the United States' reluctance to call a conference of all the powers which had participated in the 1954 Geneva cease-fire conference, as the Soviet Union suggested,[14] only one non-military avenue of approach to the Laos problem remained—the United Nations. That organization, and particularly its ever-patient Secretary-General, had received in the past two years an avalanche of Laotian notes, declarations, and requests (not to speak of unverified invasion reports) that would have tried a saint. The fiasco of the 1959 fact-finding mission was still in everyone's memory, and the reports which the "forgotten mission" of Edouard Zellweger was sending back amply justified any further refusal on the part of the UN to become involved unless Laos was ready to file a formal and full-fledged complaint of aggression against North Viet-Nam or Red China (which Laos had thus far failed to do).

What the United States wanted the United Nations to do was to send back to Laos the three members of the ICC (India, Canada, and Poland), but as a fact-finding mission under the UN rather than under the two co-chairmen of the 1954 Geneva conference.[15] That arrangement would also have satisfied the *amour propre* of the right-wing Laotians who had vowed "never" to accept again the return of the ICC to Laos. An alternate plan that was mentioned was the sending of a UN military force to interpose itself between the warring factions, but considering the fact that this had never been tried between the two major power blocs and that the contending forces were nowhere as clearly delineated as they were in the Sinai or even in the Congo (not to speak of the enormous costs of such an operation), this proposal did not meet with rousing enthusiasm in New York. In any case, both plans were quietly shelved.

For the next four months the field was open to the military activists on both sides. The United States alerted the 7th Fleet for duty in Indo-chinese waters at least three times during that period and sent at least four "strong notes" to Moscow (although they were really destined for Peking and Hanoi); Moscow was equally bellicose and Peking issued a fairly large number of "serious warnings" to the effect: "U.S. Imperialism, Get Out of Laos!"[16] And as we already have seen, the military test did not turn to the West's advantage.

Aligning the Allies

The major American objective now was to obtain sufficient cohesion in its own camp to be able to negotiate with the Communist bloc from a position of strength, or, failing this, to muster at least symbolical Allied military support in the case of an armed clash, as was the case in Korea.

This proved difficult on two accounts: (1) it would have committed to a costly ground war an outgoing administration which had, to the last, been wedded to the idea of "Peace and Prosperity," or would have saddled with a war a new administration which still smarted under the label of "war party" which had been attached to it in all American presidential elections since World War I; and (2) America's key allies in the Far East were not at all persuaded that the Laos problem could be solved by military means. Both France and Britain had gone through the experience of bitter guerrilla wars in the Far East. Britain's experience in Malaya had ended happily, but it had tied down more than 200,000 troops for twelve years and cost $2.5 billion. France's war in Indo-China had resulted in the commitment of 500,000 troops, $11 billion of her own and $2.5 billion of U.S. aid, and had ended tragically at Dien Bien Phu. And America's own experience in Korea had involved almost a million troops and cost $29 billion, only to end in a bloody draw almost exactly where it had begun.

The difference between the relatively satisfactory outcome in Malaya and the situation in Korea and Indo-China was that in the first case there had been no direct overland connection with a Chinese Communist "sanctuary," while in the case of Korea and Indo-China, that sanctuary existed in full and was, as bitter experience had shown, perfectly willing and able to play its role.

Thus, so ran the British-French argument, unless the United States was ready to "settle" once and for all her Far Eastern problems by a general-ized war with Red China and North Viet-Nam (which, considering

America's internal situation and commitments in Europe, the Middle East, and Africa, was unlikely), a satisfactory military settlement of the Laos problem was simply out of the question. This, essentially, was what the New York *Times'* noted foreign affairs specialist C. L. Sulzberger meant when he cabled his paper on January 4, 1961, that "London and Paris feel Washington is too inclined to take a tough line [on Laos] without realizing where that line may lead."

It must be considered as a total failure of British and French communications not with the Department of State, but with public opinion both in America and non-Communist Asia that this eminently sensible viewpoint was never clearly presented, or, rather, when it finally was presented (since it eventually prevailed) it was regarded as being tainted with "British lack of guts" or "French colonial intrigues" rather than simply as being a no-nonsense attempt to make the best out of a bad bargain and get the United States off the hook at the same time. Yet, against one American writer who clearly represented the European view as being one of dismay over the tendencies of certain American Government agencies to carry on "a trigger-happy papa-knows-best Laos policy at everyone else's expense. . . ."[17] there literally were dozens who, like Joseph Alsop, made any peaceful settlement of the Laos crisis look like a new "Munich," accused the French of being "pathological" and of having fostered the Kong-Lê coup, and even sideswiped the Canadians for being "approximately neutral" (a rather poor tribute to their thankless role in the three ICC's of Indo-China).[18]

Even the Pentagon, which hitherto had in fact been less sanguine about Laos than the civilian agencies (which ought to provide some food for thought for those who think that it suffices to be a civilian to be devoid of "militarism"), now began to look for convenient scapegoats upon whom to blame the bad turn the military situation was taking in Laos. Unnamed Pentagon sources now blamed the French "dominant military position [*sic*] in Laos" for the United States' allegedly not being "allowed to have military ground observers in the field," adding that the French "apparently have not sent any to the areas where the fighting is still under way," thus depriving the West of accurate information concerning the various North Vietnamese "invasions" of Laos.[19]

That, of course, was nonsense. As was stated earlier, the 500-man French mission in Laos (instead of the 5000 troops France was allowed under the 1954 cease-fire) was in no position to "allow" or not to allow the Americans to observe anything they wanted to see in Laos. In fact, the aircraft of the American military attaché in Vientiane could be seen constantly flying all over the country, and American reporters in Laos never failed to make good-natured jokes in their dispatches about the American "undercover" operative who was always to be seen (rather conspicuously, since he was Caucasian) in the immediate entourage of Prince Boun Oum and General Phoumi.[20] If, with a staff of over 750 persons in Laos in 1961, Washington was ill-informed about what was going on, then the fault lay most likely either in the reporting (which, I was told on good authority, was not the case) or in the use to which the reports were put.

As for the French Military Mission's "absence" from the battlefields, this contradicts the fact that a French seven-man team was overrun with the royal Laotian forces at the Plaine des Jarres. The fact that Kong-Lê did not mistreat the French but released them (while, on the other hand, Major Lawrence R. Bailey, the American assistant military attaché who was shot down on March 23, 1961, while flying an embassy aircraft over the Plaine des Jarres, and other American personnel were imprisoned until the formation of a "national union" government) further confirmed American and royal Laotian suspicions that the French had indeed engineered the Kong-Lê coup just as, in the international field, they were "sabotaging" Allied military intervention in the Laos struggle.

In fact, the Boun Oum government soon seemed to have completely lost sight of the international complexities which would ensue if France were to pull out of Laos, since it was only through the legal fiction of American "training aid" to the French Military Mission that the PEO and its "civilian" general, officers, and men operated in the country. Thus, when Boun Oum requested on January 17 that France withdraw forthwith all its advisers in Laos, civilian as well as military (which would have left Laos almost overnight without much of its higher school system and its public utilities), the United States intervened to calm the Laotian ire.[21] Instead, Boun Oum and Phoumi settled for the nominal occupation of parts of Séno air base, near Savannakhet, which France held by treaty.

The French made no move to prevent the Laotians from occupying a few secondary buildings on February 5, 1961. They simply stationed their armored vehicles at the entrance to the camp, leaving just enough space for the Laotians to be able to move in single file, and boycotted the takeover ceremonies which were attended both by Prince Boun Oum and General Phoumi. On March 13, the French government notified Vientiane that any further encroachments at Séno would be met with force. This had the beneficial result of clearing the air; the deteriorating military situation did the rest. When the enlarged Geneva conference on Laos opened in May 1961, Laos again banked on its traditional ties of friendship with France for support at the conference table. As will be seen, the support came forth unstintingly.

One last moment of tension over Laos occurred between France and the United States at the SEATO meeting in Bangkok at the end of March 1961. There, in the words of the *Times* of London:

> . . . The French seemed to have played a part not unlike the British one at the Geneva conference of 1954. . . . It is they who have insisted most bluntly on the dangers of precipitate action. . . .[22]

Britain's role was an equally thankless one. Fully realizing that it was far too late to influence the Eisenhower administration to change its course, it went to work with great alacrity on the incoming Kennedy team. In this effort, it enjoyed several intrinsic advantages which the French lacked: Aside from the problem of immediacy of communications, there existed an anti-French bias among the President's most immediate advisers (all admiration of Mrs. Kennedy for things French notwithstanding) because of France's past and present colonial errors, which ruled out taking French views too seriously; in contrast, the British could boast a solid record of successful de-colonization in Asia. The British, moreover, had no direct operational responsibilities in Laos and thus were cast ideally in the role of "honest broker," providing they did not too obviously rule out the idea of using force in Laos if all else failed; for the new administration, if it did not relish inaugurating its term of office with a war, would have liked even less inaugurating it with a "surrender."

Prime Minister Macmillan's own Laos policy thus operated on two planes: On one hand, he strengthened President Kennedy's military hand in the Far East by promising British support—as he did during his dramatic weekend flight of March 26, 1961, to Key West to meet with President Kennedy; and on the other, he used the very American determination which he himself had just strengthened to persuade the Russians to accept a Laotian compromise that would preclude outright surrender of all Western objectives to Soviet threats.

There is no doubt that President Kennedy's candid press conference of March 23, in which he clearly set forth America's interest in neutrality as a solution to the Laos conflict [*See* Chapter VIII], was made a great deal more forceful because British support had made a Western military counterintervention a credible possibility.

SEATO's role has been mentioned repeatedly in the course of the Laos crisis, both as an "aggressor organization" and a "paper tiger" by the Communists, and as an "indomitable shield against Communist aggression" by our own propaganda. In fact, SEATO has been neither, but it became an extremely useful clearing house for the constant exchange and sorting-out of information on what really went on in Laos, and as a sort of "chamber of reflexion" analogous to the British House of Lords, in which no decisive action is taken but in which important viewpoints can be brought to public attention.

Both the Communists and many Asian neutrals have been extremely unfair to SEATO. Deprived of permanent armed forces and a general staff of its own, like NATO, it cannot in any way be considered a military threat in itself. On the other hand it gave some of the more sanguinely anti-Communist Asian member nations—the more sanguine the less likely they are to bear the brunt of a military campaign—a chance to become aware of the regional nature of the problem of Communist subversion and of the difficulties, even for advanced Western nations, in combating that threat.

It was a thankless role that French Foreign Minister Couve de Murville played at SEATO in March 1961, when he ticked off ("with elegant disenchantment," as Joseph Alsop avers) the harsh facts that would be entailed in a military campaign in Laos. But when Couve had finished, SEATO (whose cold realism already had deflated several Laotian invasion scares) came through with a unanimous declaration which was made the more impressive because of its moderate tone.

The last ally to be whipped into line was Laos itself. There, thanks to the fact that the whole civil war, including its international consequences, seemed to have been underwritten by the United States, unbounded optimism had replaced earlier depths of despair. The Boun Oum government was found to have had $50 million worth of local currency printed, while the whole amount of local currency in circulation amounted only to $32 million,[23] and scions of the new elite again began to infiltrate many senior (and lucrative) government positions.

Utmost intransigence against any kind of negotiations with the adversary was the order of the day as long as the military situation did not have the appearance of irreversible deterioration; this explains why a solemn

Declaration of Neutrality, made in French by King Savang before the assembled diplomatic corps as well as Laotian cabinet members in Vientiane on February 19, 1961, fell on completely deaf ears. The King offered almost exactly what the Soviet bloc had asked: Full neutrality, abstention from any military bloc or alliance, and departure of all foreign bases and advisers. In addition he offered to have this full neutrality inspected by three Asian non-committed countries: Burma, Cambodia, and Malaya.[24] President Kennedy also supported King Savang's plan, but all three Asian countries rejected on February 25 the watchdog role they had been offered.

But as Kong-Lê's paratroops, supported by Soviet-made armored gun carriers, smashed into royal army defenses at Sala Phou Khoun, Muong Kassy and Sala Phou Kheng on March 10, General Phoumi Nosavan was already on his way to Phnom-Penh to talk to his archenemy Prince Souvannaphouma about peace and neutrality for Laos. To be sure, some face-saving formulas for all concerned still had to be found,[25] but on the essentials, all seemed to be agreed: Laos was going to be neutralized and Souvannaphouma was going to head its coalition government.

In the interval between the State Department White Paper of January 7 and the SEATO resolution of March 29–30, 1961, the Western nations had reached agreement on their policies on Laos. During the period of the American *interregnum,* both Britain and France had carried the Western play forward until the incoming Kennedy administration had had time to gain its bearings, hampered rather than helped in the process by holdovers from the previous administration which had been largely responsible for some of the more serious mistakes made earlier.

To be sure, there were still loose ends to be tied up in many places and ill-founded illusions to be dispelled in others.[26] But this once, almost in spite of itself, the Grand Western Alliance was working harmoniously to an extent which suggested the great Molière's comical character Monsieur Jourdain, who spoke in prose without knowing it. The fact that this which was occurring independently of American influence, was immediately hailed in some quarters as "living proof that American leadership of the West . . . had begun to be regained by a show of moral firmness,"[27] is evidence that the flower of optimism can grow even on the most dismal of soils.

In any case, on both sides signs began to appear which showed that the time for some serious negotiating had come. The road to Geneva was open.

Geneva Once More

Both the Soviet bloc and the Western Big Three agreed on the actual agenda of negotiation (albeit for diametrically opposite reasons) but the sequencing of the steps was the major stumbling block. With Britain and Russia, continuing in their role as the co-chairmen of the 1954 conference, the pre-conference arrangements were largely hammered out in Moscow and London.

In simple terms, the problem could be analyzed into the following steps: (1) cease-fire; (2) reconvening of the ICC; (3) convening of the fourteen-nation conference; and (4) creation of a neutral government in Laos. Since the non-Communist territory in Laos was shrinking with each passing day, in the minds of Western diplomats an early cease-fire was paramount. In Russian eyes, to obtain the return of the ICC seemed to outweigh all other considerations. Both sides agreed on the fourteen-nation conference. On the subject of the creation of a neutral government for Laos, Britain stated in her note of March 23 that

. . . Her Majesty's Government cannot recognize the so-called government of Prince Souvanna Phouma as being competent to represent Laos at an international conference . . . [and that] if no government of national unity had been formed by the time the international conference convenes . . . the conference will have to address itself, as its first task, to helping the parties of Laos to reach agreement on this point.

The Soviet reply of April 1 was surprisingly conciliatory in that it agreed vaguely on the resequencing of Points 1 and 2, also agreed to Point 3 and, surprisingly, though it maintained that Souvannaphouma's exile government and its representatives in Xieng-Khouang represented "the lawful government," it stated:

. . . The Soviet Government does not rule out that the conference, as moved also by the Government of Great Britain, will assume, as one of its tasks, the rendering of assistance to Laotians in reaching agreement.

This left the early application of a cease-fire as the most important point on the agenda. On April 3, Sir Frank Roberts, the British Ambassador to Moscow, once more met with Vasily V. Kuznetsov, the Soviet Deputy Foreign Minister, to press him into a more precise definition of the phrase "calling for a cease-fire," but the U.S.S.R. seemingly was in no hurry (and probably also had to consult Peking in turn). When Sir Frank was finally handed an *aide-mémoire* on the subject on April 15, it contained an extension of the powers of the ICC by authorizing the two conference chairmen to accept the Commission's finding prior to the cease-fire, which ran the risk of dragging out matters indefinitely.[28]

Finally, after the fall of Vang Vieng had completely destroyed whatever standing the Boun Oum government still had, the Soviet Union and Britain issued three messages on April 24, calling for a cease-fire in Laos prior to May 12, a meeting of the three ICC members in Delhi, and a meeting of the other twelve interested states in Geneva on May 12, "which would have the character of the Geneva Conference of 1954. . . ."

Personality clashes and the fact that the Pathet Lao was both unwilling and probably unable to harness its victorious troops in time for the cease-fire deadline marred somewhat the optimistic picture. King Savang, suddenly departing from his aloof role as constitutional monarch, declared on May 1 that the Laotian leaders should be left to work out their differences by themselves "without illegal foreign interference." Prince Norodom Sihanouk of Cambodia, the initial promoter of the fourteen-nation conference, took this to be a personal criticism of himself and declared that he no longer would support the conference.[29]

But an optimistic report by the three ICC members who met in Delhi was handed down on May 1; and when the cease-fire became effective in the field on May 3, hopes were high that the second Geneva conference would begin on schedule. On May 12, however, other last-minute snags, for which the two sides were equally responsible, delayed the convening of the conference. On the Western side, the United States refused to participate in the conference until the cease-fire had been verified fully by the ICC; the Soviet delegation, on its part, insisted upon seating the three Laotian groups on an equal basis: Phoumi Nosavan-Boun Oum, Souvannaphouma and the Pathet Lao. To make matters somewhat more confusing, America's Asian allies, South Viet-Nam, Thailand, and the Vientiane regime, were not in attendance; Cambodia, still smarting under the insult of a fortnight ago, was also absent. All things considered, this was not an auspicious beginning.

The United States delegation fought a desperate rear-guard action to prevent the seating of the other two delegations, but to little avail. The compromise solution, worked out by Britain and the U.S.S.R., provided for the seating of Laotians on an individual basis rather than as a single delegation, "as proposed by individual governments participating in the conference."[30] Finally, on Tuesday, May 16, 1961, at 5 P.M., the conference was called to order.

The Souvannaphouma Incident

While the conference was getting under way in a flurry of exchanged notes, Prince Souvannaphouma was away on a worldwide tour and was being well received in all the capitals he visited, among them Peking, Delhi, Paris, London, and Moscow. In all of them he talked with the prime minister or president (with the exception of Britain, where he had dinner with Lord Home, the Foreign Secretary). In a pithy but not inaccurate appraisal by a newsweekly, it was concluded that "Souvanna has done better in exile than most Laotian premiers have done in power."[31]

While in Delhi, Souvannaphouma had a long conversation with U.S. roving ambassador Averell Harriman, who was considerably impressed with the Prince's estimate of the situation and recommended to Washington that he be invited to visit there. Souvannaphouma was received in Paris on March 26 with considerable formality, where he had a long discussion with President de Gaulle.

It was in Paris that, on April 9, U. S. Ambassador James M. Gavin transmitted to Souvannaphouma an invitation to come to the United States in advance of his scheduled trip to Moscow, Belgrade, Prague, and Warsaw. Washington was uncertain that Souvannaphouma would accept such an invitation at this time, for he had been deeply hurt by American actions in Laos in December 1960.

In an exclusive interview granted the New York *Times* at his refuge in Phnom-Penh one month after the battle of Vientiane, Souvannaphouma had berated J. Graham Parsons as "the most reprehensible and nefarious of men" who was "the ignominious architect of [the] disastrous American policy toward Laos."

"What I shall never forgive the United States for, however," he added, "is the fact that it betrayed me, that it double-crossed me and my government."[32]

His disappointment with the United States mellowed somewhat in the succeeding months, as his political fortunes rose, and his talk with Ambassador Harriman convinced him that a new wind was blowing in Washington. Thus, when interviewed by the French press on his arrival in Paris, he did not hesitate to state that he was

. . . now convinced that the [Laotian] policy of the Democratic administration is fundamentally different from that of the Republican administration, and that our objectives are now far better understood in Washington.[33]

According to published reports, Souvannaphouma was to meet with President Kennedy and Secretary of State Dean Rusk in Washington in "private" talks which, it was hoped, "would convince Souvannaphouma of the Kennedy administration's desire for a government that would be neutral between East and West."[34]

Both the New York *Times* and the Washington *Post* editorialized favorably on Souvannaphouma's visit to the U.S., the former commending the State Department because it had "acted wisely" in inviting him; and the latter because it thought that it would acquaint Souvannaphouma "with the real objectives of American policy."

If such was the intent of the Prince's visit, he received an object lesson in diplomatic manners that he was not likely to forget in the near future. Already a few days before Souvannaphouma's projected arrival in Washington, it became known that "the Laotian Embassy would be closed to him"—a rather unusual situation since he was technically not in rebellion against the Boun Oum government and he qualified for the courtesies of the local diplomatic representative on the counts that he was (a) a prince; (b) a legislator from Luang Prabang; (c) the President of the Laotian National Assembly; and (d) in all likelihood the next Prime Minister of Laos.

It was disclosed further that, contrary to what had been the practice from Delhi to Paris, Souvannaphouma would be greeted by the lowest-ranking Foreign Service Officer dealing with Laotian affairs. In contrast, both the British and French embassies—not to speak of those of several Asian countries—had received instructions to have Souvannaphouma greeted upon his arrival by their chiefs of mission or their immediate deputies. Furthermore, the Prince, whose friendly cooperation was vital to making the next Lao government truly neutral rather than pro-Communist, was to be accommodated in a downtown hotel as if he were no more than a tourist whose main purpose in coming to Washington was to view the cherry blossoms.

To put it succinctly, the situation was building up toward the kind of diplomatic slap in the face which can also be referred to as the "Aswan-Dam Gambit," in memory of Mr. John Foster Dulles' abrupt cancellation of aid for Egypt's high dam, which caused Mr. Nasser to confiscate the Suez Canal, the British and French to launch an abortive invasion, and Soviet aid to flow into Egypt.

What happened next is not entirely clear. It may have been that Souvannaphouma suddenly became aware that he was being trapped into a well-laid snub, or perhaps things simply worked out that way by sheer accident; or, more likely, both sides were caught in a diplomatic double-snub and were simply trying to save face as the whole elaborate stratagem began to backfire.

Although Souvannaphouma's arrival in Washington was scheduled for April 18, he announced suddenly to the American Embassy in Moscow that his departure from Russia would be delayed by one day because he had to see Mr. Khrushchev in faraway Sochi, a resort on the Black Sea (although he had seen Khrushchev, several days before and was to see him again several days after his return from Washington). After a hurried consultation with the State Department, the American Embassy pointed out to Souvannaphouma that he could not see Dean Rusk on April 20 because he was heavily committed out of town.

What were Secretary Rusk's important out-of-town commitments which would prevent him from meeting with Souvannaphouma? Was it a conference with Gromyko over Berlin, with Couve de Murville over NATO, or with Hammarskjöld over the Congo?

It was none of these. The Georgian-born diplomat was to address the Atlanta Bar Association and, later during the day, attend a Cherokee County homecoming celebration on the campus of Reinhardt College at Waleska, Georgia. No one suggested that Souvannaphouma might meet with the President without Secretary Rusk, although it is likely that both leaders might have profited from the experience. On the eve of his departure for Washington, Souvannaphouma abruptly canceled his plans to come to the United States and remained in the Soviet Union to talk to Khrushchev.

The New York *Times,* which in matters oriental had in recent years developed a rather regrettable editorial tendency of shooting from the hip, immediately opined that

Prince Souvanna Phouma's pre-emptory [*sic*] cancellation of plans to visit Washington is not only irresponsible; it is tantamount to his affirming an attachment to the Communist side in the Laotian civil war. It therefore comes close to nullifying his role as a neutral nationalist. . . .[35]

Viewed objectively, it can be said that both attempts at snubbing—assuming that all this was meant to be a snub and was not simply the result of poor planning—ended in a draw. Washington could take comfort in the fact that it alone felt strong enough in Laos not to have to court the neutralist leader; and the latter could chalk up to his credit that he had been able to turn down an invitation to meet with the new leadership of the United States.

One cannot help wondering, however, as to whether Souvannaphouma was still convinced that fundamental changes had taken place in Washington's approach to his country's problems.

Three Wandering Princes

While the fourteen nations (or, rather, thirteen nations and three Laotian groups of "advisers") sat down to what was to become one of diplomacy's longer and more unimportant conferences, whatever happened at the conference table could well be outstripped by events in Laos, where various Laotian cease-fire delegations were likely to come up with yet another *arrangement à la laotienne* that could make a shambles of anything the diplomats laboriously might put together at Geneva.

The only reassuring element for the West as the conference got under way was that for once the American press shed its usual euphoria and came forth with some sober appraisals that were to prove remarkably accurate. *Time,* on the basis of the leases taken by the Communist Chinese delegation on its automobile fleet, predicted in May that the conference was to last until November; Marquis Childs, in a blunt column, stated that the Laotian mess was far greater than the Cuban one and that Dean Rusk, at Geneva, was in the unenviable position of "waiting with what grace he could muster for the rug to be pulled out from under him."[36] C. L. Sulzberger, from the New York *Times,* warned that to obtain a truly neutral Laos under the circumstances "we will need more luck than we have any right to expect in the luckless city of Geneva."

But it was the French conservative *Combat* who summed up the situation in one pithy nutshell:

Laos is a funny country [*un drôle de pays*]; it has got a funny King and a funny cease-fire; and there are funny negotiations going on at Geneva. And tomorrow, if peace were to come from them, it would be a funny peace. . . .[37]

INTERNATIONALIZING THE CRISIS

And that is precisely what was to happen at Geneva, once the first-line foreign ministers had turned over the job to their respective specialists who in turn referred more and more questions to subcommittees which, failing to come up with anything they could agree on, turned over all the deadlocked questions to the British and Soviet co-chairmen.

As the months ground on, the whole conference became a Kafkaesque nightmare in which hollow charges were hurled back and forth before the bored eyes of a few journalists, with the United States holding out for more inspection power for the ICC but without a veto, while the Soviet bloc was in favor of a weaker ICC hamstrung by a veto. Both sides found occasion to throw in a few irrelevant charges with the Communists raking up the old issue of the Chinese Nationalist Army remnants in Burma which lately had taken to seeking refuge in northern Laos from the Burmese Army which had decided to eliminate them once and for all in a bitter jungle campaign. Since Burma was one of the neutrals at the conference upon whose sympathy the United States had counted, that sideplay was not entirely without effect.

In Laos itself, the three princes upon whose eventual agreement the fate of a "national union" government depended were still haggling over a meeting place. On May 24, Souvannaphouma proposed Ban Namone, the "truce village," as a suitable meeting place, but Boun Oum, on May 26, proposed either of Laos' two capitals instead. While that point was being considered, Boun Oum left for Nice on the French Riviera to recuperate from the strains of the past months.

The first report which the reconstituted ICC issued from Laos on May 24 damned with faint praise the Vientiane regime but clearly called "provocative" American supply flights over Pathet Lao territory in support of the Méo guerrillas. This encouraged the Pathet Lao to undertake a campaign to crush the only Laotian fighters that had given a good account of themselves. The Méos at least knew what they were fighting for: Not Laos, but their own opium crops which constitute Laos' most valuable, albeit illegal, cash export.

At that moment in Geneva French Ambassador Jean Chauvel presented a two-part "Charter of Laotian Neutrality," composed of a document that was to become an appendix to the neutrality provisions of the 1954 cease-fire agreement, and in which Laos would reaffirm its rejection of military bases or forces "other than those [i.e., French] permitted under the Geneva Accords of July 20, 1954." The second declaration was to be signed by the other thirteen nations, which would subscribe to Laos' engagements under the new protocol and promise not to interfere in Laos' internal affairs.[38] That proposal, coming on the heels of an American promise to withdraw all its instructors from the country, was sufficiently vague to satisfy most delegations. But the Chinese Communists did not like it, and the conference adjourned for a week until President Kennedy had had the opportunity to talk over the deadlock with Premier Khrushchev at Vienna, but the latter did not commit himself beyond a few generalities.

When the conference resumed on June 6, it was overshadowed by the capture of Ban Padong. While it was obviously silly to compare the fall of Padong with that of Dien Bien Phu, that new military disaster knocked much of the shaky props from under the Western stand. Both Britain and the United States decided to boycott the next sessions of the conference as a means to bring pressure to bear on its Communist participants.

If anything, the conference lull had, all optimistic prognostications to the contrary, worked against the West, and the intransigence of the Soviet bloc, when the conference resumed on June 12, plainly revealed this. The only hope that remained was that the three Laotian princes, who had finally agreed to meet in close-by Zurich during the weekend of June 17–19, 1961, would succeed in reaching agreement on the formation and composition of the coalition government whose creation was part of the Geneva "package."

That hope was based, of course, on completely non-Laotian assumptions. To anyone even remotely acquainted with the history of Laos for the past decade, it was obvious that personality clashes would delay agreement for many weeks to come. After all, in 1956 when the bargaining power of the non-Communists was a great deal stronger than in June, 1961 (when the Pathet Lao was in effective control of almost all of Laos except the Mekong valley), it took almost fifteen months to come to an agreement. Finally, on June 22, the three princes signed a preliminary agreement providing for a coalition government which, bypassing the National Assembly (considered as unrepresentative by the neutralists and the Pathet Lao), would be chosen by King Savang himself. The agreement also included such obvious points as free elections, the release of all political prisoners and the promise to "honor and respect" any agreements arrived at by the conferees at Geneva. The one worrisome aspect of the agreement was a stipulation that neutral Laos would renounce the "protection of any military alliance or coalition"—a slap obviously directed at SEATO.

While the princely accord achieved nothing new, it at least served as a pretext to cease the boycott of the Geneva conference by the Vientiane regime, and Souvannaphouma's agreement on June 24 to support the Western position of a veto-free ICC helped to reinforce the Western position. At the same time, the Zurich agreements revived American fears that Phoumi, seeing that his side was losing, was selling out to Souvannaphouma and the Pathet Lao. In a hurried trip to Washington—"We have some allies to whom we have responsibilities," he was to declare before leaving Zurich on June 27—Phoumi explained to top American officials, including the President, the Secretaries of State and Defense and General Lyman L. Lemnitzer, the Chairman of the Joint Chiefs of Staff, the position of the Boun Oum regime and gained, in turn, reassurances about renewed American help should the Geneva talks break down.[39]

A similar invitation to come to Washington was extended to Souvannaphouma (since apparently no homecoming celebrations were now in the way of direct talks with senior American leaders), but the Prince merely returned the earlier snub with dividends: He stated that his schedule was now "too crowded" for such a visit and thus elected to remain in Europe, while the "Red Prince" went to Moscow and Prince Boun Oum flew back to Luang Prabang to apprise the King of what had transpired.

For all practical purposes, America's struggle to keep Laos from becoming neutral under the leadership of Souvannaphouma was over. By July 1, the United States made what was called two "forward retreats": It no longer insisted upon the need to maintain explicit SEATO protection over Laos, and it no longer gagged at the participation of Pathet Lao members in the government.[40]

The End of the Road or: This Is Where We Came In

While the diplomats in Geneva continued to split procedural hairs—a fifteen-point proposal advanced by India's Krishna Menon on July 14 ran into some Western opposition, and on July 25 a thirty-three-point proposal by Britain's Malcom MacDonald was rejected by the Soviet bloc— events in Laos itself ground on to their predictable outcome.

The still opportunistic Laotian National Assembly (as will be remembered, it had been elected on an extreme right-wing slate but had also voted the neutralists into office and out of office, and for right-wing Boun Oum after that) met in Vientiane on July 30 and adopted a constitutional amendment which permitted the sovereign to appoint a prime minister without legislative approval. Motivated by a desire to save face, Boun Oum again made a rear-guard fight for the premiership during a meeting with Souvannaphouma in Cambodia on August 4. Prince Souphanouvong did not even bother to attend, since the Pathet Lao's position was well known: No Laotian government was acceptable except one headed by Souvannaphouma.

In Geneva, in the meantime, the Chinese Communists slowly but surely whittled away at Western determination to salvage at least a measure of control over military operations in Laos. Red China remained adamant on the issue of free choice in the return of war prisoners held by either side. It balked further at authorizing the ICC to conduct a census of armament and foreign military elements present in the country, thus repeating at the Laotian level Soviet objections to arms inspection on a wide basis. But on August 24, Soviet Deputy Foreign Minister Georgi M. Pushkin himself intervened in the debate and completely undid the Chinese position by allowing the American proposal to go to the drafting committee.

By September 15, 1961, the Geneva conference had become bogged down in such a hopeless procedural quagmire that it decided to meet only once or twice a week until the various subcommittees had produced acceptable drafts.[41]

Once more the indefatigable U. S. Ambassador-at-Large and head of the American delegation to Geneva, W. Averell Harriman—a man for whom even some of the Soviet bloc diplomats would grudgingly pay homage for his resourcefulness, endless patience, and unstinting willingness to drive on until a satisfactory result was reached—flew to Southeast Asia and met Souvannaphouma in Rangoon to impress upon him the necessity of arriving at a compromise solution, lest even his middle-of-the-road policies would become unacceptable in the face of the Pathet Lao's growing political and military strength.

All three princes finally agreed to meet at the cease-fire line village of Ban Hin Heup to hammer out last details on actual cabinet seats and the selection of a candidate for the premiership. This would not have been Laos had not even that meeting of the three princes been tinged with the ridiculous. At first, the Boun Oum group refused to hold the meeting on the north bank of the river, i.e., on the Pathet Lao side, and suggested that a tent be set up instead on the rickety bamboo bridge which crosses the Nam Lik at this point. When it was pointed out that the bridge was far too flimsy to support a large tent with the princes and their staff, it was suggested that a *log float* be anchored exactly in midstream! When saner minds pointed out that this was still the rainy season and that there were good chances that such a float might be torn loose by the swollen river (which would leave Laos with no leadership at all), the parties finally agreed to hold their meetings alternately on the right and left banks of the Nam Lik. "Polarization" was again evident in the choice of transport to reach the meeting place: Boun Oum arrived at Ban Hin Heup in an American-piloted helicopter (a means of transportation which at Panmunjom had enraged the Red Chinese and North Koreans, who apparently were unable to obtain such a craft from their Soviet backers), while the other two princes had to be content with a Russian TU-4 liaison plane.

On Sunday, October 8, 1961 at 4:30 P.M., a beaming Souvannaphouma stepped out of the candy-striped negotiation tent and announced to the small group of newsmen present:

> *Messieurs,* I am very happy to announce to you that we have reached a final accord and that Prince Boun Oum and Prince Souphanouvong have agreed to our selecting my name and presenting it to His Majesty the King as Prime Minister of a provisional coalition Government.

Whether out of constitutional deference or subtle oriental revenge, Souvannaphouma then charged Boun Oum and General Phoumi Nosavan with the mission of going to Luang Prabang and requesting an audience for him. In addition to Souvannaphouma the new coalition government was to include a total of sixteen members, of whom four each would be right-wing and Pathet Lao and eight would be followers of the Prince.

Almost to the day, the Laotian crisis was exactly where it had begun four years earlier on November 2, 1957, when Souvannaphouma had formed his first coalition regime, which included two Pathet Lao leaders. There were a few far ranging differences, however. Instead of two Communists in cabinet positions, there would be four now; instead of having to deal with 1500 poorly armed Pathet Lao fighters, there were close to 10,000 now, well-armed with new Soviet weapons; instead of being neutral without ties to a Communist country, Laos now had diplomatic relations with almost all of them; in addition to assistance rendered by American and French technicians, it was now to receive aid from several Soviet bloc countries (including Red China and North Viet-Nam); and instead of being able to count on either the "umbrella clause" of

Laos

AT THE MOMENT OF THE CEASE-FIRE, 1961

The density of the hatching is proportional to the ascendancy of the Kong Lê-Pathet Lao forces.

CHINA

BURMA

VIET-NAM

THAILAND

CAMBODIA

Phong Saly

Muong Khoua

Muong-Sing

Muong Sai

Nam Tha

Nam Bac

Sam-Neua

Luang Prabang

Nong-het

Roads maintained and used by North Viet-Nam to supply the Pathet Lao.

Xieng Khouang

Vang Vieng

Ban Namone

Tha-Thom

Ban Hin Heup

Kam Kheut

Paksane

Lak-Sao

R.N.13

VIENTIANE

Muong Nhommarat

Anti-Pathet Lao Méo guerrillas active around the Plaine des Jarres.

Thakhek

MEKONG RIVER

Pathet Lao groups active in these areas.

Cease-fire talks begin on May 5, 1961 at Ban Hin Heup

Savannakhet

Séno

Muong Phalane

Tchépone

Dong Hene

Saravane

Kham

Pakseng

Attopeu

SEATO or the as yet unchallenged readiness of the West to support it, Laos was now completely isolated from effective help when it needed it most. Finally, in spite of the enormous sums of money which it had received from the United States, it is today as poor as ever and covered with the searing scars of corruption, chaos, and civil war.

In Laos, the West (and specifically the United States) has not been stabbed in the back by Communism. On the contrary, this was one theater of the Cold War where Communist intentions were clear and well known since 1953. But the West chose to commit suicide by its own stubborn unwillingness to face in time the unpleasant facts—and to face them together. Once its eyes were opened, it refused to draw the logical conclusions that the situation imposed: Total military disengagement in the hopes of being able to secure a settlement along the lines of the Austrian State Treaty or in the form of an internationally guaranteed buffer zone; or full-fledged intervention with all the necessary military forces at the disposal of the Alliance on a "hang-the-consequences" basis.

By choosing neither, the West was saddled with all the drawbacks of political "softness" without any of its few advantages (i.e., support by non-committed countries), while sporadic efforts at "hardness"—such as the covert use of training missions and full support of one political faction against the others—gave the whole effort an appearance of transparent hypocrisy that offered no moral solace and few military advantages.

The West needlessly lost a battle in Laos by succumbing to guidance by wishful thinking instead of by realism, by braggadocio instead of real strength, by concentrating on stopping "bad things" instead of coming forth with some fresh approaches of its own.

As Prince Norodom Sihanouk of Cambodia bluntly concluded when he returned from the Geneva conference in August 1961:

> As far as I am concerned, the game is over in Laos. That country will ineluctably drift toward Communism. This will certainly not be to the advantage of the West; nor will it be to the advantage of its non-Communist neighbors—Cambodia included. But I can no longer do anything about it.
>
> Laos [under the Communists] may become a strong state; but will it in fact still belong to the Laotians? That, in my view, is the only question that deserves to be asked under those sorrowful circumstances.

There is very little in Laos' predictable future that would cast doubts on the validity of that pessimistic estimate.

XII

Epilogue

by
Roger M. Smith

Bernard Fall's critique of American foreign policy in Laos ends with the succession in Washington of the Eisenhower by the Kennedy administration. Fall, in his characteristically able way, demonstrated how the United States' policy fathered by Secretary of State John Foster Dulles not only failed to achieve its objectives but in fact stimulated the proliferation of pro-Communist strength. In deliberately undermining Souvannaphouma's neutralist regime and transferring support to opportunistic and politically unsophisticated elements, the Eisenhower-Dulles administration effected an unnatural and consequently unstable polarization of power. In view of this it is not surprising that all the hundreds of millions of dollars and intrigues of American advisers on the scene, which created and tried to sustain the pro-West wing, failed to prevent the systematic extension of Pathet Lao control throughout that country. Thus it was that when Kennedy entered the White House in 1961 significantly more of Laos was under Pathet Lao jurisdiction than at the conclusion of the Geneva accords of 1954.

Faced with a situation which increasingly crossed American interests with the passage of time, President Kennedy and his advisers searched for an approach which would halt, if not reverse, Pathet Lao advances.

The bankrupt policy of the previous American administration obviously had to be abandoned, but this being done, the avenues that remained open were now limited. The alternatives were essentially three: (1) Complete withdrawal from Laos; (2) negotiations with the Pathet Lao which would lead to a mutually acceptable resolution of the conflict; and (3) all-out military escalation of the war which would necessarily involve direct participation of American military personnel. It was at this time, when these alternatives were being weighed, that the United States decided that neither the time nor the country was propitious to provoke a direct confrontation with Communist forces, and negotiations was the road chosen.[1] In the light of the *cul de sac* into which the United States had been maneuvered, it was inevitable that negotiations would culminate in the formation of a provisional national union government, composed of representatives of the three political factions and led by a neutralist.

In agreeing to the terms presented at the Geneva conference on Laos, the United States had embarked upon the only viable policy available to it from the very beginning of its presence in that kingdom. The question which rankled in the minds of those who had a stake in Laos' independence was whether the adoption of this policy had occurred too late to save the country. Prince Norodom Sihanouk in neighboring Cambodia observed sadly that it was, and Bernard Fall was moved to concur with him.

There were ample reasons for this dark outlook. For although it again fell to Souvannaphouma to attempt to hold together a divided country, his political strength had waned greatly since 1958, when the United States instigated the overthrow of his first coalition government. In the coalition which he now led, the Pathet Lao's representation constituted a substantial minority, and he had now also to contend with a recalcitrant pro-West wing, which having only recently tasted power and its accouterments was unwilling to relinquish it. Moreover, events in the intervening years had whittled away at the independence of the Pathet Lao and reduced the power of nationalists among its leadership, such as Prince Souphanouvong. Consequently, Souvannaphouma's effective authority was restricted to Vientiane and a minute portion of the country occupied by neutralist troops under Kong-Lê's command.[2]

The new, more realistic administration in Washington was clearly aware of these handicaps. At the most they hoped only to avert further domination of Laos by the Pathet Lao, even though this signified their recognition of a *de facto* partition of the kingdom which ceded to the Pathet Lao the hill and mountain areas from Nam Tha to Attopeu and which reserved for the royal Lao government the Mekong lowlands to the west. While the United States demonstrated that it was willing to and would accommodate itself to the Pathet Lao under the circumstances, at the same time it acted to prevent any misunderstanding that the new soft policy meant that it was abandoning Laos. The United States signaled its firm intention to maintain its presence by openly introducing troops and aircraft into neighboring Thailand and developing in its northeastern region the communications and transportation network which would facilitate the dispatch of American military power to Laos should the need arise.[3]

If there were any doubts on the part of anyone, including Souvannaphouma, as to the sincerity of America's avowed support of the neutralist regime, these were dispelled in April 1964, when two right-wing generals staged a coup d'état and declared the coalition regime suspended. More than anyone, perhaps, General Phoumi Nosavan, on whose behalf the generals acted, was dumbfounded to discover that the anticipated American approval was not forthcoming. The United States' reaction was to reaffirm its backing of Souvannaphouma.

This expression of America's good faith, together with the harassment of neutralist troops by Pathet Lao forces which jointly occupied the Plaine des Jarres, had the effect of encouraging Souvannaphouma to lay aside his suspicions of American intentions and to seek a rapprochement with the United States. This in turn paved the way for the subsequent reconciliation between neutralists and the right-wing.

Souvannaphouma may be accused of having departed from a neutralist policy, and he is the first to admit this. But, as he has rationalized it, Pathet Lao obstructionism and hostilities together with the unwillingness of the big Communist powers to curb them have forced him into his reluctant reliance on the United States.[4] Moreover, the complexity of the situation in Laos had been augmented by the fact that the Ho Chi Minh trail in the eastern, Pathet Lao-controlled section of the country is being utilized by North Vietnamese troops and supplies moving southward into South Viet-Nam. As has been well-publicized, the United States in retaliation has resorted to bombing this trail.

The destiny of Laos has become inextricably intertwined with events in South Viet-Nam and thus more than ever is eluding attempts of Laotians to direct it. For this Souvannaphouma blames North Viet-Nam, whose interest in Laos, he is convinced, will eventually extend beyond its usefulness as a corridor easing passage to South Viet-Nam.[5] Under these circumstances the best he can hope for is to buy time, and thus he is unwilling to permit any action which will trigger a major Pathet Lao-North Vietnamese offensive. It is for this reason that he has prudently refused to acknowledge his acquiescence to American bombing of the Ho Chi Minh trail and has resisted American plans to install defensive electronic equipment in southern Laos as well as pressures from his own generals to scrap the Geneva agreements and to invite military reinforcement by Thai and American troops.

Seven years have passed since the reversal in American policy was implemented and Bernard Fall was moved to express in writing his pessimistic appraisal of the future of Laos. During these years the new, moderate American policy has succeeded, as the alternative ones probably could not, in forestalling complete domination of Laos by the North Vietnamese-backed rebels and in bringing to the kingdom a relatively peaceful interlude. But, as Prince Sihanouk of Cambodia and Bernard Fall sadly forecasted, the American desire to deal realistically with Laos surfaced too late, for seven years later by any stretch of the imagination Laos cannot be said to be master of its own fate. The foothold established in Laos by the North Vietnamese during Dulles' tenure as Secretary of State persists and has dragged the kingdom into a stream of events which has carried it away from this goal.

After thirteen years in Laos, the United States today finds that it is unable to reverse the tragic situation which it helped to create. A tragedy on a more horrendous scale is now absorbing American attention and resources in Viet-Nam. In Thailand where American influence predominates, there have been undismissible indications that there, too, trouble is fomenting.

To many introspective Americans, it is puzzling that our good intentions, generosity, and unstinting efforts in these countries should have resulted in making more remote the very things we had hoped to help them attain: Peace, political independence, self-determination, and economic and social progress. There is no question that our avowed objectives in these countries are honorable; what is not beyond dispute is whether our efforts have always been directed toward their achievement.

One need not search far to find abundant evidence that in these countries our attention and efforts have been diverted by a more pressing concern: The threat to our interests posed by Communism. We have convinced ourselves that as long as Communism is assured of even a toehold in these countries any efforts directed toward our mutual goals

Laos
1967-1968

➤ Pathet Lao and North Vietnamese offensives

///// Communist-controlled territory

---- Roads constructed in 1961-62 by agreements with China and North Vietnam

CHINA

BURMA

Phong Saly

Royal Lao forces routed, January, 1968, from outpost captured in 1966.

Muong Khoua

Nam Tha
Muong Sai

HANOI

Nam Bac

Sam-Neua

V I E T - N A M

Luang Prabang

PLAINE DES JARRES

Xieng Khouang

Tha-Thom

Vinh

Kam Kheut
R.N.13

MEKONG RIVER

VIENTIANE Nongkhai

Muong Nhommarat

Udon Thani

Thakhek

17TH PARALLEL

THAILAND

Séno

Muong Phalane
Tchépone

Hué

Savannak et

Dong-Hene

Danang

Roi Et

Saravane

Ubon

BOLOVENS PLATEAU

Pakseng Attopeu

Khorat

C A M B O D I A

are doomed to failure. So we have dedicated ourselves to its eradication. Our fear of Communism has been so great as to be irrational. We have virtually imbued it with superhuman powers. Its very nature, in our thinking, assures it of success. We fail to see that, like other political ideologies, it can only take root among a receptive population. In our panic we have concentrated on using brute force to arrest its spread, when we should have been examining and expunging the conditions which permit it to breed. We have not taken enough to heart the reasons that Communism has succeeded where we have not. We tend to rationalize the successes of its proponents by asserting that they have been achieved through violence and the instillation of fear, that their followers are in fact captive. It apparently has not occurred to defenders of this view that similar brutalities committed by the factions which we support have failed to gain a similar following. We do not consider the possibility that our antagonists in fact may be in better tune with the needs and grievances of the people whose loyalty they seek to win, and thus have been able to promise remedies which to the latter appear realistic and just.

Communism does not attract a people among whom social equality and economic opportunities are within sight. The countries in which Communism has gained a tenacious foothold are those in which social distances are great and in which material resources are concentrated in the hands of an elect few. Ostensibly we have recognized this fact, and our most costly aid programs may be viewed as a means to combatting these conditions which cause the soul to fester. However, in practice, most of our aid has been utilized to buy the cooperation of those who profess to share our awareness of the dangers of Communism, even when this has meant undermining and incurring the hostility of selfless and politically abler men, who view as more basic the problem of creating an effective government, one which senses and responds to the needs of the people and fosters national unity.

In channeling our aid to a small clique and bringing our military might to bear in support of them, we have exacerbated internal dissension, thereby sabotaging the peace that our policy was to help secure. Moreover, through our intervention and our attempts to redirect the normal stream of politics we have been guilty of thwarting progress toward self-determination and national independence. There can be no denying that our avowed policy objectives have become overshadowed by our obsessive concern with Communism to a point where it is clear that we would rather deprive a nation of its independence and bring about its dissolution than to permit Communists or those who would seek an accommodation with them to gain a voice in its government.

Long after hostilities between Communists and Western powers cease, the urgent problems which are gnawing into the very fabric of Laos, Viet-Nam, and Thailand will persist. In addition to meeting their material needs, these include uniting behind a single government a diverse people, divided for centuries by race, religion, geography, language, and customs. For only in such a union can these countries hope to obtain internal stability and to protect themselves from the machinations of foreign powers, whatever their ideology. The partition of Laos brought on most recently by the intervention of North Viet-Nam and the United States is not a unique event in Laotian history. Indeed, for most of its past large portions of Laos were controlled by the Thais and Vietnamese, who exploited regional differences and petty rifts between rival princes eager to ascend to the throne.

In countries in which the United States is doggedly persevering in its attempts to crush Communism, it is doing worse than postponing the satisfactory resolution of these problems. America, if it is to help these countries survive, must realize this pressing need to transform diversity into unity. The nationalism which needs to be cultivated must be broad enough to include ideological as well as other differences. It is only when all voices are permitted expression in a government, and the benefits of the government are extended to all peoples within its jurisdiction, that one can expect a moderation of extreme positions and the development of immunity to the schemes of external powers.

Notes

II. Some Glimpses from the Past

1. Viravong, Sila (Maha), *Phong Savadan Lao* [History of Laos], Vol. 1. Vientiane, 1957, pp. 1–2.
2. Taboulet, George, *La Geste Française en Indochine*, Vol. II. Paris: Adrien Maisonneuve, 1956, p. 889.
3. Fall, Bernard B., "The International Relations of Laos," *in* René de Berval (ed.), *Kingdom of Laos*. Saigon: *France-Asie*, 1959, p. 472.

III. From War to War

1. Champassak, Sisouk na, *Storm Over Laos*. New York: Frederick A. Praeger, 1961, p. 5.
2. Fall, Bernard B., *Le Viet-Minh, 1945–1960*. Paris: Armand Colin, 1960, p. 312.
3. See, for example, the *Memoirs* of the late Secretary of State Cordell Hull (New York: Macmillan, 1948), those of General Claire L. Chennault, *Way of a Fighter*, ed. by Robert Hotz (New York: Putnam, 1949), and Riley Sunderland and Charles F. Romanus, *Time Runs Out in CBI* (Washington: Office of Chief of Military History, Department of Army, 1959), for details of American policy with regard to wartime aid to French Indo-China.
4. Burchett, Wilfred, *Mekong Upstream*. East Berlin: Seven Seas Book Corp., 1959, p. 225.
5. Kingdom of Laos, *L'Assemblée Constituante Laotienne*. Saigon: Imprimerie Française d'Outre-Mer, 1949, pp. 20–21.
6. *Ibid.*, p. 92.
7. It is only after the Thai government concluded an unofficial agreement with North Viet-Nam in August 1959, that the Vietnamese refugees agreed to peaceful repatriation to North Viet-Nam. The first such convoy left Bangkok on January 7, 1960.
8. Sasorith, Katay D., *Le Laos*. Paris: Berger-Levrault, 1953, p. 117. Cambodia signed its agreements with France on November 9, 1949.
9. It is not entirely clear whether Souphanouvong fled directly to North Viet-Nam. Some sources indicate that he first took refuge in Red China.
10. *Regards* [a French Communist monthly], No. 357, Paris, January 1953, p. 21.
11. Burchett, *op. cit.*, pp. 89, 239.

IV. The Road to Geneva

1. Marchand, (Gen.) Jean, *L'Indochine en Guerre*. Paris: Les Presses Modernes, 1954, pp. 299 ff.

2. U. S. War Department, Historical Division, *Merrill's Marauders*. Washington: Government Printing Office, 1948, pp. 3–5, *passim*.

3. Fall, Bernard B., *Street Without Joy*. Harrisburg: Stackpole Co., 1961, pp. 110–24.

4. Archeologists disagree as to the exact culture which carved the very well-fashioned huge jars. They appear to be over 2000 years old but no artifacts found with them seem to relate them to any of the known civilizations of the area.

5. This point alone would foredoom any partition plan of Laos, involving the surrender of the two towns, but particularly Luang Prabang, to the Pathet Lao. Yet, plans to partition Laos at the 17th or 18th parallel have repeatedly been bruited about since 1957.

6. Deydier, Henri, *Lokapâla—Génies, Totems et Sorciers du Nord Laos*. Paris: Plon, 1954, pp. 164–184. This writer was told that the Blind Bonze once ("merely for fun") predicted the winning number in neighboring Thailand's flourishing lottery. He also warned Deydier against taking a certain airplane trip—a warning which Deydier disregarded. His plane crashed, killing all occupants.

V. Phony Peace

1. Devillers, Philippe, and Lacouture, Jean, *La Fin d'une Guerre—Indochine 1954*. Paris: Editions du Seuil, 1960, p. 116.

2. United Kingdom, *Documents relating to the discussion of Korea and Indo-China at the Geneva Conference*. Cmd. 9186. London: H. M.'s Stationery Office, 1954, p. 148.

3. *Ibid.*, pp. 154–55.

4. United Kingdom. *Further documents relating to the discussion of Indo-China at the Geneva Conference*. Cmd. 9239. London: H. M.'s Stationery Office, 1954, pp. 20–21.

5. *Ibid.*, p. 10.

6. See "Agreement on the Cessation of Hostilities in Laos," Arts. 11–15, in *ibid.*, pp. 21–22.

7. Fall, *Street Without Joy*, p. 164. The French, in fact, found occasion to be grateful for Cambodia's intransigence, for it permitted them in December 1953 to pull out of Cambodia French Mobile Group No. 51 which saved the Franco-Laotian garrisons in southern Laos from annihilation.

8. *Further documents.* . . . Cmd. 9239, p. 9.

9. Souvanna Phouma, "Le Laos, avant-garde du monde libre," *France-Asie/Asia*, Vol. XVII (Nov.–Dec. 1960), No. 164, p. 1430.

10. Champassak, *op. cit.*, pp. 36–37. See also, Kingdom of Laos, *Commentaires du Gouvernement Royal Concernant le Premier Rapport Provisoire de la Commission Internationale de Surveillance et de Contrôle au Laos*. Vientiane: March, 1956, p. 13.

11. Kingdom of Laos, *Application of the Geneva Agreements in Laos—Memorandum.* Vientiane: May 1955 (mimeo.), p. 4.

12. Kahin, George McTurnan. *The Asian-African Conference.* Ithaca: Cornell University Press, 1956, p. 13.

13. Great Britain. *Third Interim Report of the International Commission for Supervision and Control in Laos.* July 1, 1955–May 16, 1957. (Laos No. 1, 1957) Cmd. 314. London: H. M.'s Stationery Office, December 1957, pp. 47–52.

14. Souvannaphouma, "Laos: le fond du problème," *Asia-France-Asie,* No. 166, March–April, 1961, p. 1825. See also Champassak, *op. cit.,* p. 43.

15. Halpern, A. M., and Friedman, H. B., *Communist Strategy in Laos,* Santa Monica: The Rand Corp., RM-2561, June 14, 1960, p. 19.

16. Souvannaphouma, *op. cit.* It is noteworthy that Sisouk, who was a member of the delegation which went to Peking, reports many of the trivia of what he saw during his trip but fails to mention at all what it accomplished diplomatically.

17. Sisouk, *op. cit.,* p. 49.

18. In Souvannaphouma's own words, "My brother has never been a Communist, only a misled patriot." *Time,* January 21, 1957.

19. *Lao-Presse* [daily mimeo. bulletin], Vientiane, January 21, 1957.

20. Arzac, Daniel N., Jr., *The 1957 Crisis over Reintegration of the Pathet Lao.* University of California, Berkeley, unpublished manuscript, 1958, p. 15.

21. *Lao-Presse,* May 29, 1957. There were at that time thirty-eight members in the National Assembly, of whom ten served in the government and did not participate in the vote.

22. Champassak, *op. cit.,* p. 60.

23. Many of the bonzes were sent for advanced Buddhist training to India and Burma; some of them at United States expense and others at the expense of an American private foundation. When they returned to Laos, some of them were found to have acquired a solid foundation of Marxism in addition to that of Buddhist texts, while others used their newly acquired English-language capability to go into more lucrative businesses than that of serving their religion.

24. Department of State, *The Situation in Laos.* Washington: September 22, 1959, p. 12.

25. New York *Times,* January 20, 1958.

26. Royal Embassy of Laos, "Background Summary: The Political Situation in Laos after Settlement of the 'Pathet Lao' Problem." Washington, January, 1958, p. 7.

27. House of Representatives, Committee on Foreign Affairs, *Hearings . . . Mutual Security Program in Laos.* Washington, May 7 and 8, 1958, p. 34.

28. Champassak, *op. cit.,* p. 62.

29. New York *Times,* May 4, 1958.

30. *Ibid.,* May 7, 1958.

31. *Ibid.,* February 5, 1959.

VI. The Pendulum

1. Champassak, *op. cit.,* p. 63.

2. *Néo Lao Hakxa Sat* [in French], No. 1 (Special Edition). Vientiane, September 1, 1958.

3. Souvannaphouma, *op. cit.,* p. 1825.

4. Halpern, A. M., *op. cit.,* p. 45.

5. Washington *Post,* January 10, 1959.

6. Royal Embassy of Laos, *News Release,* Washington, March 2, 1959.

7. Anon., *Concerning the Situation in Laos.* Peking: Foreign Languages Press, 1959, p. 14.

8. Agence Khmère de Presse [in French], *Bulletin Quotidien,* Phnom-Penh, March 31, 1959, p. xi.

9. Champassak, *op. cit.,* pp. 76–77. As Sisouk describes the events, both sides negotiated in bad faith: The Pathet Lao wanted more officers than it needed, and the royal government planned to eliminate the Pathet Lao officers from their posts by creating new education requirements which they could satisfy only in a very few cases.

VII. "The Laos Fraud"

1. Department of State, *The Situation in Laos.* Washington: September 1959, p. 20. See also the Washington *Post* of September 3, 1959.

2. Halpern, A. M., *op. cit.,* p. 51. Emphasis added.

3. Sisouk, *op. cit.,* p. 83. Here also, it is noteworthy to compare the French and English versions of the book. The French "déclenchèrent l'engrenage de la rébellion" is far less direct and forceful than the English "set in motion the mechanism of the rebellion."

4. Jones, George M. (Col.), in *Special Warfare Newsletter.* Fort Bragg, N.C.: September 1959, p. 1.

5. Halpern, Joel M., Laos Project, Paper No. 21, *Government, Politics and Social Structure of Laos—A Study of Tradition and Innovation.* Los Angeles: Department of Anthropology, University of California, (mimeo.), 1961, pp. 70–71.

6. Fall, Bernard B., *Le Viet-Minh.* Paris: Armand Colin, 1960, p. 131.

7. Halpern, A. M. and Friedman, H. B., *Communist Strategy in Laos.* Santa Monica, California: The Rand Corp., 1960, p. 4.

8. During a long march with a Laotian unit in 1959, I personally witnessed the taking without payment of food staples from Kha-Kho tribeswomen on their way to the local market. Our unit had left the army post with ample provisions, which made the act even more gratuitous.

9. New York *Times,* August 9, 1961.

10. Halpern, A. M., *op. cit.,* p. 68. On the other hand, the authors completely misjudge the rationales of North Vietnamese activities when they believe them prompted "by the development of South Vietnam into a military and political [*sic*] power" (p. 64). Considering the situation in South Viet-Nam in 1959–62, another rationale would have to be envisaged.

11. *Concerning the Situation in Laos, op. cit.,* p. 50 ff.

12. *L'Echo du Viet-Nam,* Paris, No. 4, May 1961, pp. 2–3.

13. *Concerning the Situation in Laos, op. cit.,* pp. 57–65, *passim.*

14. *France-Soir* [daily], Paris, August 2, 1959.

15. U. S. Information Agency, *Daily News Bulletin,* Vientiane, August 5, 1959.

16. Halpern, A. M., *op. cit.,* p. 101.

17. *Agence Lao-Presse.* Vientiane, August 14, 1959.

18. New York *Times,* August 16, 1959.

19. New York *Times,* August 24, 1959.

20. *Concerning the Situation in Laos, op. cit.,* p. 76.

21. Kennan, George F., *Russia and the West since Lenin and Stalin,* New York: Atlantic, Little & Brown, 1961, p. 15.

22. Ennis, Thomas E., "Operation Survival in Laos," *Current History,* March 1961, cites, for example, that France "maintained" a 1500-man training mission and a 3500-man garrison at Séno. At no time whatever did either of the two French missions reach strength figures even remotely close to those cited. The same author also alleges that France had been "relinquishing its training mission" in Laos—an assertion that was as erroneous as the previous statement about troop strengths. This is but one example of how even serious writers could be induced into error, not to speak of the more superficial news writers.

23. Champassak, *op. cit.,* p. 106.

24. *The New Republic,* October 12, 1959, pp. 6–7.

25. Champassak, *op. cit.,* p. 107.

VIII.   The American Stake

1. Several good books contain important passages on the subject, notably Sir Anthony Eden's *Full Circle;* General Ridgway's *Soldier;* or John Beal's *John Foster Dulles,* etc.

2. Sulzberger, C. L., "An Embarrassing Diet of Principles," in the New York *Times* (International Edition) of October 4, 1961.

3. *Comments by the Department of State and ICA on the Report "U.S. Aid Operations in Laos,"* [henceforth referred to as *Comments*] (mimeo.), Washington, June 15, 1959, p. 2.

4. The use of an underdeveloped country's armed forces as a reform element has been espoused by a whole school of political scientists. Examples of "good influences" in government that are currently cited are General Ne Win (Burma), Marshal Ayub Khan (Pakistan), General Nasution (Indonesia), Marshal Sarit (Thailand). The list of nefarious military influences in government is somewhat longer.

5. Unpublished typescript of hearings, Senate Foreign Relations Committee, May 26, 1959, p. 15.

6. House of Representatives, 86th Congress, Committee on Government Operations, *U.S. Aid Operations in Laos.* Washington: Government Printing Office, June 15, 1959, p. 8.

7. See, for example, Miller, Haynes, "A Bulwark Built on Sand," *The Reporter,* November 13, 1958; Beech, Keyes, "How the U.S. Fumbled in Laos," *Saturday Evening Post,* April 22, 1961; Karnow, Stanley, "The Mess in Laos," *Life,* November 19, 1960.

8. Champassak, *op. cit.,* p. 64.

9. *Comments, op. cit.,* p. 19.

10. *Hearings, op. cit.,* p. 8.

11. Beech, *loc. cit.*

12. *Mutual Security Programs in Laos, op. cit.,* p. 11.
13. *U.S. Aid Operations in Laos, op. cit.,* p. 48.

IX. New Turmoils

1. New York *Times,* October 25, 1959.
2. New York *Times,* November 4, 1959.
3. Inagaki, René Georges, "Laos Moving Toward Neutralist Policy," Washington *Post,* December 20, 1959.
4. Champassak, *op. cit.,* p. 132.
5. *Time,* January 18, 1960.
6. New York *Times,* January 12, 1960.
7. See, for example, "Southern Laos 'Seething' with Reds," Washington *Post,* October 18, 1959; or "Reds in Laos Raid Key Southern Town," New York *Times,* October 22, 1959.
8. New York *Times,* November 17, 1959.
9. For a good study of the legal aspects of the Laos "UN presence" problem, see Gross, L., "The Question of Laos and the Double Veto in the Security Council." *American Journal of International Law,* Vol. 54, January 1960, pp. 118–31. For a view of Soviet objections, see New York *Times,* November 17, 1959.
10. Typescript of speech made by UN Secretary Ralph J. Bunche before the 9th General Assembly of the International Press Institute at Tokyo, March 25, 1960, pp. 1–2.
11. *Ibid.,* p. 4.
12. *Ibid.,* p. 5. Emphasis supplied, except for the word "be."
13. New York *Times,* November 18, 1959.
14. *Ibid.,* January 9, 1960.
15. *Ibid.,* March 26, 1960. Also, personal correspondence between writer and UN Secretariat-General, August 1961.
16. Champassak, *op. cit.,* p. 140. He calls this procedure "a trick."
17. *Bangkok World,* April 22, 1960, and New York *Times,* April 23, 1960.
18. Champassak, *op. cit.,* p. 142, and Washington *Post,* April 23, 1960.
19. AP dispatch quoted in Washington *Post* of April 27, 1960 and New York *Times,* April 26, 1960.
20. Chef d'Escadrons [Major, Armored Cavalry] D . . . , "Le Laos, Etat tampon ou satellite?" in *Revue de Défense Nationale,* October 1961, p. 1631.
21. Washington *Post,* June 1, 1960. See also Champassak, *op. cit.,* p. 145.

X. Coup and Countercoup

1. For a more detailed view of the development of the Laotian elite, see the excellent study by Joel M. Halpern, *Government, Politics and Social Structure in Laos: A Study of Tradition and Innovation.* Los Angeles, 1961: Department of Anthropology, U.C.L.A.
2. Zukrowski, Wojcech, *et al., Sous le ciel du Laos,* Hanoi: Editions en Langues Etrangères, 1961, p. 17.

3. *Ibid.*, p. 20.

4. New York *Times*, August 17, 1960.

5. *Ibid.*, August 11, 1960.

6. Halpern, *op. cit.*, p. 74.

7. *Time*, March 17, 1961.

8. Chef d'Escadrons D . . . , *op. cit.*, p. 1632.

9. Washington *Post*, September 9, 1960.

10. New York *Times*, September 6, 1960.

11. New York *Times*, September 17, 1960.

12. On September 21, Colonel Khamkhong Vongnarath, commanding officer at Sam-Neua, declared (New York *Times*, September 22) that there was "no evidence" of North Vietnamese troops operating around Sam-Neua.

13. New York *Times*, September 20, 1960.

14. AP, Bangkok, September 26, 1960.

15. New York *Times*, October 4, 1960.

16. *Ibid.*, October 8, 1960.

17. On October 10, 1961, i.e., almost exactly one year to the day after the aid crisis, the New York *Times* printed a news story stating that

> . . . it is now widely accepted that General Phoumi Nosavan was persuaded to spurn his post in the [Laotian] government and rebel against it by agents of the Central Intelligence Agency and United States military officers stationed in Laos to run the Laotian Army.

This augurs well for any future settlement of the Laos crisis on the basis of a coalition.

18. New York *Times*, October 15, 1960.

19. *Ibid.*, November 16, 1960.

20. *Ibid.*, November 20, 1960.

21. See, for example, the articles by Max Clos in the conservative *Le Figaro;* or by Robert Favart (a former Catholic missionary in Indo-China now reporting for *Paris-Match* and other French papers) in *Réalités Cambodgiennes*, December 1960–January 1961.

22. This writer had several from perfectly reliable sources who were in Vientiane during the battle. One of them was pinned down in the middle of the street with a year-old child in his arms while a machine gunner laughingly sprayed the street around him from atop his tank turret.

23. Favart, *op. cit.*

24. New York *Times*, December 17, 1960.

XI. Internationalizing the Crisis

1. Beech, Keyes, "Laotians Aren't Wasting Enthusiasm Over Americans," Washington *Post*, December 26, 1960.

2. Those Frenchmen, as will be seen, were unharmed. Others, such as several French Catholic missionaries, were kidnaped and were not heard from again.

3. *Time*, January 27, 1961.

4. New York *Times,* February 28, 1961.

5. *Ibid.,* April 18, 1961.

6. Fall, Bernard B., *Street Without Joy,* Harrisburg: Stackpole, 1961, pp. 249–51. According to news reports, South Vietnamese commando forces were operating under cover in southern Laos, trying to stamp out infiltrating Viet-Minh forces.

7. Those circumstances, of necessity, exclude thermonuclear wars. But under other conditions, it should be remembered that Hitler considered attacking Sweden but desisted when his General Staff apprised him of the prospective cost of the operation.

8. See, for example, the remarkable book by Annette Baker Fox, *The Power of Small States.* Chicago: University of Chicago Press, 1960.

9. Fall, Bernard B., "Cambodia's International Position," *Current History,* March, 1961, pp. 164–70.

10. New York *Times,* October 14, 1960. It is noteworthy that Sihanouk rejected the "troika" system which Russia had proposed to supervise such a neutralization and proposed three fully neutral commissioners instead (cf. *Réalités Cambodgiennes,* December 9, 1960).

11. Washington *Post,* December 27, 1960.

12. For full text of Sihanouk's note, see *Réalités Cambodgiennes,* January 1, 1961.

13. Washington *Post,* December 31, 1960.

14. New York *Times,* December 26, 1960. Britain likewise was cool to the idea of a new Geneva conference.

15. Washington *Post,* December 25, 1960.

16. See, among others, various issues of the *Peking Review,* notably Nos. 2, 6, 7, 18, 19 and 22, January–June, 1961.

17. Unna, Warren, "Allies Force U.S. Review of Laos Policy," Washington *Post,* January 5, 1961.

18. Alsop, J., "The Yawning Drain," New York *Herald-Tribune,* January 6, 1961. On April 5, Alsop was to accuse the French of outright "sabotage."

19. Washington *Post,* January 5, 1961.

20. Cf. Warren Unna's articles in the Washington *Post* of April 5 and 7, 1961.

21. New York *Times,* January 18, 1961. Ironically enough, the Communist "Voice of the Lao People" denounced on the following day those anti-French moves as "a plot of the American imperialists . . ."

22. *Times,* London, March 30, 1961.

23. Oka, Takashi, "Official Corruption in Laos Tries U.S.," *Christian Science Monitor,* January 31, 1961. In his defense, Boun Oum declared that the printer had offered him a cheaper price for a larger quantity of bills to be printed.

24. New York *Times,* February 20, 1961.

25. Secretary Rusk was quoted on March 13 to have told Sir Harold Caccia, the British Ambassador to Washington that the "United States could not now accept the idea of reactivating the ICC." It was reactivated six weeks later.

26. For example, the three maps shown by President Kennedy at his press conference of March 23, 1961, which purported to show the progressively worsening situation in Laos, were so grossly inaccurate in their optimism as to be completely meaningless. At a time when most of the Laotian uplands were more or less under Communist control, the map purporting to show the "present" situation gave the Com-

munists credit for holding only parts of three provinces and one small isolated spot around Kam Kheut. The question remains open as to whether the inaccuracy was deliberate (so as not to worry public opinion) or whether the research services which provided the maps for the President were fooled as well.

27. Alsop, J., "Leadership Regained," Washington *Post*, March 31, 1961.

28. New York *Times*, April 19, 1961.

29. *Le Monde*, May 2, 1961.

30. New York *Times*, May 16, 1961.

31. *Time*, April 7, 1961.

32. New York *Times*, January 20, 1961.

33. *Le Monde*, January 27, 1961.

34. New York *Times*, April 19, 1961.

35. *Ibid.*, April 20, 1961. The word "pre-emptory" (unless it were a misprint for "peremptory") would mean that Souvannaphouma *forestalled* an American snub by one of his own—which was precisely his view of the whole affair.

36. Childs, Marquis, "Bungles in Laos also Laid to CIA," Washington *Post*, May 17, 1961.

37. *Combat*, Paris, May 16, 1961.

38. French Ministry of Foreign Affairs, typescript, 2 pp. It is noteworthy that Mao Tse-tung, in an interview granted François Mitterrand, a French Left-wing legislator, in the spring of 1961 stated that Red China had no objections to France's retaining bases in Laos (cf. *France-Observateur*, March 30, 1961).

39. New York *Times*, June 29 and 30, 1961.

40. Washington *Post*, July 1, 1961.

41. *Le Monde*, September 16, 1961.

XII.   Epilogue

1. See Roger Hilsman, *To Move a Nation, The Policies of Foreign Policy in the Administration of John F. Kennedy*. New York: Doubleday, 1967, pp. 142–49.

2. See Arthur J. Dommen, *Conflict in Laos, The Policies of Neutralization* (New York: Praeger, 1964), pp. 242–43, and E. H. S. Simmonds, "Breakdown in Laos," *The World Today*, Vol. 20 (July 1964), No. 7, *passim*.

3. The background to and the assumptions underlying this new policy for Laos have been discussed by one of the men who participated in its development: Roger Hilsman, in his *To Move a Nation . . . , op. cit.*, pp. 142–49, 152–54. Major criticisms of the United States position at Geneva are to be found in Dommen, *op. cit.*, and George Modelski, *International Conference on the Settlement of the Laotian Question, 1961–62*. Australian National University, Department of International Relations. Canberra, 1962.

4. See the text of Souvannaphouma's letter to President de Gaulle in "The Status of Neutrality in Laos," Royal Embassy of Laos, News Release, Washington, July 30, 1964.

5. *New York Times* dispatch by Drew Middleton, April 7, 1967. Phoui Sananikone also shares these views. See the *Bangkok Post*, December 30, 1966, for an account of an interview with the former prime minister.

Appendixes

APPENDIX I

MESSAGE FROM THE CO-CHAIRMEN DATED APRIL 24, 1961, APPEALING FOR A CEASE-FIRE*

The Co-Chairmen of the Geneva Conference on Indo-China, represented by the Governments of the Soviet Union and Great Britain, are following with great concern the situation which has developed in Laos.

They proceed from the fact that if this situation is not changed the position in Laos may become a serious threat to peace and security in South-East Asia. They note at the same time that real conditions exist for normalising the situation in Laos in accordance with the national interests of the Laotian people, on the basis of the Geneva Agreements of 1954. The Co-Chairmen have in view the understanding already reached that an international conference to settle the Laotian problem is to be called in Geneva on May 12 this year.

The Co-Chairmen call on all military authorities, parties and organizations in Laos to cease fire before the convening of the international conference on Laos, and they call on appropriate representatives to enter into negotiations for concluding an agreement on questions connected with the cease-fire.

The Co-Chairmen call on the people of Laos to cooperate with the International Commission for Supervision and Control in Laos and to render it assistance, when it arrives in the country on their instructions, in exercising supervision and control over the cease-fire.

* United Kingdom, *International Conference on the Settlement of the Laotian Question*. Laos No. 1 (1962). Geneva, May 12, 1961–July 23, 1962. Cmd. 1828. London: H.M.'s Stationery Office, October 1962, p. 6.

APPENDIX II

MESSAGE FROM THE CO-CHAIRMEN DATED APRIL 24, 1961,
INVITING PARTICIPANTS TO AN INTERNATIONAL CONFERENCE*

The Co-Chairmen of the Geneva Conference on Indo-China, represented by the Governments of the Soviet Union and Great Britain, have examined the situation which has developed in Laos and taken note that at present there exist real conditions for the normalization of the situation in that country. They have in view that the Governments of Burma, Cambodia, Canada, the Chinese People's Republic, the Democratic Republic of Vietnam, France, India, Laos, the Polish People's Republic, the Republic of Vietnam, Thailand, the Union of Soviet Socialist Republics, the United Kingdom and the United States, have expressed agreement to participate in an international conference, which would have the character of the Geneva Conference of 1954 with the broader membership proposed by the Head of State of Cambodia, Prince Norodom Sihanouk, for the settlement of the Laotian problem.

The Co-Chairmen have addressed to all military authorities, parties and organizations in Laos a call for a cease-fire and for the carrying out by appropriate representatives of negotiations for concluding an agreement on questions connected with the cease-fire and have also sent to the Government of India a message with a request to convene in Delhi the International Commission for Supervision and Control in Laos.

The Co-Chairmen express the hope that the Government of —— will send its delegation to the International Conference on the Laotian question, which will be held in Geneva and will begin its work on May 12 this year. They have in view that the participating countries will be represented at the conference by Ministers of Foreign Affairs.

* *Ibid.,* pp. 6–7.

APPENDIX III

JOINT COMMUNIQUÉ OF THE THREE PRINCES ON THE PROBLEM OF ACHIEVING NATIONAL CONCORD BY THE FORMATION OF A GOVERNMENT OF NATIONAL UNION*

As agreed between them on 18 June last, the three Princes, Souvanna Phouma, Boun Oum and Souphanouvong, being the high representatives of the three parties in Laos, met at Zurich on 19 June and thereafter to discuss the problem of achieving national concord by the formation of a Government of National Union. The three Princes discussed successively the political program of the provisional Government of National Union and its immediate tasks.

With regard to these two matters, the three Princes agreed as follows:

I. *Political Program*

The Kingdom of Laos is resolved to follow the path of peace and neutrality in conformity with the interests and aspirations of the Laotian people and with the Geneva Agreements of 1954, in order to build a peaceful, neutral, independent, democratic, unified and prosperous Laos. A provisional Government of National Union will be formed, which will give effect to this policy of peace and neutrality, by carrying out the following political program:

Domestic Policy:

(1) To implement the cease-fire agreement concluded between the three parties concerned in Laos and to see that peace is restored in the country.

(2) To give full effect to democratic freedoms for the benefit of the people and to abrogate all provisions contrary to such freedoms; to bring back into force the law on the democratic freedoms of citizens and the electoral law approved by the National Assembly in 1957.

(3) To preserve the unity, neutrality, independence and sovereignty of the nation.

(4) To ensure justice and peace for all citizens of the Kingdom with a view to appeasement and national concord without discrimination as to origin or political allegiance.

* *Ibid.,* pp. 13–14.

(5) To bring about the unification of the armed forces of the three parties in a single National Army in accordance with a program agreed between the parties.

(6) To develop agriculture, industry and crafts, to provide means of communication and transport, to promote culture and to concentrate attention on improving the standard of living of the people.

Foreign Policy:

(1) Resolutely to apply the five principles of peaceful coexistence in foreign relations, to establish friendly relations and to develop diplomatic relations with all countries, the neighboring countries first and foremost, on the basis of equality and the sovereignty of Laos.

(2) Not to join in any alliance or military coalition and not to allow the establishment of any foreign military base on Laotian territory, it being understood that a special study will be made of what is provided in the Geneva Agreements of 1954; not to allow any country to use Laotian territory for military purposes; and not to recognize the protection of any alliance or military coalition.

(3) Not to allow any foreign interference in the internal affairs of Laos in any form whatsoever; to require the withdrawal from Laos of all foreign troops and military personnel; and not to allow any foreign troops or military personnel to be introduced into Laos.

(4) To accept direct and unconditional aid from all countries that wish to help Laos build up an independent and autonomous national economy on the basis of respect for Laotian sovereignty.

(5) To respect the treaties and agreements signed in conformity with the interests of the Laotian people and of the policy of peace and neutrality of the Kingdom, in particular the Geneva Agreements of 1954, and to abrogate all treaties and agreements which are contrary to those principles.

II. *Immediate Tasks*

The provisional Government of National Union will carry out the following immediate tasks:

(1) Formation of a Government delegation to take part in the International Conference on the settlement of the Laotian question.

(2) Implementation of the cease-fire and restoration of peace throughout the country.

(3) Fulfilment of the undertakings entered into on behalf of Laos at the International Conference on the settlement of the Laotian question

and faithful execution of the agreements concluded between the three parties concerned in Laos.

(4) Release of all political prisoners and detainees.

(5) Holding of general elections to the National Assembly for the formation of the definitive Government.

(6) During the transitional period, the administrative organs set up during the hostilities will be provisionally left in being.

As regards the formation of the Government of National Union the three Princes agreed on the following principles:

(1) The Government of National Union will include representatives of the three parties and will be provisional.

(2) It will be formed in accordance with a special procedure by direct designation and nomination by His Majesty the King, without reference to the National Assembly.

Exchanges of views on this matter will be continued between the three Princes at further meetings, in order to achieve national reconciliation as soon as possible.

Done at Zurich, This Twenty-second Day of June 1961.

Signed:

PRINCE SOUVANNA PHOUMA
PRINCE BOUN OUM
PRINCE SOUPHANOUVONG

APPENDIX IV

DECLARATION ON THE NEUTRALITY OF LAOS*

The Governments of the Union of Burma, the Kingdom of Cambodia, Canada, the People's Republic of China, the Democratic Republic of Viet-Nam, the Republic of France, the Republic of India, the Polish People's Republic, the Republic of Viet-Nam, the Kingdom of Thailand, the Union of Soviet Socialist Republics, the United Kingdom of Great Britain and Northern Ireland, and the United States of America, whose representatives took part in the International Conference on the Settlement of the Laotian Question, 1961–1962;

Welcoming the presentation of the statement of neutrality by the Royal Government of Laos of July 9, 1962, and taking note of this statement,

* *Ibid.,* pp. 15–18.

which is, with the concurrence of the Royal Government of Laos, incorporated in the present Declaration as an integral part thereof, and the text of which is as follows:

THE ROYAL GOVERNMENT OF LAOS,

Being resolved to follow the path of peace and neutrality in conformity with the interests and aspirations of the Laotian people, as well as the principles of the Joint Communiqué of Zurich dated June 22, 1961, and of the Geneva Agreements of 1954, in order to build a peaceful, neutral, independent, democratic, unified and prosperous Laos,

Solemnly declares that:

(1) It will resolutely apply the five principles of peaceful coexistence in foreign relations, and will develop friendly relations and establish diplomatic relations with all countries, the neighboring countries first and foremost, on the basis of equality and of respect for the independence and sovereignty of Laos;

(2) It is the will of the Laotian people to protect and ensure respect for the sovereignty, independence, neutrality, unity, and territorial integrity of Laos;

(3) It will not resort to the use or threat of force in any way which might impair the peace of other countries, and will not interfere in the internal affairs of other countries;

(4) It will not enter into any military alliance or into any agreement, whether military or otherwise, which is inconsistent with the neutrality of the Kingdom of Laos; it will not allow the establishment of any foreign military base on Laotian territory, nor allow any country to use Laotian territory for military purposes or for the purposes of interference in the internal affairs of other countries, nor recognize the protection of any alliance or military coalition, including SEATO;

(5) It will not allow any foreign interference in the internal affairs of the Kingdom of Laos in any form whatsoever;

(6) Subject to the provisions of Article 5 of the Protocol, it will require the withdrawal from Laos of all foreign troops and military personnel, and will not allow any foreign troops or military personnel to be introduced into Laos;

(7) It will accept direct and unconditional aid from all countries that wish to help the Kingdom of Laos build up an independent and

autonomous national economy on the basis of respect for the sovereignty of Laos;

(8) It will respect the treaties and agreements signed in conformity with the interests of the Laotian people and of the policy of peace and neutrality of the Kingdom, in particular the Geneva Agreements of 1962, and will abrogate all treaties and agreements which are contrary to those principles.

This statement of neutrality by the Royal Government of Laos shall be promulgated constitutionally and shall have the force of law.

The Kingdom of Laos appeals to all the States participating in the International Conference on the Settlement of the Laotian Question, and to all other States, to recognize the sovereignty, independence, neutrality, unity, and territorial integrity of Laos, to conform to these principles in all respects, and to refrain from any action inconsistent therewith.

Confirming the principles of respect for the sovereignty, independence, unity and territorial integrity of the Kingdom of Laos and non-interference in its internal affairs which are embodied in the Geneva Agreements of 1954;

Emphasizing the principle of respect for the neutrality of the Kingdom of Laos;

Agreeing that the above-mentioned principles constitute a basis for the peaceful settlement of the Laotian question;

Profoundly convinced that the independence and neutrality of the Kingdom of Laos will assist the peaceful democratic development of the Kingdom of Laos and the achievement of national accord in that country, as well as the strengthening of peace and security in Southeast Asia:

1. Solemnly declare, in accordance with the will of the Government and people of the Kingdom of Laos, as expressed in the statement of neutrality by the Royal Government of Laos of July 9, 1962, that they recognize and will respect and observe in every way the sovereignty, independence, neutrality, unity and territorial integrity of the Kingdom of Laos.

2. Undertake, in particular, that

(a) they will not commit or participate in any way in any act which might directly or indirectly impair the sovereignty, independence, neutrality, unity or territorial integrity of the Kingdom of Laos;

(b) they will not resort to the use or threat of force or any other measure which might impair the peace of the Kingdom of Laos;

(c) they will refrain from all direct or indirect interference in the internal affairs of the Kingdom of Laos;

(d) they will not attach conditions of a political nature to any assistance which they may offer or which the Kingdom of Laos may seek;

(e) they will not bring the Kingdom of Laos in any way into any military alliance or any other agreement, whether military or otherwise, which is inconsistent with her neutrality, nor invite or encourage her to enter into any such alliance or to conclude any such agreement;

(f) they will respect the wish of the Kingdom of Laos not to recognize the protection of any alliance or military coalition, including SEATO;

(g) they will not introduce into the Kingdom of Laos foreign troops or military personnel in any form whatsoever, nor will they in any way facilitate or connive at the introduction of any foreign troops or military personnel;

(h) they will not establish nor will they in any way facilitate or connive at the establishment in the Kingdom of Laos of any foreign military base, foreign strong point or other foreign military installation of any kind;

(i) they will not use the territory of the Kingdom of Laos for interference in the internal affairs of other countries;

(j) they will not use the territory of any country, including their own, for interference in the internal affairs of the Kingdom of Laos.

3. Appeal to all other States to recognize, respect and observe in every way the sovereignty, independence and neutrality, and also the unity and territorial integrity, of the Kingdom of Laos and to refrain from any action inconsistent with these principles or with other provisions of the present Declaration.

4. Undertake, in the event of a violation or threat of violation of the sovereignty, independence, neutrality, unity or territorial integrity of the Kingdom of Laos, to consult jointly with the Royal Government of Laos and among themselves in order to consider measures which might prove to be necessary to ensure the observance of these principles and the other provisions of the present Declaration.

5. The present Declaration shall enter into force on signature and together with the statement of neutrality by the Royal Government of Laos of July 9, 1962, shall be regarded as constituting an international agreement. The present Declaration shall be deposited in the archives of the Governments of the United Kingdom and the Union of Soviet So-

cialist Republics, which shall furnish certified copies thereof to the other signatory States and to all the other States of the world.

In witness whereof, the undersigned Plenipotentiaries have signed the present Declaration.

Done in two copies in Geneva this twenty-third day of July one thousand nine hundred and sixty-two in the English, Chinese, French, Laotian and Russian languages, each text being equally authoritative.

For the Union of Burma:
    U THI HAN
For the Kingdom of Cambodia:
    NHIEK TIOULONG
For Canada:
    H. C. GREEN
    CHESTER RONNING
For the People's Republic of China:
    CHEN YI
For the Democratic Republic of Viet-Nam:
    UNG-VAN-KHIEM
For the Republic of France:
    M. COUVE DE MURVILLE
    JACQUES ROUX
For the Republic of India:
    V. K. KRISHNA MENON
For the Polish People's Republic:
    A. RAPACKI
For the Republic of Viet-Nam:
    VU VAN MAU
    THANH
For the Kingdom of Thailand:
    DIRECK JAYANÂMA
For the Union of Soviet Socialist Republics:
    A. GROMYKO
For the United Kingdom of Great Britain and Northern Ireland:
    HOME
    MALCOLM MACDONALD
For the United States of America:
    DEAN RUSK
    W. AVERELL HARRIMAN

APPENDIX V

PROTOCOL TO THE DECLARATION ON THE NEUTRALITY OF LAOS

The Governments of the Union of Burma, the Kingdom of Cambodia, Canada, the People's Republic of China, the Democratic Republic of Viet-Nam, the Republic of France, the Republic of India, the Kingdom of Laos, the Polish People's Republic, the Republic of Viet-Nam, the Kingdom of Thailand, the Union of Soviet Socialist Republics, the United Kingdom of Great Britain and Northern Ireland and the United States of America;

Having regard to the Declaration on the Neutrality of Laos of July 23, 1962;

Have agreed as follows:

Article 1

For the purposes of this Protocol

(a) the term "foreign military personnel" shall include members of foreign military missions, foreign military advisers, experts, instructors, consultants, technicians, observers and any other foreign military persons, including those serving in any armed forces in Laos, and foreign civilians connected with the supply, maintenance, storing and utilization of war materials;

(b) the term "the Commission" shall mean the International Commission for Supervision and Control in Laos set up by virtue of the Geneva Agreements of 1954 and composed of the representatives of Canada, India and Poland, with the representative of India as Chairman;

(c) the term "the Co-Chairmen" shall mean the Co-Chairmen of the International Conference for the Settlement of the Laotian Question, 1961–1962, and their successors in the offices of Her Britannic Majesty's Principal Secretary of State for Foreign Affairs and Minister for Foreign Affairs of the Union of Soviet Socialist Republics respectively;

(d) the term "the members of the Conference" shall mean the Governments of countries which took part in the International Conference for the Settlement of the Laotian Question, 1961–62.

Article 2

All foreign regular and irregular troops, foreign paramilitary formations and foreign military personnel shall be withdrawn from Laos in the shortest time possible and in any case the withdrawal shall be completed not later than thirty days after the Commission has notified the Royal Government of Laos that in accordance with Articles 3 and 10 of this Protocol its inspection teams are present at all points of withdrawal from Laos. These points shall be determined by the Royal Government of Laos in accordance with Article 3 within thirty days after the entry into force of this Protocol. The inspection teams shall be present at these points and the Commission shall notify the Royal Government of Laos thereof within fifteen days after the points have been determined.

Article 3
The withdrawal of foreign regular and irregular troops, foreign paramilitary formations and foreign military personnel shall take place only along such routes and through such points as shall be determined by the Royal Government of Laos in consultation with the Commission. The Commission shall be notified in advance of the point and time of all such withdrawals.

Article 4
The introduction of foreign regular and irregular troops, foreign paramilitary formations and foreign military personnel into Laos is prohibited.

Article 5
Note is taken that the French and Laotian Governments will conclude as soon as possible an arrangement to transfer the French military installations in Laos to the Royal Government of Laos.

If the Laotian Government considers it necessary, the French Government may as an exception leave in Laos for a limited period of time a precisely limited number of French military instructors for the purpose of training the armed forces of Laos.

The French and Laotian Governments shall inform the members of the Conference, through the Co-Chairmen, of their agreement on the question of the transfer of the French military installations in Laos and of the employment of French military instructors by the Laotian Government.

Article 6
The introduction into Laos of armaments, munitions and war material generally, except such quantities of conventional armaments as the Royal Government of Laos may consider necessary for the national defense of Laos, is prohibited.

Article 7

All foreign military persons and civilians captured or interned during the course of hostilities in Laos shall be released within thirty days after the entry into force of this Protocol and handed over by the Royal Government of Laos to the representatives of the Governments of the countries of which they are nationals in order that they may proceed to the destination of their choice.

Article 8

The Co-Chairmen shall periodically receive reports from the Commission. In addition the Commission shall immediately report to the Co-Chairmen any violations or threats of violations of this Protocol, all significant steps which it takes in pursuance of this Protocol, and also any other important information which may assist the Co-Chairmen in carrying out their functions. The Commission may at any time seek help from the Co-Chairmen in the performance of its duties, and the Co-Chairmen may at any time make recommendations to the Commission exercising general guidance.

The Co-Chairmen shall circulate the reports and any other important information from the Commission to the members of the Conference.

The Co-Chairmen shall exercise supervision over the observance of this Protocol and the Declaration on the Neutrality of Laos.

The Co-Chairmen will keep the members of the Conference constantly informed and when appropriate will consult with them.

Article 9

The Commission shall, with the concurrence of the Royal Government of Laos, supervise and control the cease-fire in Laos.

The Commission shall exercise these functions in full cooperation with the Royal Government of Laos and within the framework of the Cease-Fire Agreement or cease-fire arrangements made by the three political forces in Laos, or the Royal Government of Laos. It is understood that responsibility for the execution of the cease-fire shall rest with the three parties concerned and with the Royal Government of Laos after its formation.

Article 10

The Commission shall supervise and control the withdrawal of foreign regular and irregular troops, foreign paramilitary formations and foreign military personnel. Inspection teams sent by the Commission for these purposes shall be present for the period of the withdrawal at all points of withdrawal from Laos determined by the Royal Government of Laos in consultation with the Commission in accordance with Article 3 of this Protocol.

Article 11

The Commission shall investigate cases where there are reasonable grounds for considering that a violation of the provisions of Article 4 of this Protocol has occurred.

It is understood that in the exercise of this function the Commission is acting with the concurrence of the Royal Government of Laos. It shall carry out its investigations in full cooperation with the Royal Government of Laos and shall immediately inform the Co-Chairmen of any violations or threats of violations of Article 4, and also of all significant steps which it takes in pursuance of this Article in accordance with Article 8.

Article 12

The Commission shall assist the Royal Government of Laos in cases where the Royal Government of Laos considers that a violation of Article 6 of this Protocol may have taken place. This assistance will be rendered at the request of the Royal Government of Laos and in full cooperation with it.

Article 13

The Commission shall exercise its functions under this Protocol in close cooperation with the Royal Government of Laos. It is understood that the Royal Government of Laos at all levels will render the Commission all possible assistance in the performance by the Commission of these functions and also will take all necessary measures to ensure the security of the Commission and its inspection teams during their activities in Laos.

Article 14

The Commission functions as a single organ of the International Conference for the Settlement of the Laotian Question, 1961–1962. The members of the Commission will work harmoniously and in cooperation with each other with the aim of solving all questions within the terms of reference of the Commission.

Decisions of the Commission on questions relating to violations of Articles 2, 3, 4 and 6 of this Protocol or of the cease-fire referred to in Article 9, conclusions on major questions sent to the Co-Chairmen and all recommendations by the Commission shall be adopted unanimously. On other questions, including procedural questions, and also questions relating to the initiation and carrying out of investigations (Article 15), decisions of the Commission shall be adopted by majority vote.

Article 15

In the exercise of its specific functions which are laid down in the relevant articles of this Protocol the Commission shall conduct investigations (directly or by sending inspection teams), when there are reasonable grounds for considering that a violation has occurred. These investigations shall be carried out at the request of the Royal Government of Laos or on the initiative of the Commission, which is acting with the concurrence of the Royal Government of Laos.

In the latter case decisions on initiating and carrying out such investigations shall be taken in the Commission by majority vote.

The Commission shall submit agreed reports on investigations in which differences which may emerge between members of the Commission on particular questions may be expressed.

The conclusions and recommendations of the Commission resulting from investigations shall be adopted unanimously.

Article 16

For the exercise of its functions the Commission shall, as necessary, set up inspection teams, on which the three member-States of the Commission shall be equally represented. Each member-State of the Commission shall ensure the presence of its own representatives both on the Commission and on the inspection teams, and shall promptly replace them in the event of their being unable to perform their duties.

It is understood that the dispatch of inspection teams to carry out various specific tasks takes place with the concurrence of the Royal Government of Laos. The points to which the Commission and its inspection teams go for the purposes of investigation and their length of stay at those points shall be determined in relation to the requirements of the particular investigation.

Article 17

The Commission shall have at its disposal the means of communication and transport required for the performance of its duties. These as a rule will be provided to the Commission by the Royal Government of Laos for payment on mutually acceptable terms, and those which the Royal Government of Laos cannot provide will be acquired by the Commission from other sources. It is understood that the means of communication and transport will be under the administrative control of the Commission.

Article 18

The costs of the operation of the Commission shall be borne by the members of the Conference in accordance with the provisions of this Article.

(a) The Governments of Canada, India and Poland shall pay the personal salaries and allowances of their nationals who are members of their delegations to the Commission and its subsidiary organs.

(b) The primary responsibility for the provision of accommodation for the Commission and its subsidiary organs shall rest with the Royal Government of Laos, which shall also provide such other local services as may be appropriate. The Commission shall charge to the Fund referred to in sub-paragraph (c) below any local expenses not borne by the Royal Government of Laos.

(c) All other capital or running expenses incurred by the Commission in the exercise of its functions shall be met from a Fund to which all the members of the Conference shall contribute in the following proportions:

The Governments of the People's Republic of China, France, the Union of Soviet Socialist Republics, the United Kingdom and the United States of America shall contribute 17.6 per cent each.

The Governments of Burma, Cambodia, the Democratic Republic of Viet-Nam, Laos, the Republic of Viet-Nam and Thailand shall contribute 1.5 per cent each.

The Governments of Canada, India and Poland as members of the Commission shall contribute 1 per cent each.

Article 19

The Co-Chairmen shall at any time, if the Royal Government of Laos so requests, and in any case not later than three years after the entry into force of this Protocol, present a report with appropriate recommendations on the question of the termination of the Commission to the members of the Conference for their consideration. Before making such a report the Co-Chairmen shall hold consultations with the Royal Government of Laos and the Commission.

Article 20

This Protocol shall enter into force on signature.

It shall be deposited in the archives of the Governments of the United Kingdom and the Union of Soviet Socialist Republics, which shall furnish certified copies thereof to the other signatory States and to all other States of the world.

In witness whereof, the undersigned Plenipotentiaries have signed this Protocol.

Done in two copies in Geneva this Twenty-third day of July One thousand nine hundred and sixty-two in the English, Chinese, French, Laotian and Russian languages, each text being equally authoritative.

For the Union of Burma:
U THI HAN

For the Kingdom of Cambodia:
NHIEK TIOULONG

For Canada:
H. C. GREEN
CHESTER RONNING

For the People's Republic of China:
CHEN YI

For the Democratic Republic of Viet-Nam:
UNG-VAN-KHIEM

For the Republic of France:
M. COUVE DE MURVILLE
JACQUES ROUX

For the Republic of India:
V. K. KRISHNA MENON

For the Kingdom of Laos:
Q. PHOLSENA

For the Polish People's Republic:
A. RAPACKI

For the Republic of Viet-Nam:
VU VAN MAU
THANH

For the Kingdom of Thailand:
DIRECK JAYANÂMA

For the Union of Soviet Socialist Republics:
A. GROMYKO

For the United Kingdom of Great Britain and Northern Ireland:
HOME
MALCOLM MACDONALD

For the United States of America:
DEAN RUSK
W. AVERELL HARRIMAN

Bibliography

AGENCE LAO-PRESSE. *Bulletins Quotidiens.* Vientiane: 1955–

ANON., *Concerning the Situation in Laos.* Peking: Foreign Languages Press, 1959.

BEECH, KEYES, "How Uncle Sam Fumbled in Laos." *Saturday Evening Post,* April 22, 1961.

BERVAL, RENÉ DE, ed., *Kingdom of Laos.* Saigon: Editions France-Asie, 1959. (Published originally in Nos. 118–20, March–May 1956, of the French cultural monthly, *France-Asie.*)

BURCHETT, WILFRED G., *The Furtive War: The United States in Vietnam and Laos.* New York: International Publishers, 1963.

—— *Mekong Upstream.* Berlin (Soviet Sector): Seven Seas Publishers, 1959.

CHALERMNIT PRESS CORRESPONDENT, *Battle of Vientiane of 1960.* Bangkok: Charlermnit Press, 1961.

CHAMPASSAK, SISOUK na, *Storm Over Laos.* New York: Praeger, 1961. (Also published in French as *Tempête sur le Laos.* Paris: La Table Ronde, 1961.)

DEYDIER, HENRI. *Introduction à la Connaissance du Laos.* Saigon: Imprimerie Française d'Outre-Mer, 1952.

—— *Lokapâla.* Paris: Plon, 1954.

DISCHAMPS, J. M., *Tam-Tam sur le Mékong—Avec les guérillas laotiens.* Saigon: Ardin, 1948.

DOMMEN, ARTHUR J., *Conflict in Laos, The Politics of Neutralization.* New York: Praeger, 1964.

—— "Laos: The Troubled 'Neutral,'" *Asian Survey,* Vol. VII (January 1967) No. 1.

Douze Années d'Intervention et d'Agression des Impérialistes Américains au Laos. Editions du Neo Lao Haksat, Juillet, 1966.

DURDIN, PEGGY, "The Grim Lesson of Laos." *The New York Times Magazine,* May 21, 1961.

FALL, BERNARD B., *Le Viet-Minh, 1945–1960.* Paris: Armand Colin, 1960.

—— "The International Relations of Laos," *Pacific Affairs,* Vol. XXX (March 1957) No. 1.

—— "The Laos Tangle." *International Journal,* Vol. XVI (Spring, 1961) No. 2.

—— "The Pathet Lao: A 'Liberation' Party," in Robert A. Scalapino, ed. *The Communist Revolution in Asia: Tactics, Goals, and Achievements.* Englewood Cliffs, New Jersey: Prentice-Hall, 1965.

—— "Reappraisal in Laos," *Current History,* Vol. 42 (January, 1962) No. 245.

—— *Street Without Joy.* Harrisburg: Stackpole, 1961.

FIEDLER, ARKADY, *Im Lande der wilden Bananen.* Leipzig: Brockhaus Verlag, 1961.

FIELD, MICHAEL, *The Prevailing Wind, Witness in Indo-China.* London: Methuen, 1965.

GENTIL, PIERRE, *Remous du Mékong.* Paris: Charles-Lavauzelle, 1950.

HALPERN, A. M. and H. B. FRIEDMAN, *Communist Strategy in Laos.* Santa Monica, Calif.: The Rand Corp., 1960. RM-2561.

HALPERN, JOEL M., *Government, Politics, and Social Structure in Laos. A Study of Tradition and Innovation.* Yale University Southeast Asia Studies. Monograph Series No. 4. New Haven, 1964.

—— *America and Laos: Two Views of Political Strategy and Technical Assistance.* Los Angeles: published by author, 1959.

HILSMAN, ROGER, *To Move a Nation, The Politics of Foreign Policy in the Administration of John F. Kennedy.* New York: Doubleday, 1967.

LACOUTURE, JEAN and PHILIPPE DEVILLERS, *La fin d'une guerre, Indochine 1954.* Paris: Editions du Seuil, 1960.

LARTEGUY, JEAN, *The Bronze Drums* (translated from the French, *Les Tambours de bronze* by Xan Fielding). New York: Knopf, 1967.

LEBAR, FRANK M. and ADRIENNE SUDDARD, eds., *Laos, its people, its society, its culture.* New Haven: HRAF Press, 1960.

LE BOULANGER, PAUL, *Histoire du Laos français: Essai d'une étude chronologique des principautés Laotiennes.* Paris: Plon, 1931.

LEDERER, WILLIAM J., *A Nation of Sheep.* New York: Norton, 1961.

LÊ KHAM, *Truo'c Gio No Sung* [Before the Attack]. Hanoi: Van Hoc, 1960.

LEWIS, NORMAN, *A Dragon Apparent.* London: Jonathan Cape, 1951.

MEIRING, DESMOND, *The Brinkman.* Boston: Houghton Mifflin, 1965.

MODELSKI, GEORGE, *International Conference on the Settlement of the Laotian Question, 1961–2.* Australian National University, Department of International Relations. Canberra, 1962.

QUANG MINH. *Au Pays du Million d'Eléphants.* Hanoi: Editions en Langues Etrangères, 1961.

SASORITH, KATAY DON, *Le Laos.* Paris: Berger-Levrault, 1953.

SIMMONDS, E. H. S., "A Cycle of Political Events in Laos," *World Today,* Vol. XVII (February, 1961), No. 2.

—— "Breakdown in Laos," *World Today,* Vol. 20 (July, 1964) No. 7.

—— "Independence and Political Rivalry in Laos, 1945–61," in Saul Rose, ed.,

Politics in Southern Asia. London: Macmillan; New York: St. Martin's Press, 1963.

—— "Laos and the War in Vietnam," *World Today,* Vol. 22 (May, 1966) No. 5.

—— "Laos: A Renewal of Crisis," *Asian Survey,* Vol. IV (January, 1964) No. 1.

—— "The Evolution of Foreign Policy in Laos since Independence," *Modern Asian Studies,* Vol. II (1968) No. 1.

SMITH, ROGER M. "Laos," in GEORGE McT. KAHIN, ed., *Governments and Politics of Southeast Asia.* 2d. ed. Ithaca: Cornell University Press, 1964.

—— "Laos in Perspective," *Asian Survey,* Vol. III (January, 1963) No. 1.

TOYE, HUGH, *Laos, Buffer State or Battleground.* London: Oxford University Press, 1968.

Une Année pour l'Application des Accords de Genève de 1962 sur le Laos. Le Comité Central du Neo Lao Haksat, 1963.

UNITED KINGDOM, *Documents Relating to British Involvement in the Indo-China Conflict, 1945–1965.* Miscellaneous No. 25 (1965). Cmd. 2834. London: H. M.'s Stationery Office, December, 1965.

—— *Documents Relating to the Discussion of Korea and Indo-China at the Geneva Conference, April 27–June 15, 1954.* Cmd. 9186. London: H. M.'s Stationery Office, 1954.

—— *Further Documents Relating to the Discussion of Indo-China at the Geneva Conference, June 16–July 21, 1954.* Cmd. 9239. London: H. M.'s Stationery Office, 1954.

—— *International Conference on the Settlement of the Laotian Question, Geneva, May 12, 1961–July 23, 1962. Laos No. 1 (1962).* Cmd. 1828. London: H. M.'s Stationery Office, 1962.

—— *Progress Report of the International Commission for Supervision and Control in Laos . . . : Laos No. 1 (1955) et sqq.* Cmd. 9445, 9630; Cmd. 314, 541. London: H. M.'s Stationery Office, 1955–58.

UNITED NATIONS. SECURITY COUNCIL, *Report of the Security Council Sub-Committee under Resolution of 7 September 1959.* S/4236, November 5, 1959. New York: Security Council, 1959; mimeographed.

UNITED STATES, CONGRESS, HOUSE OF REPRESENTATIVES. *U.S. Aid Operations in Laos: Seventh Report by the Committee on Government Operations.* 86th Cong., 1st Sess. Washington: Government Printing Office, June 15, 1959.

—— DEPARTMENT OF STATE. *The Situation in Laos.* Washington: September, 1959.

WYATT, DAVID K., "Siam and Laos, 1767–1827," *Journal of Southeast Asian History,* Vol. 4 (September 1963) No. 2.

ZUKROWSKI, WOJCECH, et al., *Sous le ciel du Laos.* Hanoi: Editions en Langues Etrangères, 1961.

Index

Abramov, Aleksandr, 190, 194–95
Adenauer, Konrad, 65
Afghanistan, 89, 209
Aid programs. *See* Foreign-aid programs; specific countries, programs
Aircraft (airplanes; airfields), 17, 147; Geneva Agreements (1954) on, 60, 73; and 1959–61 conflict, 96, 105, 109, 117, 128, 138, 191, 197, 203, 204, 205, 206, 207; Royal Laotian Air Force, 96, 105, 117, 128; and Viet-Minh offensive (1953–54), 47, 49, 50, 51, 54, 55
"Air Laos," 128
Alakh tribes, 31, 41
Algeria, 35, 162, 185
Alsop, Joseph, 135–40, 147, 155–56, 214, 217
American Foreign Policy, 1900–1950 (Kennan), 157
American Military Advisory Group, 133, 173. *See also under* Military advisers
Amkha Soukhavong, General, 33, 131, 135, 137; and Kong-Lê, 188
Annam Cordillera, 24, 54
Anou, King, 27
Arabs, 68
Argenlieu, Admiral, 38
Argentina, 141, 143, 145
Artillery, 49, 54, 55, 111, 117, 191, 198, 206

Asian-African Conference. *See* Bandung Conference
Associated Press reports, 130, 132, 141, 150, 173
Aswan Dam, 222–23
Attopeu, 116, 118, 234
Auriol, Vincent, 42
Australia, 107, 151, 176, 195
Austria, 81, 89; and neutrality, 208, 209, 210, 231
Austrian State Treaty, 210, 231
Automobiles, 163, 185
Ayub Khan, G., 245

Bailey, Lawrence R., 215
Balkans, 209
Ban Dan, 137
Bandung Conference, 63, 65, 69–70, 72–73, 113
Bangkok, 27, 141, 143, 151, 191, (*see also* Thailand); Lao-Issara in, 38, 40, 41, 42, 43
Ban Hat Bo, 207
Ban Hin Heup, 205, 206, 228–29
Ban Keun, 207
Ban Mai, 105
Ban Namone, 225
Ban Napa, 125
Ban Padong, 207, 226
Ban Pak Ca-Dinh, 130–31
Ban Pa-Thi, 56
Ban Sanoth, 106
Ban Sot, 197
Ban Tian Kha, 63
Base areas, Pathet Lao use of, 115–16, 117, 118–19

Bassac, 31, 118
Battalion Commanders' School, Laotian, 117
Beech, Keyes, 167
Belgium, 208
Berlin crisis, 11–12
Bernadotte, Folke, 68
Black T'ai, tribal group, 18, 19, 21, 25, 111, 116, 127
Black market operations, 95, 112, 165
Blind Bonze, 53–54, 242
Bodard, Lucien, 148
Bolovens Plateau, 24, 31, 41, 55, 116
Bong Souvannavong, 181, 182
Bonnet, Gabriel, 110
Bonzes, 53–54, 82, 242, 243
"Booster Shot" (Operation), 85–86
Bouavan Norasing, 205
Boun Oum, Prince, 111, 159, 172; Kong-Lê coup and, 190–91, 192, 198; post-World War II status of, 38–39; regime of, 172, 190–91, 192, 198, 203 ff., 208 ff., 215 ff., 222, 225, 227 ff.; and World War II, 33
Boyle, Andrew Jackson, 206
Boy Scout movement, 32
British. See Great Britain
"Brotherhood" (Operation), 168
Brown, Winthrop G., 169
Budapest, 198–99
Buddhism, 25, 26, 49, 121, 138, 153, 173; temples, 27, 85
Bulganin, N. A., 113
Bunche, Ralph J., 177–78
Burke, Arleigh, 150
Burma, 17, 26, 28, 31, 89, 99, 225; Japanese conquest of, 46, 50; neutrality of, 209, 210; Ne Win and reform in, 245

Caccia, Sir Harold, 248
Cambodia, 23, 25, 26, 33, 52, 57, 94, 97; Communists in, 44–45, 55;

foreign relations of, 64–65; French in, 28, 31, 32, 35, 162; and Geneva Conference (1954), 58–59, 60–62, 64, 69; and neutrality, 69, 209, 210, 211, 218, 231
"Cambodian National Liberation Committee," 44
Canada, 107, 214; members of ICC from, 60, 66, 68, 88, 211, 212, 214
CARE, 165
Castro, Fidel, 210
Catry, Captain, 136
CDIN, 93 ff., 100 ff., 109 ff., 150 (see also "Young Turks"); and crisis of 1960, 174–76; and elections of 1960, 181–83; and Kong-Lê coup, 188, 194
Central Intelligence Agency, U.S. See CIA
Chagla, M. A. C., 212
Cham Niem, 104, 105–6, 109
Champa, 25
Champassak (principality), 27, 29, 33, 38–39
Champassak (province), 116
Champassak, Sisouk na. See Sisouk na Champassak
Chao Phraya valley, 25
Chapman, Christian G., 169n
"Charter of Laotian Neutrality," 225–26
Chasseurs Laotiens, 33, 50, 52, 55. See also specific units
Chauvel, Jean, 225
Chen-La, 25
Chennault, Claire L., 241
Chen-Yi, 98
Chiang Kai-shek, 157–58
Chicago Daily News, 167
Childs, Marquis, 224
China, 24, 25, 26, 29, 32 (see also Communist China; Nationalist

China (cont'd)
    China); Méo tribe from, 25;
    pirates and raiders from, 18, 28
Chinaimo, Camp, 174, 187, 198
Chou En-lai, 60, 69–70, 72, 73
Chu-Teh, 52
CIA, 139–40, 167, 170, 175; and
    Kong-Lê, 189; and Phoumi No-
    savan, 247
CINCPAC, 194
"Civic Action" groups, 116
Civil service, 31, 39
Clans, 24, 26
Clos, Max, 148, 247
Cold War, 195, 199, 231
Combat, 224
Commando groups, 56
Committee for the Defense of Na-
    tional Interests (CDIN). See
    CDIN
Committee system, Pathet Lao, 113–
    14
Communications, army, 187
Communist China, 37, 70–76; Ameri-
    can foreign policy and, 3, 157–
    58, 213; and CDIN, 95; and
    conflict of 1959–61, 95 ff.,
    108 ff., 121, 127, 132, 140, 143,
    148, 154, 189, 211, 213, 226,
    228, 229; and five principles
    agreement, 72–73; and Geneva
    Conference (1954), 60, 63, 69–
    70, 76; and Geneva Conference
    (1961), 226, 228; Kong-Lê and,
    189; and neutrality in Laos, 211,
    213, 226, 228
Communist Viet-Minh. See Viet-Minh
"Condor" (Operation), 56–57
Conflict in Laos . . . (Dommen),
    46n
Congo, 177
Congress, U. S. See United States
    Congress
Constitutent Assembly, Laotian, 39–
    40. See also National Assembly

Constitution, Laotian, 39–40, 71, 121
Constitution Day, 101–2
Corruption, and aid programs, 85–
    86, 87, 165–66, 194, 231; and
    crisis of 1959, 111–12; Kong-Lê
    and, 185; and swing to right, 93,
    94
Counterpart funds, 164
Coups, military, 174–75, 179, 234;
    and countercoups, 184–99
Cousins, Norman, 23
Couve de Murville, Maurice, 217
Crèvecoeur, Boucher de, 47, 56
Cuba, invasion of, 139–40; missile
    crisis, 107, 108
Currency, 95, 164, 165, 171, 217, 231
Customs, Directorate of, 174–75

Dala Savang Vathana, Princess, 125
Declaration of Independence (April
    1945), 34, 37
Declaration of Neutrality of Laos,
    218; text of, 257–61; text of
    protocol to, 262–68
De Gaulle, Charles. See Gaulle,
    Charles de
Delhi, 220, 221
"Denial value" concept, 209
Déo family, 18
Déo Van Khoun, Lieutenant, 19–22
Déo Van Tri, 29
Deydier, Henri, 242
Dien Bien Phu, 18, 29, 45, 56; battle
    of, 18, 45, 53, 54, 55, 56–57,
    130, 147, 148; overrun by Viet-
    Minh, 55, 130, 204, 213
Dillon, Douglas, 141
Dollar import licenses, 84
Dommen, Arthur, 46n
Dong-Hene, 47, 55
Dudman, Richard, 149–50
Dulles, Allen, 140
Dulles, John Foster, 65, 83, 170, 222–
    23, 232, 235
Durdin, Tillman, 86

East Asia, as first priority of Red China, 73
East Germany, 11–12
Economic aid, 87, 94–95, 116, 163 ff., 194, 195, 231. *See also* Foreign-aid programs
Education, 30, 32 (*see also* Schools); Ministry of, 37
Egypt, 222–23
Eisenhower (Dwight D.) Administration, 126, 132, 142, 155, 161, 162, 166, 167, 216, 232–33; and Kong-Lê coup, 192–99, 211 ff.; and neutralization of Laos, 211 ff.; sends Parsons to Laos, 171, 194
Elections, 80, 181–83, 226; introduction of universal suffrage, 40; of 1946, 39; of 1955, 71; of 1958, 81–87, 88; of 1960, 175, 176, 181–83, 188
Elite, 93 ff., 184 ff., 217
Emerald Buddha (temple), 27
Ennis, Thomas E., 245
European Free Trade Area ("The Outer Seven"), 209

Fabre, Major, 37
Fa Ngum, King, 26
Favart, Robert, 148, 247
Faydang (Phai-Dang), 43, 120
Felt, Harry D., 155
Festival of the Dead, Buddhist, 138
Finland, 89, 208–9
1st Lao Infantry Battalion, 33, 50
1st Lao Parachute Battalion, 204
1st UCPL Battalion, 96–97, 99–106, 110–11, 116, 125
5th Lao Infantry Battalion, 52
Flag(s), Laotian, 44
"Force 136," 33, 35, 56, 207
Foreign-aid programs, 63, 82, 84, 95, 97, 121, 154, 171–72, 179, 191, 193, 194 (*see also* specific countries, programs); corruption in

administration of, 85–86, 87, 165–66, 231
Foreign Commerce Directorate (Laos), 174
Foreign Legion, French, 53, 55
Foreign policy (foreign diplomacy relations), Laotian (*see also* specific aspects, countries, events); "gentle firmness," 41; negotiating processes (diplomacy), 64 ff., 139, 141 ff., 154
Foreign policy, U.S. *See* United States policies
Formosa, 95. *See also* Nationalist China
France and the French, 18, 28, 30–45, 73, 76, 80, 82, 89, 101, 111 (*see also* French Indo-China; specific individuals); and aid to Laos, 82, 97, 111 (*see also* Foreign-aid programs; specific aspects, programs); and Geneva Conference (1954), 58 ff., 61, 65, 66, 67, 72, 111; and ICC, 67, 68 ff.; and Indo-China (*see* French Indo-China); and Laos conflict (1959–61), 18–19, 101, 107, 108, 111, 125, 128, 133, 141, 143, 162–66, 168–69, 176, 182, 192, 193, 195–98, 203, 204, 214–20, 222, 225; and neutralization of Laos, 208, 211, 225; and press reports, 107, 108, 125, 144, 148–50; and "revolutionary warfare," 110, 111; and Thailand, 28–29, 31, 32, 41; and training programs, 60, 73, 111, 112, 117, 133, 147, 162, 169, 185, 204, 214–16, 245; and U.S. in Laos, 37, 107, 108, 125, 144, 146 ff., 162, 166, 168–69, 192, 214 ff.; and Viet-Minh in Laos (1953–54), 46–57; and World War II, 31–35
"Free Laos" (*Lao-Issara*), 34–43, 59

French Foreign Legion, 53, 55
French Indo-China, 13, 18, 26, 28–57 *passim*, 65, 146, 158, 162, 213 (*see also* Dien Bien Phu); and Geneva Conferences (*see* Geneva Conference [1954]; Geneva Conference [1961]); Japan and, 31–32, 33 ff.; map of Laos in, 13; post-World War II, 35–43; World War II and, 31–35
French Military Mission, 60, 73, 111, 112, 117, 133, 162, 169, 185, 204, 214–16
French Union, 30–33, 40, 42, 56, 59, 65, 146
Fulbright, Senator J. William, 139
Fu-Nan, 25

Gassouin, Olivier, 147
Gaulle, Charles de, 35–36, 65, 87
Gavin, Ambassador James M., 221
"General Franco-Laotian Convention," 42, 43
Geneva Conference (1954), 58 ff., 73, 87–88, 97, 98, 111, 156; cease-fire provisions, 59–62, 66 ff., 87; ICC and, 60, 66 ff., 87–88; Laotian negotiation process at, 64–66
Geneva Conference (1961), 216, 218, 219–28, 233; cease-fire appeal, text of, 253; invitation to participants, text of, 254
Germany, 11–12, 31, 32, 33, 209, 248
Giap. *See* Vo Nguyen Giap
Graft, 94, 165–66, 174, 185. *See also* Corruption
Great Britain and the British, 28, 29, 31, 76, 80, 101, 213; and conflict in Laos (1959–61), 123, 141, 143, 144, 147, 151, 176, 192, 193, 195, 196–97, 198, 203, 207, 208, 211, 214, 216–18, 219 ff.; and French in Indo-China, 33, 34–35; and Geneva Conference (1954), 71–72, 88, 98, 216; and

Geneva Conference (1961), 219 ff.; in Malaya, 31, 213; and neutralization of Laos, 208, 211, 214, 216–18, 219 ff.; and press reporting, 107, 108; and U.S. in Laos, 168, 214, 216–18
Grew, Joseph C., 196
Gromyko, Andrei, 98
Guerres insurrectionelles et revolutionnaires, Les (Bonnet), 110
Guerrilla warfare, 33, 34–35, 45, 47, 110–11, 213 (*see also* specific aspects, individuals, places, units); and conflict of 1959–61, 100 ff., 109 ff., 117–18, 124, 125, 138, 192, 193, 197, 205 ff., 213; nature of, 109–12

Haiphong, 32
Hammarskjöld, Dag, 99, 123, 127, 131, 139, 142; and "UN presence" in Laos, 177–81
Hanoi, 63, 74, 185. *See also* North Vietnam
Harriman, Averell, 221, 228
Heintges, General ("Mister"), 133, 215
Helicopters, use of, 205, 206, 207, 229
Herter, Christian A., 194, 212
Hindu kingdoms, 25
Hitler, Adolf, 248
Ho Chi Minh, 37, 41, 43, 132, 199
Ho Chi Minh trail, 234, 235
Home, Lord, 221
Ho pirates, 27, 28–29
Hua-Muong, 50
Hull, Cordell, 241
Hungary, 198–99, 209
Huong-Lap, 96

ICA, 166
ICC (International Commission for Supervision and Control), 66 ff.,

ICC (cont'd)
    96, 99, 211, 262; and accords of
    1957, 80, 82, 83; and crisis of
    1959, 99, 119, 120, 123, 143;
    dissolution of, 87–88, 119, 143,
    171; establishment of, 60; and
    Laotian neutrality, 211, 212; re-
    convening of (1961), 219–20,
    225, 227, 228
Ilyushin-14's (Soviet aircraft), 204
Imfeld, Colonel, 37
Impeng Suryadhay, 153
Implementation of the Geneva Agree-
    ments in Laos (government
    "White Book," 1955), 68, 69
Independent Party, 84, 86, 87
India, 25, 31, 66, 69, 70, 73, 99; and
    ICC, 60, 66, 68, 88, 211, 212;
    and neutrality, 209, 211, 212
Indochinese Union, 30–33. See also
    French Union
Indonesia, 245
Infantry, Laotian, 33, 50, 52, 55. See
    also specific units
Interparliamentary Union, 99
Irawaddy valley, 25
Insisiengmay, Leuam, 72
"Internal war," 110
International Commission for Super-
    vision and Control. See ICC
Irwin, John N. II, 194
Israel, State of, 68
"Is There Aggression?" (Alsop arti-
    cle), 139–40
Italy, 141, 143, 145

Japan, 31–35, 36; and Burma con-
    quest, 46, 50; and France in
    World War II, 31–32, 33–35;
    and Laos conflict of 1959, 141,
    143, 145, 152–53
Jars, 51, 242
Joint Chiefs of Staff, United States,
    163–64, 227. See also U. S. De-
    partment of Defense

Jordan, 177
Judd, Walter H., 169

Kambuja, 25
Kam Kheut, 207, 249
Kashmir, 177
Katay Don Sasorith, 36, 66, 70, 72,
    78, 89; on Communism as "num-
    ber one enemy," 94; and con-
    flict of 1959, 122, 123, 154, 156;
    death of, 156; and elections of
    1958, 84, 87; and Pathet Lao ac-
    cords, 77, 84
Kaysone Phoumvihan, 112n
Kene Sane, 114–15
Kennan, George F., 145–46, 157,
    167, 171
Kennedy (John F.) Administration,
    159, 160, 167, 211, 216, 232–
    35, 248; and Laos neutrality,
    211, 216–17, 218, 226–31, 232–
    35; retains Parsons, 172; and
    Souvannaphouma, 222–23
Kennedy, Mrs. John F., 216
Key West, Florida, 216
Khamkhong Vongnarath, Colonel,
    247
Khamking Souvanlasy, 210
Khammao, Prince, 36, 38, 40, 42
Khammouane province, 41
Khamphan Panya, 119, 120, 123,
    141, 142; speaks before UN, 152,
    153
Kha tribes, 43, 100, 104, 127, 184,
    244
Khmer (linguistic family), 24, 44
Khmer Empire, 25, 26, 28
"Khmer Resistance Government," 58,
    59, 62
Kho, tribal group, 244
Khommouane, 118
Khosla, J. N., 66
Khou Abhay, 176, 181
Khrushchev, Nikita S., 126, 144, 209,

Khrushchev (cont'd)
210, 223; and Kennedy on Laos, 226
Khun Borom (or Bolom), King, 26
Khun-Lo, King, 26
Kingdoms, early Lao, 25, 26–27
Kip, devaluation of, 95, 171
Komadone (tribal leader), 63
Komadone Military Academy, 63
Kong-Lê, Captain (later General), coup d'etat by, 111, 174, 184–99, 203 ff., 214, 215, 218, 230, 233; appointed President of Supreme Military Command, 205; background and description of, 184–86
Korea, 157–58, 162, 211, 213
Kouprasith Abhay, 174
Kou Voravong, 77
Kuznetsov, Vasily V., 219

Lafont, Bernard, 130
Laniel, Joseph, 65
Lan-Xang, 26, 118
"Lao," meaning of term, 24
Lao (lowland) tribes, 100, 104. See also Lowlands; specific groups
Lao Hak Sat, 119n
Lao Hakxa Sat, 94, 103, 119n
Lao-Issara ("Free Laos"), 34, 43
Lao People's Party, 112n
Laos, description (geography; early history; people) of, 17–22, 23–28
Laos, maps of: in Indo-China, 13; Viet-Minh invasion (1953–54), 48; Pathet Lao attacks (1959), 124; at cease-fire (1961), 230; in 1967–68, 236
Lao-Thai war of 1828, 29
Laotian Armed Forces (Laotian Royal Army), 21, 32–33. See also Royal Laotian Army; specific units
Laotian Military Academy, 47, 55

Lebanon, 177
Lederer, William J., 107, 138
Lemnitzer, Lyman L., 227
Liaison Training Advisory Group (LTAG), U. S., 206
Liberia, 143
Liên-Viêt, 44
Linguistic families, 24
Lloyd, Selwyn, 98
Lolo Kha Kho, 25
London Times, 216
Lové tribe, 31
Lowlands (lowlanders; lowland people), 24–25, 36, 41, 56, 112, 116, 189, 234. See also specific tribal groups
LTAG, 206
Luang Prabang, 18–19, 25, 26, 27, 28–29, 36, 37, 38; conflict of 1959–61 and, 102, 118, 123, 125, 129, 132, 186, 188, 193, 194, 195, 196, 204; ICC in, 68; French in, 30, 35; Japanese in, 34, 35; Kong-Lê coup and, 186, 188, 193, 194, 195, 196; Viet-Minh offensive against, 47, 52–55, 57; World War II and, 34, 35
Lü tribesmen, 96
Lwa (or La-Wa), 24

MAAG, 196, 206
MacDonald, Malcolm, 227
Machine guns, 173
Macmillan, Harold, 216
Malaya, 31, 213
Malaya-Polynesian group, 25
Man, tribal group, 24
Manila, 193
Mansfield, Michael J. (Mike), 142
Mao Tse-tung, 72, 110, 249
Maps: Laos in Indo-China, 13; Viet-Minh invasion of Laos (1953–54), 48; Pathet Lao attacks (1959), 124; Laos at cease-fire,

Maps (cont'd)
    (1961), 230; Laos (1967–68),
    236
Maquis, 207
Marlic, Major, 53
Marold, Leopold, 136
Massive retaliation, U.S., concept of,
    158
Mekong River, 17, 23, 31, 38, 180
Mekong Valley, 25–26, 37, 42, 130,
    195, 207, 226, 234
Mendès-France, Pierre, 60, 61, 62
Menon, V. R. Krishna, 227
Méo (Miao) tribe, 18, 24, 25, 41, 43;
    and conflict of 1959–61, 96, 100,
    104, 105, 118, 189, 190, 206–7,
    225; and Viet-Minh offensives,
    49, 50, 51, 56, 57
Mercedes-Benz automobiles, 164, 185
Merchant, Livingston T., 212
"Merrill's Marauders," 46
Messinesi, Philip, 179
Miller, Haynes, 165–66, 168
Mobile Groups, French, 55, 242; No.
    51, 242
Military advisers, 45 (see also spe-
    cific groups); French, 60, 73,
    111, 112, 117, 133, 162, 169,
    185, 204, 214–16; U.S., 112,
    117, 133, 162, 173, 185, 196,
    197, 206, 215
Military Assistance Advisory Group,
    Laos (MAAG/Laos), U.S., 196,
    206. See also Military advisers;
    PEO
Military coups, Laotian, 174–75, 179;
    and contercoups, 184–99
Mitterand, François, 249
Molotov, V. M., 58–59, 61–62, 64
Monaco, 208
Mongols, 25
Monsoon rains, 189. See also Rainfall
Moroccan troops, 53
Mortars, 47, 82, 117, 137, 144, 150,
    197, 206

Mountain people (mountaineers), 24,
    25, 31, 36, 51, 56, 207 (see also
    specific places; tribal groups);
    and conflict of (1959), 100, 111,
    116, 118; used by Communists,
    41, 100
Mountains, 24, 25
Mukdahan, 113
Muong Het, 134–35, 136–37
Muong Hiem, 122
Muong-Kassy, 206, 218
Muong Khoua, 18–19, 20, 49, 55,
    127
Muong-Lap, 50
Muong Ngam, 52, 105, 106
Muong Nhommarat, 207
Muong-Peun, 50, 122, 129–30
Muong Phalane, 207
Muong Sai, 21, 55
Muong-Sing valley, 96
Muong Sone, 63, 122
Muong Song, 127
Mutual Security program, 167
Myre de Villers, Le, 28

Nagy, Imré, 198
Nalane, 125
Nam Bac, 55
Nam Ca-dinh, 197
Nam-Hou, 17–19, 20, 47, 52, 55
Nam-Houa, 17–18, 56
Nam Lik, 205, 206, 228–29
Nam Ma, 134, 135, 138
Nam Sane, 52
Nam-Tha, 118, 233
Nam-Yum, 18
Nan-Chao, 26
Na-San, 45
Nasser, Gamal A., 223
Nasution, General, 245
Nation of Sheep, A (Lederer), 107,
    138
National Assembly, France, 39–40
National Assembly, Laos, 39–40, 75–
    80, 94, 175; and crisis of 1959–

National Assembly, Laos (*cont'd*) 61, 102, 120, 121, 175 ff., 181–83, 188, 226, 227–28; and 1958 elections, 84–87; and 1960 elections, 181–83
National Defense Committee, French, 57
National Defense Committee, Laotian, 102
"National Front for the Liberation of South Viet-Nam," 122
Nationalism, geography and absence in Laos of, 23–24; U.S. policies in Far East and need for cultivation of, 238
Nationalist China, 32, 35, 36, 73, 95; U.S. foreign policy and, 157–58
Nationalist Party, 84, 86, 87
National Union (Party), 181
National Union government, 225, 233; text of three princes on problem of achieving, 255–56
NATO (North Atlantic Treaty Organization), 217
Navarre, Henri, 55, 57
Nehru, Jawaharlal, 69, 70, 73
Neo Lao Hak Xat. See NLHX
Neo Lao Issala ("Free Laos Front"), 44
Nepal, 89, 209
Neutrality (neutralism; neutralization), Laos, 175–76, 187, 192, 208 ff.; Cambodia and, 69, 209; CDIN and, 95, 99; conflict of 1959–61 and, 95, 99, 121, 175–76, 178, 179, 187, 192, 193–94, 197, 198, 208 ff.; Geneva Conference (1954) and, 61; Geneva Conference (1961) and, 216, 218–28; plans for, 208 ff.; Souvannaphouma and, 170, 171, 193–94, 197, 198, 210, 211, 218, 224 ff., 227, 228 ff., 232, 233, 234; U.S. policy and, 167, 168,

170, 171, 187, 192, 193–94, 197, 198, 208 ff.
New Delhi, 70
Ne Win, General, 245
Newspapers (news media; press), and reporting of events in Laos: Communist, 119 n (*see also* specific journalists, news agencies, periodicals); western (France; Great Britain; U.S.), 97–98, 107–8, 116, 122–26, 130–43, 144, 145, 148–50, 154–56, 167, 171, 180, 198–99, 210–11, 224–25 (*see also* specific countries, journalists, periodicals)
New York *Herald Tribune,* 135
New York *Times,* 78, 83, 86, 97, 126, 130, 131, 133–34, 144, 145, 146, 149, 150, 152, 155, 214; on CIA and Phoumi Nosavan, 247; on conflict of 1960–61, 176, 199, 211, 214; on French in Laos, 173; on Geneva Conference (1961), 224; on neutralization of Laos, 211, 224; and Souvannaphouma, 221, 222, 223
New Zealand, 151
Ngo Dinh Diem, 196
Ngon Sananikone, 125, 126, 127
Nhouy Abhay, Thao, 37, 40
93rd Division, Nationalist China, 35
NLHX (*Neo Lao Hak Xat*), 78, 79, 85, 86; and conflict of 1959–60, 101, 102, 103, 108, 109, 112–18, 120, 121, 196, 197; and election of, 1960, 182; organization of, 112–18
"Noel" (Operation), 206
Nong-Het, 96
Nongkhai, 42
Norodom Sihanouk, Prince, 64, 69, 231, 233, 254; and neutrality plan, 210, 211, 220; on U.S. policy in Laos, 231, 233, 235
North Korea, 157–58

North Viet-Nam, 17, 18, 19, 32, 43–45, 73, 74, 95 ff., 207, 213, 229, 234–35, 244; and Bandung Conference, 69–70, 72–73; CDIN and, 95 ff.; and Geneva Conference (1954), 63–68, 69–76; and invasion of Laos (1953–54), 46–57; and Kong-Lê coup, 189, 204; and Laos conflict (1959–61), 95 ff., 107–56 *passim*, 189, 204, 211, 213, 229; and Laos offensives (1967–68), 236; and Pathet Lao, 43–45, 234, 235, 236
Nouhak Phoumsavan, 43, 75, 79, 113
Nu, U, 69

148th Independent Regiment (Viet-Minh), 55
"Operation Brotherhood" hospital project, 168
Opium, 19, 20, 51, 225
Orient, L', 142
"Otter" aircraft, 128, 138
Ouane Rathikoun, 101–2, 103, 104, 135, 137; given Defense post, 190
Oudone Sananikone, 146

Pakistan, 245
Pak Lat, 207
Paksane, 52, 191, 193
Paksé, 36
Pakseng, 125, 132
Palestine, UN and, 177
Palmer, Williston B., 193
"Panhandle" area (Laos), conflict of 1959–61 and, 122, 138, 147, 154, 176, 207
Paphay, 125
Paratroops, French, 37, 52, 53, 57
Paratroops, Royal Laotian, 111, 112, 129–30; and Kong-Lê military coup (1960–61 conflict), 174, 185–99, 203, 204

Parliament, Laotian. *See* National Assembly, Laotian
Parsons, J. Graham, 83–84, 86, 132, 163, 166, 170–72; as Ambassador to Laos, 170–71, 194; and Laotian neutrality, 167, 170–71, 194–95; retained by Kennedy, 172; and Souvannaphouma, 170, 194–95, 196, 211
Pathet Lao, 74–80, 180, 181, 232–38; and accords of 1957, 75–89; administration and organization of, 112–18; and Bandung Conference, 70–71; and conflict of 1953–54, 47, 50, 54, 56, 57; and conflict of 1959–61, 11, 19, 96–172 *passim*, 185–99, 203 ff., 225, 228–31; creation of, 43–45; and elections of 1958, 83–87; and elections of 1960, 181–83; fighting forces of (*see* UCPL); and Geneva Conference (1954), 58 ff., 66, 68, 70 ff.; and ICC, 66, 68; and Kong-Lê, 185, 188–99; and military coups, 173, 185–99 *passim;* and program of July 1959, 121–22; strength of, 118; U.S. policy and, 157–72, 232–38
"Pathet Lao Fighting Units," 62 ff., 69. *See also* UCPL
Patriotism, 24
Pavie, Auguste, 28
Paxasangkhom (PSK), 182
Peking, 63. *See also* Communist China
Peng Te-huai, 154
Pentagon. *See* United States Department of Defense
PEO, 133, 167, 169, 206, 215
"People's Committee," 36
Phai-Dang (Faydang), 43, 120
Phak Khon Ngan Lao (PKNL), 112–18
Phak Phasason Lao (Lao People's Party), 112n
Pham Van Dong, 59, 69

Phetsarath, Prince, 34, 35, 36, 40, 42, 76; death of, 156

Philippines, 33, 185, 186, 193

Phnom-Penh, 174, 218

Phone Kheng police camp, 183

Phong Saly, province, 21, 78, 79–80, 81, 82; conflict of 1959–60 and, 117, 118, 154, 191; Geneva Conference (1954), and, 59, 62, 63, 71, 72; Kong-Lê coup and, 191

Phong Satone, 122

Phong-Savane, 51

Pho Sathou, 53–54

Phoui Sananikone, 78, 249; conflict of 1959 and administration of, 94, 95, 96, 97, 98–103, 108, 112, 120–23, 125–26, 141, 150, 153–54; and elections of 1958, 84, 87; as figurehead in own government, 96; and Geneva agreements (1954), 58, 59, 97; government replaced, 122; military coup against, 174–76

Phoumi Nosavan, General, 94, 141, 143, 215, 227, 247; and coup of 1964, 234; and Kong-Lê coup (1960–61 conflict), 185, 188, 189, 190–98, 205, 215, 218, 220, 227, 229, 247; military coup by, 174, 175–76, 179; military reverses (1961), 159

Phoumi Vongvichit, 75, 79, 81–82

Phouthai tribe, 31

Piromoteurs, 17

PKNL (*Phak Khon Ngan Lao*), 112–18

Plaine de Jarres, 24, 28, 73, 234; conflict of 1959–61 and, 99–100, 101–6, 174, 204, 205; described, 51; Viet-Minh offensives (1953–54), 47–49, 50–52, 53

Poland, 82; members of ICC from, 60, 66, 67, 68, 88, 211, 212

"Polarization," 189, 190, 191, 195–99, 203–4, 229, 232

Political parties, in elections of 1958, 84–87; in elections of 1960, 181–83 (*see also* specific parties)

Porters, use by Viet-Minh of, 47

Pothisarath, King, 26

Potsdam Conference, 35

Prasad, Rajendra, 99

Pravda, 195

Press. *See* Newspaper

Prisoners, military, 68, 144, 150, 152–53, 228; political, 226

Program Evaluation Office (PEO), 133, 167, 169, 206, 215

Progressive Party, 84, 86–87

Propaganda, 44, 82 (*see also* Newspapers; Psychological warfare); conflict of 1959 and, 101, 112–18, 119n, 127, 150

Proto-Indochinese, 24

"Provisional Executive Committee," 188

"Provisional Government of Free Laos," 43

PSK, 182

Psychological warfare, 110, 115, 148, 181. *See also* Propaganda

Pushkin, Georgi M., 228

Quang-Yen, 185

Quinim Pholsena, 188, 197

Radio communications, 188

Radio Hanoi, 119n

Radio Peking, 119n

Radio Vientiane, 187

Rainfall (rainy season), 19–20, 54, 130, 189

Rally of the French People (1948), 87

Rally of the Laotian People (RPL). *See* RPL

Rand Corporation study, 95, 113, 123, 126

Rangoon, Burma, 46, 71

Recoilless rifles, 137, 173

Red River Delta and Valley, 25, 54
Reform(s), 87, 163 ff.; CDIN and,
    94–95, 116; use of army for,
    163 ff., 245
Regionalism, 24
Religion, 25, 26, 49. *See also* Bud-
    dhism
Reuters news agency, 142
"Revolutionary Committee Against
    the Coup d'Etat," 191
"Revolutionary warfare," 109–12,
    140
Reymond, M. de, 40
Rice, 18, 19, 24
Rifles, 137, 173
Riley, Herbert, 194
Rivers, 17–18, 25, 26. *See also* by
    name
Roads, 17, 189; No. 4, 52; No. 7,
    117; No. 9, 55, 207; No. 12, 54
Roberts, Sir Frank, 219–20
Robertson, Walter S., 83, 170, 171
Royal Laotian Air Force, 96, 105,
    117, 128
Royal Laotian Army (Lao Armed
    Forces), 43, 45 (*see also* specific
    individuals, places, units); and
    conflict of 1959–61, 18–21, 95–
    97, 99–106, 107 ff., 122 ff.,
    174 ff., 185–99 *passim*, 203 ff.;
    and conflict of 1967–68, 236;
    and elections of 1960, 181; and
    Geneva Conference (1954), 63,
    69, 72; and integration of UCPL
    into, 78–79, 80, 82–83, 96–97,
    99–106; and Kong-Lê coup,
    185–99 *passim*, 203 ff.; morale
    problem in, 111–17; and training
    programs, 162–66, 169, 173 (*see
    also* Training missions); U.S. aid
    to, 95, 110, 111, 117, 162 ff.,
    (*see also* under U.S. aid pro-
    grams, specific programs); and
    Viet-Minh invasion (1953–54),
    46–57

RPL (Rally of the Laotian People),
    87, 93, 94, 174, 176; and elec-
    tions of 1960, 181–82
Rural Affairs Department, establish-
    ment of, 95
Rusk, Dean, 222, 223, 224, 248
Russia. *See* Union of Soviet Socialist
    Republics
Russia and the West (Kennan), 145–
    46, 157

Saigon, 36, 38, 196. *See also* South
    Viet-Nam
St. Louis *Post-Dispatch*, 149–50
Salan, General, 52
Sala Phou Kheng, 218
Sala Phou Khoun, 205–6, 218
Salween valley, 25
Sam-Neua (city), 49–50, 51, 52, 56,
    128, 135, 137
Sam-Neua (province), 78–82; conflict
    of 1959–61 and, 113, 117, 118,
    122, 127–35 *passim*, 138, 141,
    142, 153, 182, 191–92, 207; Ge-
    neva agreements (1954) on, 59,
    62, 63, 71, 72
Sam Teu, 142, 145, 149–50
Sananikone. *See* Phoui Sananikone
San Marino, 81, 208
Santiphab ("Neutralist") Party, 85,
    86, 87, 181, 182
Saravane, 116
Sarit Thanarat, Marshal, 143, 179,
    191, 245
Sasorith, Katay D. *See* Katay Don
    Sasorith
Savang Vathana, King, 34, 70, 88,
    125; and conflict of 1960–61,
    176, 180, 182, 188, 189, 190,
    193, 194, 195, 218, 220, 226,
    227, 229; Declaration of Neu-
    trality by, 217; Kong-Lê coup
    and, 188, 189, 190, 193, 194,
    195; replaces Sisavang Vong as
    king, 128–29, 134

Savannakhet, 55, 118, 174, 189, 190, 191, 198

Sayaboury, 31, 118

Say Pethrasy, 118

"School 44," 63

Schools, 30, 32, 37; aid program and, 85, 89; military, 113, 115, 118; Pathet Lao, 113, 115, 118, 119

SEATO (Southeast Asia Treaty Organization), 73, 88, 98, 216; and Laos conflict of 1959, 123, 141, 142, 151–52, 156, 178; and Laos conflict of 1960–61, 196, 208, 216–18, 226, 231; meeting of March, 1961, 216–18, 226, 231; U.S. foreign policy and, 160, 161, 208

2nd Lao Infantry Battalion, 55

2nd Lao Paratroop Battalion (BPL), 183, 186–99

2nd UCPL Battalion, 96–97, 99–106, 107, 116, 117, 119, 120

Sen, Samar, 66

Séno, 54, 55, 60, 73, 147, 215–16

Setthathirat, King, 26

7th Fleet, U.S., 155–56, 213

Shan states (Burma), 99

Shibuzawa, Shinachi, 152–53

Shuff, Charles H., 81

Siam. See Thailand

Sieu Heng, 44

Sihanouk. See Norodom Sihanouk, Prince

Singkapo, Choulamany, 79, 101, 183, 197

Sino-Tibetans, 24

Sisavang Vong, King, 29, 34, 35–36, 37, 38, 39, 42, 44, 52, 88; and conflict of 1959, 128–29, 132; cremation of, 186; death of, 132, 146, 156; described, 128; and Geneva Conference (1954), 59; replaced by son, Savang Vathana, 128–29; signs Constitution, 40

Sisouk na Champassak, 67, 95, 113, 243; and conflict of 1959–61, 98, 100, 103, 113, 142, 146, 147–48, 153, 165; on accords of 1957, 81; on elections, 181; as Information Minister, 98, 103; quoted on black market operations, 165

Sithone, Komadone, 43, 55

6th Lao Infantry Battalion, 52

Smith, Horace H., 86, 148, 167, 169

Smith, Walter Bedell, 203

Sobolev, Arkady A., 141

Sochi, 223

Social Democratic Party, 182

Sop Bau, 134, 135

Sop Hao, 134

Sop-Nao, 18–21

Sop Sai, 134

Sop-Sang, 125

Sorre, Colonel, 68–69

Sounthone Patthammavong, General, 174, 197

Souphanoubong, Prince, 35–36, 37–38, 70, 113, 233; and accords of 1957, 75–76, 80, 81–82; chosen as Prime Minister of Pathet Lao, 44; communism of, 75–76; and conflict of 1959–61, 96, 101, 102, 109, 113, 126, 192, 193, 227, 228 ff.; and elections of 1958, 85, 86; escapes from prison camp, 183; expelled from Lao-Issara, 43; moves to left, 40–42; Souvannaphouma and, 75–76; and Viet-Minh offensive (1953–54), 47; visits Moscow (1961), 227

South Korea, 157–58

South Viet-Nam, 57, 95, 98, 119, 121–22, 146, 156, 162, 185, 211, 234, 235, 244

Southeast Asia Treaty Organization. See SEATO

Souvannaphouma, Prince, 35, 36, 40, 73, 75–76, 82–84, 87–88, 95, 113, 175, 197, 233; and coalition government (1961), 229–30; and conflict of 1959, 95, 120; and conflict of 1960–61, 170, 171, 174, 175, 180, 182, 188–99 *passim*, 210, 211, 218 ff., 227–30; and elections of 1958, 83, 84, 85, 87; and Geneva Conference (1954), 62, 63–64, 66, 87–88; moderate position of, 42, 43; neutrality policy of, 170, 171, 193–94, 197, 198, 210, 211, 218, 224 ff., 227 ff., 232–34; and Pathet Lao accords, 75–80, 81, 82, 83 ff.; as President of National Assembly, 182, 222; resigns (1958), 88–89; returns to power (1956), 71–72; returns to power (1960), 174; and U.S., 72, 75, 82, 83–84, 89, 221–24, 227, 228, 232, 233, 234

Soviet bloc, 63, 89 (*see also* specific countries); conflict of 1959–61 and, 97 ff., 110 ff., 121 ff., 140, 150, 207, 208–31 *passim* (*see also* specific countries); and Laos neutrality, 208 ff., 218–31 *passim;* Pathet Lao accords and, 75, 80, 82, 88, 89; U.S. foreign policy and, 11–12, 161 ff., 208 ff., 232–38; vis-à-vis U.S. in Laos as compared to Berlin, 11–12

Soviet Union. *See* Union of Soviet Socialist Republics

Spanish Civil War, 196

Special Forces, U.S., 185, 206, 207

Stilwell, Joseph W., 50

"Strange War on Laos' Border, The" (Alsop article), 135–38

Students, World War II and increase in, 32. *See also* Schools

Suffrage (universal), introduction of, 40. *See also* Elections

Sukhothai, 26

Suliyavongsa, King, 26, 27

Sulzberger, C. L., 214, 224

Sweden, 208, 248

Switzerland, 208, 209; Zurich agreements, 226, 227, 255

Tachen islands, 158, 162

T'ai-Lü tribesmen, 96, 100

T'ai tribes, 18, 19, 21, 24, 25, 26, 29, 41, 56, 96, 100

Taiwan, 95, 158. *See also* Nationalist China

Tali, 25

Tass news agency, 198

Ta Viang, 105, 106

Taxes, 44

Tchépone area, 96, 120

Temples, 27, 85

Thadeua, 185

Thai (linguistic family), 24

Thailand, 17, 24, 26, 52, 54, 113 (*see also* Bangkok); and early Lao history, 17, 24, 26, 27, 28, 29; and France, 28–29, 31, 32, 41; and Geneva Conference (1954), 65, 72; and Laos (World War II era), 31, 32, 38, 40, 41, 42; and Laos conflict (1959–61), 95, 98, 113, 120–21, 143, 151, 191, 192, 193, 196, 208, 211, 234; and neutrality, 208, 211; Sarit and reform in, 245; U.S. policies and, 234, 235, 238

Thakhek, 34, 37, 39, 54, 123

Thanat Kjoman, 120

Thao Khé, 101, 103, 104–5

Thao Nhouy Abhay, 37, 40

Tha-Thom, 52, 138, 204, 205

That Ong-Tu, 134

That Sen Pagoda, 53

3rd Foreign Legion Regiment (French), 55

304th Infantry Division (Viet-Minh), 47–49, 53

308th Infantry Division (Viet-Minh), 47, 55
312th Infantry Division (Viet-Minh), 47
316th Infantry Division (Viet-Minh), 47, 49, 52, 53, 55, 127; 98th Regiment, 50, 52, 53
"330th Division" (North Viet-Nam), 146
351st "Heavy Division" (Viet-Minh), 55
Tiao Somsanith, 174, 182, 188
Tibet, 99
Time magazine, 167, 189, 205; on Geneva Conference (1961), 224
Times of London, 216
Tito, Marshal, 209
Tokyo, 21. See also Japan
Ton Duc Thang, 44
Touby Lefoung, 49, 190
Training missions (military training), 231 (see also Military advisers; specific organizations); French, 60, 73, 111, 133, 147, 162, 169, 245; North Viet-Nam, 63; Soviet, 63; U.S., 73, 133, 162 ff., 173, 206; Viet-Minh, 63
Tran-Ninh, 118
Treaty of Sovereignty (1941), 31, 32
Tribes (tribesmen), 24–25, 31, 63, 128. See also Lowlands; Mountain people; specific tribal groups
T-6 aircraft, U.S., 204
Tunisia, 140, 141, 143, 145
Tuomioja, Sakari Severi, 178–79
Tuyên-Quang, 43
20th Indian Division, 35
25th Infantry Battalion, Laotian, 65

Ubon, 42
UCPL (Pathet Lao army), 62, 63, 170; Battalion 1, 96–97, 99–106, 110–11, 116, 125; Battalion 2, 96–97, 99–106, 107, 116, 117, 119, 120; and conflict of 1959, 96–97, 99–106, 107 ff., 122–35; integration into government army of, 78–79, 80, 82–83, 96–97, 99–106; military coups by, 173 ff.; and revolutionary (guerrilla) warfare, 109–12; strength of, 118; training of, 116–17, 118
Ulbricht, Walter, 12
UNEF, 177
Union of Soviet Socialist Republics, 145 (see also Soviet bloc); and aid to Laos, 117, 171, 172, 174, 195, 197, 203 ff.; airlift of supplies to Laos (1961), 117, 174, 197, 204; and conflict in Laos (1959–61), 126, 127, 140, 141, 142, 144, 146, 189–90, 194–95, 197, 198, 203 ff.; and Geneva Conference (1954), 58–59, 60–62, 63, 71–72, 88; and Geneva Conference (1961), 219 ff., 228 ff.; and Kong-Lê, 189–90, 194–95, 197, 198, 203; and neutrality of Laos, 208 ff.
United Kingdom. See Great Britain and the British
United Nations, 131, 141, 151, 152–55, 210; Development Program, 180; Emergency Force (UNEF), 177; Fact-Finding Committee (1959), 130, 133–34, 139–51, 152–55, 178, 212; and Laos (1958), 99; and Laos (1959–61), 122, 123, 125–26, 127, 130, 131, 133–34, 139–51, 152–55, 176–81, 182, 192, 210, 212; and neutralization of Laos, 210, 212; observation mission in Laos, 177–81; observer group (UNOGIL), 177, 192; "presence" of, 177–81, 182, 192; Truce Supervisory Organization (UNTSO), 68, 177
United States aid programs, 63, 75, 81, 82, 84, 89, 97, 154, 162–

United States aid programs (cont'd)
68, 171–72, 191, 193, 194, 237;
corruption in administration of,
85–86, 87, 165–66, 194; military, 95–96, 97, 110, 111, 138,
162–68, 171–72, 191, 193, 194,
203 ff.

United States Air Force, 95

United States Army Special Forces,
185, 206, 207

United States Army Special Warfare
Center, 110

United States Congress, 83, 138, 140,
159–60, 163, 167, 169, 171, 194;
Appropriations Committee, 81;
Foreign Relations Committee,
171, 194; Government Operations Committee, 163; reports on
Laos to, 58–59, 83–84, 108, 138,
171, 192

United States Department of Defense,
81, 159, 163, 169–70; and 1961
conflict, 193, 214 ff., 227

United States Department of State,
157–72; and accords of 1957,
80–89; and conflict of 1959–61,
120, 131–32, 140, 141, 157–72,
193–99, 211–12, 214, 218; and
Kong-Lê coup, 193–99; and policy in Far East, 157–72 (see
also United States policies);
White Papers on Laos, 160, 161,
218

U. S. Military Assistance Advisory
Group, Laos (MAAG/Laos),
196, 206. See also Military advisers; PEO

United States Operation Mission
(USOM), 85

United States policies, 11–12, 53,
73 ff., 157–72, 232–38 (see also
specific administrations, agencies,
aspects, departments, individuals); accords and elections of
1957 and 1958, 73–89 passim;

and bases in Laos, 93, 95, 98;
"bastion" ("bulwark") concept,
159, 160, 170, 194; and communism in Laos compared to Berlin
crisis, 11–12; and Cuba, 107,
108, 139–40; "firmness" policy,
155, 158, 162; and French in
Indo-China, 33, 34, 213; and
French in Laos, 37, 107, 108,
125, 144, 146–51, 162, 166,
168–69, 192, 214 ff.; and Geneva
Conference (1954), 58–59, 65;
and Geneva Conference (1961),
216–28 passim; and Laos conflict
(1959–61), 94–97, 101, 107 ff.,
116, 117, 120–56 passim, 157–
72, 173 ff., 185, 187–88, 189–
99, 203–31, 232–35; and neutralization of Laos (see Neutrality); reasons for presence in
Laos, 161 ff.; Souvannaphouma
and, 72, 75, 82, 83–84, 89, 221–
24, 227, 228, 232

United States press reports, 97–98,
107–8, 116, 125–26, 127–28,
130–43, 149–50, 154–56, 171,
180 (see also specific journalists,
periodicals); on Geneva Conference (1961), 224; on 1960–61
crisis, 192, 198–99, 210, 214,
215; on neutralization of Laos,
210–11, 224

UNOGIL, 177, 192

UNTSO, 68, 177

USOM, 85

U-2 crisis, 107, 108

Vang Pao, 207

Vang Vieng, 204, 205–6; fall of, 220

Vattay airfield, 187, 194, 197, 198

Veha Akhat (airline), 128

Vienna, Austria, 226

Vientiane, 19, 21, 25–29, 35, 36, 37,
38, 39, 73, 76, 93 ff.; "battle for"
(1960), 198, 203, 204; captured

Vientiane (cont'd)
in coup, 174; and conflict of 1959–61, 93 ff., 108, 118, 119 ff., 133–34, 144, 174, 180, 184, 186–88, 191, 192, 195–99, 203 ff.; described, 26–27; Kong-Lê coup and, 186–88, 189, 191, 192, 195–99, 203 ff.; Viet-Minh offensive (1953–54) and, 49, 52, 53, 57; and World War II, 34, 35, 36

Viet-Minh, 18–19, 21, 41, 42, 207; and Bandung agreement, 70; and Geneva Conference (1954), 58 ff., 69; and Laos conflict of 1959–61, 108, 113, 120, 123, 126, 127, 132, 145, 148–56 passim, 170, 199, 204; and Laos invasion (1953–54), 46–57, 58 ff.; overrun Dien Bien Phu, 58, 204; Pathet Lao and, 44, 45, 74

Viet-Nam, 31, 32, 35, 36, 38, 41, 43–45, 57, 196 (see also North Viet-Nam; South Viet-Nam); and early Laos history, 17, 26, 27, 28; and Geneva Conference (1954), 59–60, 65, 69; refugees in Thailand from, 113; U.S. policies and, 235, 238; and World War II, 32, 33, 35

"Vietnamese United Front" (Liên Viêt), 44

Villages (villagers), 23, 24, 25; aid programs and, 85–86, 95; Pathet Lao (NLHX) and, 112–18, 119; UN and, 180

Vishinski, Andrei, 61

Vittel, 146

Voeunesai, 55

"Voice of America," 193

Voix du Peuple, La (French language newspaper), 122–23, 154

Vo Nguyên Giap, 45, 47, 55

Washington Post, 125, 135, 138, 173, 190; advocates neutralization of

Laos, 210

Weapons (armament), 41, 191 (see also specific battles, kinds); accords of 1957 and, 82–83, 89; conflict of 1959–61 and, 109, 110, 111, 117, 137, 138, 206; Geneva Conference (1954) and, 60, 62–63; Geneva Conference (1961) and inspection of, 228; Pathet Lao, 44, 109, 117, 204; U.S. aid programs and, 95–96, 110, 111, 173, 191; and Viet-Minh offensives (1953–54), 47, 49, 51, 60

West Berlin, 11–12

"White Book" on the Implementation of the Geneva Agreements in Laos, 68, 69

White T'ai tribes, 25, 116

"Why They Called Off the Dogs" (Alsop article), 155–56

Wiener Zeitung, 142

World Congress for the Defense of Peace, 63

World War II, 29, 31–35

World Youth Congresses, 63

Xieng Kho, 134, 135, 136, 137

Xieng-Khouang, 51, 52, 102, 105, 118, 147, 205, 207

Xieng-Ngeun, 99, 102, 103, 111, 125

Yao tribesmen, 96

Year of the Buffalo, 173

"Young Turks," 93, 96, 100, 115, 139, 143, 147, 150, 152 (see also CDIN); and conflict of 1960, 175, 176, 179, 181

Youth movements, 32

Yugoslavia, 82, 110, 209

Yunnan province, China, 24, 25, 26, 30; refugees in Laos from, 96

Zellweger, Edouard, 178, 179, 180, 192

Zurich agreements, 226, 227, 255

DATE DUE